Thank you to all of the soldiers, civilians, and volunteers who trusted
me to tell their stories.

WHAT WAR DID TO US

Volume II

UKRAINE

THE FIRST 150 DAYS OF COMBAT

FEBRUARY 24 - JULY 24, 2022

Nicholas Laidlaw

Contents

Dedicated to the tortured souls, both living and dead, who were witnesses, participants, and victims of this war.

"We have done everything possible and impossible."

-     Anton Kryl. KIA May 14th, 2022. Siege of Mariupol

What you are about to read is a collection of stories I gathered day by day during the Russian Invasion of Ukraine in 2022. This is the first 150 days of war. These stories were gathered from Ukrainian soldiers, Russian soldiers, Ukrainian civilians, and Western volunteers from multiple countries across the world. The majority of these stories were documented online through several different messaging apps, during phone calls, or online video conference interviews.

As stated in my last book, "What War Did To Us", published in November of 2021; I am not a professional author. I am not a professional historian and nor am I a member of any mainstream media. I am simply trying to preserve oral history as best I can.

The majority of these stories were documented anonymously for the protection of those submitting them. At the time of publication, this war is still ongoing, and people are still in harm's way. For their safety, all names, units, and locations have been removed unless explicitly stated otherwise by the author of the anecdote. Some stories were documented the same day as the date mentioned, others were documented weeks or months later.

These stories were submitted to me oftentimes from the scene of the same battlefield they took place in, minutes or hours after they occurred. I have done my best to verify each and every single story as best I could; however, it is impossible for me to verify any story completely. Every single war story ever told has had parts left out, pieces of it redacted, or is embellished in some major or small way.

I have corrected only major spelling mistakes and grammatical errors, and I have left the stories exactly how they are told. This is my attempt to give you an experience that I had. Reading these messages and stories as if they have been texted or emailed directly to you from the source. All of the foul words, language, and ways of speaking have been left intact to protect their original authenticity.

There are actions, language, and other derogatory terms used in these stories that some may find disturbing, disgusting, and distasteful. These words, views and actions do not necessarily represent the beliefs and actions of the organization or nation from where they originated. If these stories offend you; they should. War is dirty, and often brings out the worst in those who participate in it. It can also bring out the best. For these reasons, I will not be censoring anything. This is my attempt to show the world what war really is, and how complex, heroic, and vile it can be. The world is not black and white, and neither are the hearts of the men and women in these stories. Try to keep in mind that too often in history the evil henchman and helpless victim have often been the same man.

This book is not a collection of Pro-Ukrainian or Pro-Russian stories. It is simply a large collection of experiences presented as evidence and testaments of what it was like to experience these historical events. I ask readers to take any opposing views to theirs as this: simply stories in a book. This collection is not intended to promote or denounce any ideology or political belief. Everything you read beyond this point has the potential to offend, disgust, or disappoint you. Nothing beyond this point is my own personal belief, or experience.

For all of us that worked on this project, myself, my co-author Ilya, and our artists João "J-Dot" Alves, and Mike Liu, this book has been an intense labor of love. Documenting these stories as they happened was a tough task to try to remain unbiased in. I myself lost several friends during the course of this conflict, and we tried our best to stay true to our original mission to document the stories of both sides equally and without bias. I hope that by reading these stories, you can see that effort.

I will remind you all again, we are not authors or historians. Instead, think of us more like carrier pigeons. Relaying stories to all of you as we find them. Thank you for your support, trust, and confidence.

- Nicholas Laidlaw
  Author
  Battles and Beers: War Stories
  US Marine Veteran

- Ilya Rudyak
  Co-Author
  Battles and Beers: War Stories
  US Marine

FOREWORD

Written by Ilya Rudyak

As *What War Did To Us: Volume II* is a work of non-fiction, it is important to include historical pretext, overview, and analysis of the events that have led to this conflict, and this terrible invasion, or, as the Kremlin refers to it as a 'Special Military Operation'. As someone who has spent a significant portion of his childhood in Russia, whose family was almost entirely from the Ukraine, and friends and relatives on all four sides of the conflict (Russian Federation, Donetsk People's Republic, Ukraine, and Western volunteers on the side of Ukraine), I believe I am qualified enough for the following crash course. Even with all my modesty, I have got to put an emphasis on the impressive level of neutrality that I have expressed on the political aspect of this conflict, despite having certain biases from cultural clashes and history, especially being a Jew, whose family suffered a tremendous amount through generations of residing in the region, as well as having relatives and friends caught in this war for the past eight years.

We started documenting this invasion from its very first hour, following it daily and in detail. At some point, part of our team, including myself, was on the ground conducting interviews and refugee assistance in the war zone. Those details will not be exposed in this book in order to preserve OPSEC (Operational Security) of our acquainted efforts. Perhaps those will be included in the next book, or when the conflict reaches a conclusion.

I had the honour of the author, a man I take great pleasure in calling my friend and an elder comrade of the Marine Corps Infantry, Sergeant Nicolas Laidlaw, in allowing me to write this foreword and the preface, as well as participate in various portions of the book. I take great pride in the countless hours that I have spent alongside Nick working on this project.

This is our best attempt at relaying our on the ground examination of the first 150 days of war.

PREFACE

With the propaganda machines of all sides hard at work, it can be difficult for someone who isn't well versed in the history and geography of Eastern Europe to wade through the lies and manipulated truths, and I am not talking about the Ghost of Kiev or the defiant and undoubtedly ballsy troops who were stationed on Zmeyinni (Snake) Island. I am referring to the geopolitical deceptions of the Russo-Ukrainian peoples, some of which are over a millennial old. For example, Kiev did in fact come first, by hundreds of years. And yes, the Kievan-Rus, also known as Ancient Rus, was the predecessor to the Russian Empire, but it actually was the successor to the Rurik Kingdom and the Rus Khaganate, the original states that united and more or less created the Slavic identity. Kiev being Moscow's forerunner was not suppressed in Russo-Soviet teachings, it was not downplayed either. In the Ukrainian national narrative, on the other hand, the influence of the sibling peoples' on each other's identity has been minimized, especially since the Revolution of Dignity of 2014, an event that I'll ease my way up to. In this foreword my priority is to address the historical events that are undoubtedly true, and the fallacies that have been used to twist those events to advance certain agendas.

The subjects of territory and language are heavily intertwined; therefore, I will address them together, with as much chronological simplicity as the wannabe scholar in me will allow. It is also important to note that when I am referring to the peoples that make up the Easter Slav group (Russia, Ukraine, and Belarus), that I am referring to the Ukrainians east of the Chmelnitskaya/Chmelnitskiy Oblast (an 'oblast' is pretty much an administrative region or a province), and Russians west of the Urals. This is a very rough demographical estimate, but it is adequate enough to paint a picture generalizing the root ethnic group, I will explain this in further detail later on.

The Ukrainian nationalistic ideology believes that the Ukrainian language outdates modern Russian, due to Kiev being the elder of the two cities (Kiev and Moscow are often used to address their respective countries). Russo-enthusiasts, on the other hand, believe that modern Ukrainian is just old Russian that was diluted with Polish. The latter theory is more accurate in account with the era of the Kievan and Ancient Rus. The truth is that the people that lived there spoke the successor to the

Ancient Slavic and Proto Slavic languages; Ancient Russian. The reason that the language name ended up being 'Russian' is because the 'Rus' eventually overtook the 'Kiev', as Kiev served as an adjective in the name. The word 'Rus' originated from the Ancient Scandinavian word 'Ruotsi', which roughly meant 'those who row' in reference to the Vikings that settled and organized the modern-day Northwestern Russian and Baltic lands. With time the term was coined by the Ruriks and eventually all the city states settled on the name. The Kievan Rus' was Baptized in the year 988 and Orthodox Christianity has been the main religion of the Eastern Slavs since, serving as an obvious split with the predominantly Catholic Western Slavs (Poles, Czechs, etc.).

Language and identity fractured around 1240, when forces of the Mongol-Tatar and Central Asian peoples, known as the Golden Horde, began advancing their conquest onto the Rus' Lands. The Horde peaked in area in the early 1300s, with its western conquest encompassing nearly all of modern Ukraine, Belarus and Western Russian lands, even reaching Poland and butting heads with the Holy Roman Empire. Citizens of the Rus' lived under the Rus' Vassal of the Golden Horde, a time of great occupation and deprivation, however it is important to note that many of the Slavs living under the Mongols benefited from the new government. Collaboration and treason were not uncommon, as with every armed conflict with prolonged durations of occupation. In 1380, after a long-planned battle to get their lands back, forces led by a unity of Rus' dukes fought with the Horde's forces at the Battle of Kulikovo. While losses were great for both sides, and the battle did not immediately end the occupation, it signaled the beginning of the Horde's downfall. From this battle, came the rise of Moscow, the vassal state that did not gain much power in the century since its origin (mid-1200s), until after the battle.

The Grand Duchy of Moscow, or Moscovite Rus', quickly replaced its predecessor. The two headed eagle, the symbol that represented the Russian Empire and today's federation, came from Moscow, replacing the (Ukrainian) trident. Yes, the trident representing the Ukrainian Coat of Arms originated from the Ancient Rus' and is a significantly older symbol than the Russian two headed eagle. The Great Stand at the Ugra River of 1480 was the victory that symbolized the end of the Horde's control over Rus' Lands. It took another seven decades of turbulent and short-term rule by various factions until the Rus' lands united once again into the new Tsardom of Russia. During these years, new foes, who themselves fought the Mongol-Tatars, expanded their own conquest into the Rus'. By 1526, Poles and Lithuanians, later united into one Commonwealth of Poland and Lithuania, controlled majority of modern-day Ukraine's territory, significantly farther east then Kiev, almost reaching the Caucasus in the south! Eventually they were pushed back, and the Tsardom of Russia ruled consistently within the borderlines I described earlier; east of the Chmelnitskaya/Chmelnitskiy Oblast, but to dumb it down even farther, a little west of Kiev and all the way east with the continuous expansion into modern day Asiatic Russia.

This is perhaps the most influential part of Eastern Slavic history, and the origin of today's cultural divide between Russians and Ukrainians.

Centuries under Mongol-Tatar occupation, as well as centuries of conquering and reconquering of the western Rus' lands created differentiating identities. Modern day Russians are significantly more mixed with Mongol, Tatar and Central Asian blood than Ukrainians are, as they lived longer under occupation and were geographically closer to the heart of the Horde's empire. Ukrainians living in the central and eastern oblasts are more consistently of the same blood as Western Russians, perhaps the most 'clean' blood when it comes to those peoples that lived in the Kievan and Ancient Rus'. Western Ukrainians are mostly of Polish blood, with hints of Hungarian, Lithuanian and Slovak due to centuries of warfare, migration, and conquest.

This is the bottom-line of the cultural divide. As Boris Nemtsov, a great opposer of the Putin regime and a strong supporter of liberal reforms in Russia who was assassinated in 2015, once said in a 2008 interview with Ukraine's Dmitry Gordon,

"I can explain to you the difference between Russia and Ukraine... you were part of the empire but never the centre, which is why you have way less of this bullshit attitude of great autocracy and servility than we do. Reason number two, you don't have the Caucasus and the Muslim factor... which leads into my third point, if you ask Ukraine if Ukraine is a European country, Ukraine will answer yes. You for yourselves have decided that you're a Christian country, that you are a fully European country without major internal conflicts of multi-nationality.

In Russia, not only geographically but mentally, there isn't a general an agreement on these questions."

This is also the origin of the linguistic divide. It was only in the 16th century that the first real cases of the modern Ukrainian language surfaced, after years of living under Polish-Lithuanian rule. An interesting example that perfectly explains this controversial and touchy subject was in the early 90s when Leonid Kravchuk, the first president of Ukraine, was trying to register the Ukrainian language in the diplomatic community. He was given a response that said roughly the following,

'Ukrainian language is not an independent language, it is a language comprised of 70% Russian, 12% Romanian, 12% Polish, with the rest being a Central European mixture. Ukrainian is nothing more than a patois; a unique dialect.'

While this anecdote may seem politically biased, it serves as a good example of how the Ukrainian language was treated upon the dissolution of the Soviet Union, before the three decades have passed and created the new Ukrainian identity with at times illusory details about its origin. It is also important to note that the modern-day Russian and Ukrainian languages only share about 60% similarity with each other.

Throughout 18th and 19th centuries, suppression of the Ukrainian language became officially aligned with the monarchial doctrines of the Russian and Austro-Hungarian Empires, including the occupied Polish lands, split by the two empires at the time. Czar Nicholai II allegedly even said,

"There is no Ukrainian language, just illiterate peasants speaking Little Russian."

Successfully continuing his predecessors' repressive linguistic policies of *Russifying* the kingdom. By the turn of the century, it was borderline forbidden to speak Ukrainian in the empire. Monarchial persecution and suppression of the Ukrainian language dealt a huge blow to the speaking population that took all of the twentieth century to re-teach and recover.

After the Russian Tsardom came the Russian Empire, the state that lasted until 1917 when the Russian Revolution overthrew the monarchy. Over the centuries leading up to the First World War the borders shifted with the continuous wars the empire would partake in. By 1914, prior to the Great War breaking out, the Russian Empire expanded far west, engulfing almost of modern-day Poland's territory. The empire crumbled

12

in 1917, with two revolutions setting the country into chaos. By November 15th the

Bolsheviks took Moscow and the empire had ceased to exist. Five days later the Ukrainian Republic was proclaimed; marking the first time in the nation's history that it truly became independent, but not for long.

On December 15th, 1917, Vladimir Lenin, in order to pull Russia out of the war, signed an armistice with the Central Powers, which led to the Treaty of Brets Litovsk (ratified on the March 6th). This treaty was comprised of Soviet Russia ceding Ukraine, Poland and other territories to the German Empire. With the Central Powers losing the war, Ukraine's independence became a reality.

During the Russian Civil War (1918-1922), Ukraine consisted of different warring factions. Besides those fighting for the White and Red Forces, many fought for their own visions, including anarchists led by the famous Batko Mahno (a personal hero of mine, mainly due to his acceptance and inclusion of Jews, which was anomalous at the time), and Ukrainian Peoples' Army, led by Simeon Petlyura, as well as others. It is important to note that during the civil war, pogroms (an intentional massacre of Jews), a subject that deserves its own section, were rampant across Ukraine and most of the atrocities were committed by the Ukrainian Peoples' Army. The Russian Civil War throughout Ukrainian lands is a very dense and massive subject of its own. The Bolsheviks triumphed across the former empire's lands and all resistance forces were crushed. The Ukrainian Socialist Soviet Republic was proclaimed in 1919, and officially joined the USSR on December 30th of 1922.

During the two decades leading up the Second World War, the most infamous event that took place in Ukraine was the *Holodomor.* While some historians claim that tragedy was caused by the Kremlin's miscalculation with collectivization of agriculture, most scholars agree that the famine was intentional, and its purpose was to starve the Ukrainian people into submission to the Soviet government. The Holodomor started in 1932 (my grandfather was born in the Vinitskaya Oblast in 1933), and lasted almost two years and resulted in the deaths of millions of Ukrainians. The Holodomor is often considered a genocide. What I personally find interesting is how the Holodomor is portrayed as Russia's fault, and how the Soviet Union's faults are portrayed as synonymous with Russia. It is important to never forget, for accurate historical analysis, that Soviet Union and Russia were not the same country. Yes, it is true that the

Russian Soviet Federative Socialist Republic was the supreme republic of the union, but to say that it was Russian in the sense of ethnicity and nationality would be an ambiguous statement. After all, in 1933, four of the eight incumbents of the highest federal governmental positions weren't even Russian. Two were from Ukraine, including the famous Marshall of the Soviet Union, Kliment Varashilov, who was born in Bakhmut, where currently, as I am writing this, fierce fighting is going on. That list doesn't even include Lavrentiy Beria, the head of the NKVD, the KGB's (even more) evil predecessor, who was an ethnic Georgian, just like the supreme commander Joseph Stalin. A very convenient detail to forget when rallying the world against your oppressor.

Fast forward six years. It is 1939, the Soviet Union and Nazi Germany have signed the Molotov-Ribbentrop Non-Aggression Pact and successfully invaded, and consequently split Poland in two. A large chunk of former (constantly disputed and fought over throughout the centuries) Russian Empire's (hence Ukrainian) territory was once again under 'Russian' rule, this time under the communist regime. Lwow (Lvov or Lviv) was once again a Polish city under Eastern Slavic occupation.

The pact didn't last long, and at four in the morning on June 22nd of 1941, Hitler betrayed Stalin and launched Operation Barbarossa; the invasion of the Soviet Union. By October 12th, all of Soviet Ukraine was under Axis occupation, it took less than four months. Some local factors contributing to Germany's speedy success was that not all Ukrainians were patriots of the Soviet regime, especially after the horrors of the 30s. Many Ukrainians saw the advancing Axis troops as liberators, and did not resist, many even immediately volunteering to aid and fight for the Reich. Ukrainians fighters that didn't retain their loyalty to the Red Army or join the Axis forces joined the newly recreated Ukrainian Insurgent Army (The UPA), which fought the Reds and collaborated heavily with the Nazis throughout the beginning and final years of the war. During this time, the infamous Stepan Bandera rose to fame as one of the leaders of the Ukrainian Insurgent Army.

Germany capitulated in May of 1945, but the UPA continued its fight even though Bandera fled to Germany. Using guerrilla warfare tactics against the victorious Red Army until 1956, hiding out in the Western Ukrainian forests until they were actively hunted down and either captured or exterminated by the regime's forces. Stepan Bandera was assassinated by KGB agents in Western Germany in 1959, but his spirit lived on and has often been used as a symbol of Ukrainian resistance ever since, often completely ignoring his collusion with Nazis and the horrors that he himself along with his forces has perpetrated, massacring hundreds of thousands of Jews as well as thousands of ethnic Poles. It is important to mention that the UPA did have a falling out with the Germans at some point in the war, leading to dozens of engagements and even arresting Bandera (whose power was seen as a legitimate threat to the Reich) in 1941 and sending him to a concentration camp, but was released in 1944 as Germany needed all the help it could get against the advancing Reds, reigniting the shaky alliance. The fall out between the Nazis and the UPA did not stop the insurgents targeting and massacring Jews and Poles, which shows that these genocidal ambitions were shared between the two factions and was not exclusive to the Reich with the UPA merely 'collaborating'. Also, it was from the UPA that the famous motto *Slava Ukraini* (Glory to Ukraine) and the marching song *Oi U Luzi Chervona Kolina* (Red Viburnum in the Meadow) originated. Both of which have been used extensively since. The term 'Bandervites' has been used derogatorily since the war to categorize nationalistic Ukrainians.

There was not much action in post war Soviet Ukraine. Once the insurgency was crushed there was not much of an organized resistance except for the occasional assassination of local Communist Party officials. The USSR reclaimed the territories Lenin ceded during the First World War, and Eastern Bloc went into full effect. In 1954, the leader of the Soviet Union, Nikita Kruschev issued an order transferring the Crimean Oblast into the Ukrainian Soviet Republic from the Federative Russian Republic. Historians are still disputing the reason as to why he made such a decision, but that does not change the fact that at the time it made absolutely no difference which republic Crimea was part of, as every republic was just a part of the USSR. In 1991, the Soviet Union ceased to exist, and on the 24th of August the Ukrainian Soviet Socialist Republic declared its independence from the Union, and Ukraine, for once without any antecedents in its name, was born.

Some topics that I did not cover in chronological order include the Cossacks, territorial titles, and Anti-Semitism.

Since the start of the invasion, I have noticed that the Cossacks have been used extensively as an ancestral Ukrainian symbol. This is not entirely accurate, and this is coming from a man whose birth name literally derives from the Ukrainian Cossacks of the Zaporozhia Region. The Cossacks were not exclusive to the modern-day Ukrainian territory. The Cossacks had their named derived from an old Central Asian Turkic language, which is ironic in the Ukrainian peoples' attempt to distance themselves from their Central Asiatic ancestors and kinsfolk. The term in the original language is believed to have meant 'free person', which is logical and consistent with the nomadic and warrior lifestyle. Cossacks evolved and lived all across the Rus' and its successor, from the Ukrainian steppes to the mountains of the Caucasus's to the taigas of Siberia. Claiming the Cossack heritage as purely of Ukrainian culture is incorrect.

I have also not mentioned that throughout the imperial centuries Ukraine was split into two governorates.

Malorossya, translating to literal 'Little Russia' was the northern half of Ukraine starting in the 14th century.

Novorossiya, translating to literal 'New Russia' was the southern half of Ukraine starting in the 18th century.

Both of these titles lasted until the Bolshevik takeover when Ukraine was united into one official republic under the Soviet Regime.

On top of those two, literally, lay *Belarusya,* translating to 'White Russia'.

Quite hard to miss this pattern. One may say that this is a perfect example of imperialistic oppression. But is it really oppression if it is literally how the area and people were referred to and identified as for the vast majority of the peoples' history?

The topic of Anti-Semitism and the Holocaust is extremely personal to me; therefore, I will simplify and cover the subject in relation to the main topic; the history of Ukraine.

Anti-Semitism is a cancer that has plagued our planet since the days of The Old Testament. Very few places in the world where Jews have not been abused and persecuted for the sole reason that they were Jews. The Russian Empire was no exception. The Jewry in the empire was the largest in the world, and experienced horrendous persecution throughout the centuries. Anti-Semitism in Ukraine was almost always rampant and was by far the worst out of all the empire's territories. However, it is important to include the fact that there were more Jews living in the Ukrainian lands than in Russia. Hundreds of thousands were killed throughout the centuries in Pogroms, an organized massacre of Jews, and during World War Two over a million and a half of the two million Jews living in Soviet Ukraine were killed. That means that about one in every four Jews that was killed in the Holocaust died in Ukraine, and don't let simplified history fool you, hundreds of thousands were killed at the hands of local Ukrainian collaborators. It is hard to get exact statistics of the perpetrators in relation to the total amount of murders, but through collection of anecdotal and specific, case by case evidence we can paint ourselves a rough picture. In one of the most infamous massacres of the war, just outside of Kiev in Babiy Yar, over 33 thousand Jews were executed in just two days. Most of the executioners were local collaborators, not Germans...

***

In my family the word Holocaust was not foreign. The horrors of this racism and xenophobia fueled genocide did not pass over my ancestors. My grandparents were children in Western Soviet Ukraine when the Germans invaded, grandpa was eight and grandma was three. My grandfather's family could not evacuate in time like my grandmother's had and were forced to remain in an enclosed 'ghetto'. My grandfather survived the war and is now a published author living in the United States. Within his literary works he includes multiple accounts of life in the occupied territories during the Holocaust, with stories about how the local populace, people that he and his family lived with in peace for years, suddenly began participating in horrendous, evil acts. One story that would put an average American history teacher in a stupor follows. During another mass execution in his area, where dozens of Jewish elderly, women and children were shot into a mass grave, only one of the executioners was a German, a soldier left in charge as the Wehrmacht continued their advance east.

While his story may be anecdotal, it connects with a theme that thousands of others share, painting a common picture of the significance of Ukrainian perpetrators of the genocide we now know as the Holocaust.

***

Independence was not easy for the brand-new nation. The 90s were turbulent years for all the members of the Commonwealth of Independent States, the organization created to retain the unity and cooperation of the former Soviet republics. 12 of the 15 republics joined, with the three Baltic states declining. Many experienced civil wars, as well as the Central Asiatic republics dealing with the consequences of the Soviet Afghan War and the newly founded Taliban forces engaging in border skirmishes. Transitioning to free market economies (allegedly) after almost a century of controlled economies was not easy for the newly independent states.

In 1994, Ukraine, encouraged by the United States, United Kingdom, and the Russian Federation, destroyed the nuclear weapons it had retained on its territories after the breakup of the union. This is arguably the first major mistake that Ukraine made in relation to securing its sovereignty, a mistake heavily sponsored and motivated by the West. The 2000s were also full of internal strife in the country, with political factions clashing on multiple occasions.

For the most relevant events in relation to the ongoing armed conflict I will be focusing on the rift between Russia and Ukraine, cultural as well as political. While still part of the union, the Ukrainian Soviet Republic signed the 'Law of the Languages', which established Ukrainian as the official state language, a position that no language held prior. The law also included protection for the use of Russian and other minority languages. In 1996, the *Verhovna Rada* (Ukraine's Parliament) signed the law into the state's new official constitution.

Throughout the 2000s, the rift between the sides continued growing, with Western and Eastern Ukraine's differences showing their colours. The event that began heating the kettle to the boiling point was in 2012, when members of the *Verhovna Rada* introduced and passed a language bill that would allow Russian and other minority languages to be officially used in government institutions (courts, schools, etc.) in regions of the country where the minority population of given language exceeded ten percent. `The bill, with the official title being *On the Principles of the State Language Policy*, was signed into law in August by President Viktor Yanukovych, who was seen by many as Kremlin's puppet for his preference of not distancing his politics too far from Moscow, which ultimately led to his downfall. The bill had a real basis, after all, over thirty percent of the country spoke Russian as their main language with much of Ukraine being fluent in the language as well. A large proportion of citizens felt like their cultural and linguistic rights were heavily encroached on by their western countrymen.

The kettle reached a boiling point in November of 2013 when Yanukovych rejected a much-awaited agreement with the European Union, hence showing his discontent with shifting away from the Kremlin's hands. This sparked the Maidan Uprising, fighting ensued in the streets of Kiev, with protests into riots. Even the chamber of parliament broke out into a brawl, with members fist fighting over their political views. By March of next year Yanukovych was ousted and fled the country for Russia's safe haven. This period is now known as the Revolution of Dignity.

On February 20th, 2014, Russian troops secretly began the annexation of Crimea. While the official reason for the annexation was to protect the Russian population of the peninsula, the strategic and not as voiced reason was to secure the Black Sea Fleet, which Russia had stationed in Crimea since the dissolution of the Soviet Union (The Russian Federation retained majority of the Soviet fleet and leased the Sevastopol port from Ukraine).

This marked the beginning of the Russo-Ukrainian War, which was a proxy war between the Russian Federation and NATO up until this year's invasion, when it turned into a full-scale conflict, disregarding the Kremlin's insistence on the technicality that they are conducting a 'Special Military Operation' never declaring war.

Just as we, the United States, haven't officially declared war since World War Two.

Just like our involvement in Vietnam, Iraq, and Afghanistan...
same as Russia's in Ukraine...
It is damned war, that's for sure.

Discontent with the newly formed government in Ukraine caused great discontent in the southern and eastern regions. Separatist groups quickly emerged in the Donetsk, Lughansk, Kharkov, and Odessa Oblasts, the Kremlin saw this and quickly began expressing its support for the dissidents. The separatists lost their spark in Kharkov and Odessa, and the regime loyalists retained control over the Oblasts. The proxy war was in full effect, with Russia initially insisting that it was not involved in the fighting, even though Federation personnel were exposed in a wide variety of positions, from combat advisors to front line fighters. After it became obvious that Russian troops were directly involved in fighting, the Kremlin scaled back the denying of the allegations of involvement.

The Lughansk and Donetsk Oblasts declared their independence, naming themselves respectfully as the Lughansk and Donetsk Peoples' Republics, running Kremlin sponsored referendums where the alleged majority vote was to cede from Ukraine. Crimea also had a referendum, but the outcome was to join Russia, not seek independence. We may never know the legitimacy of these referendums. It is easy to say that they were fake and fraudulent, but from personal connections and utilization of critically thinking, I tend to believe that majority of the citizens in those three regions did in fact vote to leave Ukraine. After all, many of the citizens believed a full-scale war was coming, and in 2014 there was a crystal-clear idea of who the winner of that war would be.

Afterwards, a negotiation took place, agreements were drawn up, seize fires declared. All of these were failed as all parties violated the seize fires. These are known as the 'Minsk Accords', and they obviously did not work out. On February 15th, the Kremlin officially recognized the LNR and DNR, and fighting between the two factions increased significantly. In the early hours of the 24th of February, Putin addressed his citizens on his decision to conduct the 'Special Military Operation' on the territory of Ukraine. His stated goals were to demilitarize and 'de-nazify' Ukraine, while ensuring the protection of the people of Donbass (historically what the LNR and DNR areas are known as). What started next is ongoing as we are producing this book, and the end does not appear to be in sight.

***

This preface consisted of a relatively brief summarization of Ukraine's history. Hopefully, it was detailed enough to paint a decent picture on the country's past, its relationship with its neighbors, and the events leading up to this conflict. I understand that many of you reading this have been subjected by western media clickbait, as a result refusing to even consider a different viewpoint in this conflict, but even as a rookie journalist I believe it is of outmost importance to step in other peoples' shoes, even if the shoes belong to Vladimir Putin. I spent a decent chunk of my childhood in Russia, had great holidays and trips to Ukraine, seeing the impoverished and disease ridding conditions that my grandfather's lived in. To me this is soul shattering. I have friends and family on both sides of the conflict.

Millions of formers Soviets, including the diaspora as well as those who stayed, view this conflict as a civil war, myself included. Even though, by definition, this conflict falls under the category of an 'undeclared war between two sovereign nations', some people still see it as a civil war since literal friends and family are fighting each other. Many of us see it as a delayed civil war across border lines that are a mere three decades old. A civil war delayed by the relatively peaceful and, to an extent, unexpected dissolution of the USSR.

I also ask of you, as a reader, and as an appreciator of history to consider all factors leading up to this invasion. It is easy to point your fingers at one man, and believe me, I am not a Putin apologist. I do not hide my beliefs, I was a supporter of Crimea's annexation, as well as a supporter of Donbass's independence, but that does not make me a Kremlin kook. Millions of people share these opinions with me while not being fans of Putin. While the final button was pushed by Vladimir, it is crucial to not forget that NATO's expansion east, as well as Kiev's reluctance to come to an agreement in order to prevent this awful development. Imagine being an American citizen, starring across the Niagara or Rio Grande, and seeing Russian tanks conducting military training, would you feel like the aggressor? That is me putting you in the shoes of Russian villagers starring across the border at their Baltic neighbors. NATO's encroachment on Russia's sovereignty was very real and looking at it from a neutral perspective it is very difficult to not take that into account.

I also believe Kiev did not commit enough to prevent the Kremlin from getting away with the brainwashing of Russia's populace, convincing them that Ukraine is run by a bunch of Neo-Nazis. Kiev also did not put enough effort in suppressing Bandera era rhetoric, who quickly rose back to popularity after the revolution in 2014. The 2015 'Decommunization Law', which was really a 'de-Russfication' and white washing of Soviet Ukrainian history, further aided the Kremlin's agenda. Russian language was swiftly and carefully removed from key public institutions, starting with railroad transport and airports. In 2017, an education law was passed that set all public secondary education to be taught in Ukrainian, pretty much banning Russian as the educator's main language. These legislations were passed on the national level, region legislation was free to go much farther, the Oblast of Lvov banned Russian cultural products in 2018, including books and films. The Hungarian speaking minority in Southwestern Ukraine was also affected by the passing of this law, which significantly deteriorated the friendly relations between Hungary and Ukraine. This development proved to be significant as Hungary has been fairly reluctant on supporting Ukraine since the invasion in February, not sending any of its weapons to aid Kiev in its fight against Moscow.

President Zelensky's election gave the people hope for better change, and I truly admire him and his cabinet! He was a brilliant comedian who I personally watched prior to his political stunt, but that does not take away from the fact that he's obligated to give in to certain Western demands, a price to pay when seeking an uneven partnership. Zelensky turned out to be quite an authoritative ruler who expanded executive power even farther than it was before, borderline outlawing his opposition. Regardless, he turned out to be a great war time leader, not bailing when the threat was near as well as rallying the West against the invader. Him being a Jew also significantly undermined Putin's rally against hyperbolic Ukrainian neo- Nazism. Even though Ukraine has one of the worst Anti-Semitic histories in the world, electing a Jew for president definitely shows progress in the right direction. However, it does not mean that there isn't any Anti- Semitism or neo-Nazism present in modern day Ukraine at all, after all, the election of President Obama didn't mean all of America's racists were suddenly gone... perhaps, the other candidate was just too weak of a choice, just food for thought.

This war is a proxy war between the West and the Russian Federation. While Ukraine's stand is admirable and incredibly impressive, it is crucial to remember the amount of military aid the West has poured into the conflict, using Ukrainian forces to fight their *New Cold War.*

Perhaps, this war has been brewing for much longer than thirty years. Perhaps it is a cultural clash that has been brewing for much longer. The very name of the country suggests this, as 'Ukraina' means two different things in the two respective languages. The Ukrainian definition of the term is believed to have started around the 1930s.

At the edge in Russian, referring to the territory as the edge of the empire:
(U)-(Kraina)
(At)- (the edge)

And

Country, or state in Ukrainian:

(U/V)-(Kraina)

(In)-(Country)
(The U and V are actually interchangeable as both letters mean 'in', the result being 'in the country' either way.

I feel compelled to reiterate, this war has been absolutely heart breaking. Growing up over there, both countries were the same to me. Crossing the borders was a fairly meaningless event. Growing up in a post-Soviet mindset of the 2000s, both nations seemed pretty much as one whole, so when I refer to Russia and Ukraine as the motherland, I truly mean both. My motherland is burning, and it is has not been easy being in contact with both sides and having friends and family on both sides. My role as a self-proclaimed journalist has made this dilemma significantly simpler, as I treat the interactions and interviews as work, minimizing the emotional attachment, all the while retaining the bias that lays deep in my subconscious. How can it not? We as humans often develop biases on instinct, a natural response. Growing up in Western Ukraine my mother involuntarily participated in regular games of *Cossacks and Jews,* an equivalent of *Cowboys and Indians* in the States, on her way to school. Often getting physically assaulted in the process, one time she got bashed in the head with a rock, the scar on her scalp remains even though decades have passed. How can I as a boy, and later as a man, simply shove this knowledge under the rug? I cannot.

I have had the absolute honour working with both sides, relatives, friends new and prior, new colleagues and associates made along the way as well. Could not think of a better to end this foreword as to state the following,

Most reasonable people will agree that Ukraine is a sovereign nation, with a right to self-determination. Question posed is, where does Ukraine start? And where does it end?

Ilya Rudyak, Co-Author

Илья Рудяк, Соавтор

Ілля Рудяк, Співавтор

The following pages are the results of these historical events.

Every witness and participant of war has a story, and every story deserves to be told.

2014 - 2021

Ukrainian Soldier
51st Guards Mechanized Brigade
Battle of Ilovaisk. 2014

Fighting men in cities and streets is stressful. The adding of armored cars and tanks such as IFV's and T-72B's is another thing. In the fighting for Ilovaisk, we lost hundreds of soldiers. During the fighting, we were surrounded completely that is a helpless feeling. I have read many books, and for moments it felt reality was we were to be the German 6th Army fighting at Stalingrad. Surrounded. Destroyed and beaten to nothing.

They even flew Ukrainian flag to trick us. All of our units agreed to use tape on arms as insignia to identify each other. Green, red or white. The Russians used our insignia too. White tape.

Our commanders and the separatists and Russians made a deal. We could leave the city and be unharassed. Our lives could be spared, we just had to go. So, we went. They left a path for us to go.

I don't know what happened, but they fired at us still! Wounded and dead men were coming with us, and they still fired. Men in the front were carrying white flags. By the end, over 350 men had died and were resting with God or whoever else they prayed to during those hours.

"Krusader"
Western Volunteer - Ukrainian Marines
Svitlodarsk sector. 2017

I arrived in Ukraine in 2017 to fight with the Georgian National Legion on the Svitlodarsk sector. During my first month on position "олені" Two of my comrades were gravely wounded by a sniper and one more would be KIA with a direct shot to the head. Fire fights where not only daily but would happen around the clock.

Our worst fear was shelling. As soon as our sector started to get smashed up by artillery the mood changed. Our position was only 150 meters away from the enemy and partially hidden in the wood line we shared.

Nighttime guard duty was tense with the constant threat of an enemy patrol sneaking up on us to do us in during our sleep. After the first two months I became hardened by the combat. The firefights started to not to phase me and my adrenaline all but disappeared. Later in I would lose two more friends to a mortar attack that destroyed half our position. This position was no "Hilton" it had no running water, no electricity, the roof above our head made up of wooden logs leaked snow onto our sleeping bags. The winter was brutal and fighting more.

I would go on to becoming the position commander and even the platoon leader of the foreign legion. Then in 2019 I would enlist in the Ukrainian Marines and go onto do a 13-month deployment on the Mariupol sector. This was only the beginning and first phase of my war in Donbass and the war against the Russian Federation.

"Carlo"
British Army veteran from Northern Ireland.
Donbas 2015-17.

I arrived in Kyiv early 2015 I had two options to fight in Donbas one with the Azov Battalion and one with the Right Sector 'volunteer guard' I opted for right sector as I was told they had an abundance of javelin missiles which I later found out to be an exaggeration. I took the 7-hour night train to Krasnoarmisk near Donetsk City and was met with RS fighters who took me to their permanent base.

After getting my kit checked and being ran through some basic weapon handling skills, I was sent off with a group of other foreigners to a village called Adiivka. The battle was happening on the outskirts in the forest. Trench warfare. At that time 2015 to 17 it was only us and some other volunteer battalions fighting in the east. The Ukrainian Army and Marines just sat about and drank from my experiences of them.

I fought under 'Santa' to begin with and then 'Da Vinci' when Santa left us. We never had the world's media supporting us then, or the weapons. Just a large group of Ukrainians not willing to be pushed about by its bullying neighbor and small group of westerner's sick of seeing the west's weakness towards Russia.

Ukrainian Soldier
Svitlodarsk Frontline Trenches
January 2022

I am a history teacher serving in the army of Ukraine. I must be truthful. Some moments are very exciting for me. My favorite time to learn and teach is the First World War. Living in trenches now is such a similar time. We live much as the soldiers of France and Germany and England did. At night, I sleep in a dugout underground. I have my small bed and some books. During the day we stand watch and shovel snow away. The ground becomes mud and cold. I look at my feet and think that millions of men were here before I was. (In WW1)

Danger is always close. We keep our heads below the parapet and listen for mortars in the distance. Our snipers sometimes lie still near us, and we can hear them work. We have gotten many new things from our friends in Europe. I received a new spade and pants for the snow yesterday. The small things help us here. I must confess that it is scary, even though it is exciting. I know how World War One started. Many men in the army in 1914 were with God in 1918. It is scary knowing history and finding I am in similar situations.

Art by João "J-Dot" Alves

Russian Soldier
Russian – Ukrainian Border
January 2022

     I don't know why we are here. (Ukrainian border) We were moved here weeks ago and have just been sitting. The Ukrainian's say we are going to war soon supposedly. I know several will read this. I don't want to fight you. Several units here do want a fight, but most don't. Why should we fight and kill? What is the point? We should not be fighting.

     The West fears us. I know this. But we are not conquerors anymore. Russian soldiers want peace, not war. NATO treats us like Soviets. We are Russians. If this conflict happens, it was not our (the soldiers) choice for it to happen. Most of us here are good boys. We have families and would like to return home. God be with all of us.

Ukrainian Soldier
Donbas Frontline
January 2022

(In response to the Russian soldier)

     We do not seek conflict either. Many months now we have lived in trenches. In the rain, snow, sunshine and dark. This is our home. My family has lived and bled in this ground since the Mongols. If necessary, my blood will wet it also. We are ready for you. Are you ready? You know I want to go home? I miss my home and my family. You stay over there. We stay over here. We do not want you here. Go home and maybe we can be friends someday. We should only fight in the Olympics. As well. Thank you for the drone. Ha ha.

Ukrainian Soldier
Donbas Frontline
January 2022

     Russian men. We are waiting for you. We are dug in with clean weapons. Machine guns, and artillery. If you cross over the border, we are waiting for you. We have trained for this moment. I will admit, I am frightened to fight, but we, are ready. I am new here. I have never fought. The others have more experience. Some have taken lives; others have seen men die. They said sometimes separatists are so close you can hear them talk in the trenches.

I don't want to kill any of you. We want to be in peace and go back to our homes. I question if you'd like the same? I've been here in the trench for weeks. My children's picture hangs next to my bunk. I want to see them but will die for them if I must. Russian men. We are waiting for you. I hope you don't, but if you do, we are waiting for you.

Aiden Aslin, @CossackGundi
Western Volunteer - Ukrainian Marine
Donbas Frontline/Mariupol
January 2022

It's hard to tell if this is actually going to happen and Russia will invade. For the past month and a half, the political atmosphere between the West and the Russian government has only gone downhill without any real outcome or direction. It's starting to look like it might happen. If the worst happens, it's going to be a very violent and brutal fight. The frontline units in Donbas and Luhansk will be hit hardest if we think logically about it.

I'm typing this from a trench myself and I don't want it to happen. More war won't solve anything and create more hatred. We had the same feeling in Syria and then eventually Turkey invaded. And as I'm aware I do have Russian observers so I figure I should clarify my stance since it's the norm. I don't hate you or your family nor do I want to fight you. You have a family same as me and everyone else.

I'm pretty sure if we were in a pub we would probably drink, politics aside. If we cross paths on the battlefield, then we will do what we were tasked with doing, which for me is Defending Ukraine and for you attacking Ukraine.

Ukrainian Soldier
Frontline
January 2022

Before this I was a schoolteacher. I teach history to children. In 2014 I saw destruction in Donbas, and I knew history would repeat. I joined the Army of Ukraine in 2018 to do my duty. We have just come from the front positions for scheduled rest but can return any moment. We spend our days digging deep and better defenses. The experienced soldiers say, "These holes will not protect us from the sky." but still our minds are in good shape.

Separatists can be seen through binoculars. Soon, the Russians will replace them, I think. I know my rifle as well as I know my old history books. At night in the defenses, I speak to other soldiers. I tell them all the great battles in the past where little forces defeated big ones. We are all praying to go home. I want to teach again. If the war gets worse, and the Russians stand where I stand now, I don't think I'll be a teacher. I don't think I'll be anything.

Ukrainian Soldier
79th Air Assault Brigade
Frontline
February 20th

Tonight, we were told the Russians crossed over the border of Ukraine controlled by separatists. We do not know what is going to happen here. Our weapons are loaded, our positions are ready, and we are waiting. Orders right this moment are to wait.

The eyes (of the world) are on us now. It feels like a moment history is about to be made. The future? I'm not sure. I know no matter what outcome; many people will die. Truthfully, I am tired of wondering. I want it to happen, or to just end. I don't want to be unaware any longer. The waiting is the most difficult part. It makes me sick.

But I am ready. I am ready to fight. Ready to die. Ready to defend our homes. I just do not want to wait any longer. God be with all the soldiers of Ukraine.

Russian Soldier
Logistics Unit
Ukrainian – Russian Border
February 22nd

I said goodbye to them (his friends) last night as they left. (Across the border) I will not accompany them for medical reasons. I remind myself this feels like when my mother said goodbye when I left for the army 4 years ago. She said, 'Be safe. Have an adventure and then come home. You are needed here deeply.'

I said those same words to my friends. 'Be safe. Have an adventure and I'll see you soon.'

I don't know what is going on around here. Most of the tanks and vehicles have left, and I am with a supply truck now sitting with other sick soldiers or ones who have injuries. They say when I am better, I will rejoin them. (His unit)

Many of the countries of the world must be watching what is happening here. I am just a soldier. I do not know what is happening or what is going on or what might happen. Some soldiers have family from Ukraine and another I know has a grandmother in Kiev. Everywhere is chaos, my hands are cold, and my throat is sore to swallow with a temperature.

Ukrainian Soldier
Frontline
February 23rd

Last night I went to sleep and woke up being shaken. 'Wake up. The Russians are on their way.' I didn't believe him. I thought it was trash news and not to be believed. So much the last few days has happened. He showed me his phone and I saw on the news before our commander told us. 'We are being activated. Get ready.' And so, we did. Our drills to prepare we have rehearsed over and over were not drills anymore.

We ran to fetch our rifles and to stand ready. 'We will hold positions here as reserve in a deep defense in case it escalates.' I heard artillery fire away from us. Russian artillery was shooting. This brought memories of earlier battles back. We do not distinguish from Russians and separatists anymore; they are all the same.

My sergeant was at the airport, same as me. (Battle of Donetsk Airport, 2014) and has seen combat before. I have as well. But I suspect I will again soon. We get in a Gaz-66 toward the front. My sergeant is sitting across from me. He says, 'Every man dies someday.' I did not like this statement. I do not want to die, but I will fight if I have to.

Today we drove past civilians waving to us. They call out 'Good luck!' 'Glory to Ukraine!' as we drive past. Luck will not be enough. We must count on our training.

Dymtrus
Ukrainian Civilian
February 23rd

My brother was killed at the Donetsk airport in 2014. My big brother. I was 11 when he was killed. I am 19 now and I will join the army today. My mother asked me to not go, and my father said nothing. Last week I said, 'Enough time has been wasted. I must join the army. I cannot stay home while men like my brother suffer.' My mother cried and said to stay. My father as I said, did not say anything. He gave me a hug and I felt he knew I couldn't be turned from this.

My family is unique. Every war our country has been in someone has died in our family. I am afraid, but I know it is right. Boys younger than me are fighting now. Why shouldn't I? I can do it too. I know I can. I am strong and ready to endure. I worry for my mother. My father has a strong mind and heart. My mother I hope does not have to carry anymore sadness. I will do what I must and hope she can accept my action to join.

Week One: Feb 24 – March 2

Hadeon
Ukrainian Civilian
Kyiv
February 24th

This is madness! Why! Bombs are falling on us! My neighbor and his house with his family! Gone tonight! Blown up. I drove into the city deeper and am taking shelter. I can hear the bombs still. Babies are crying. Women are crying. Men and boys are crying! A man in this store has a rifle with him.

A truck with soldiers in drove by not long ago. Heading toward the explosions. God bless them. I am scared for what is happening and for the people who will die. Why is this happening? Yesterday was normal and this last night is hell erupting from the earth and sky. My country and home are in ruins. Why?

Anastasiia
Ukrainian Civilian
Kyiv Suburbs
February 24th

The explosions are continuing. We are packing our bags. Fuck this is so scary. We have been hearing the explosions since four in the morning. The shockwaves are beating our windows. Ukraine has entered a state of emergency. The fighting is in Donetsk and Luhansk. Here we are seeing volleys of Russian rockets that are hitting the military compounds. Military compound near us is in flames. I'm unable to reach my best friend who lives somewhere in the fighting zone. There is panic outside.

As of now we can only see drones and rockets (affecting our area). Right now, we are at home and will go to the bomb shelter when are given the command. We are not leaving the city. Most of the rockets are being repelled by the anti-air weaponry. There is mixed information about civilians being hit but it could be mass panic caused by texts and social media. I personally haven't seen any hit civilian areas. Still can't reach my friend. Service is malfunctioning. We are holding on. The obnoxious carwash next to our building is finally quiet. Only good thing

Ukrainian Soldier - Reservist
Frontline
February 24th

I am a reservist. Being trucked to the front. This is hell. There are explosions all over. This does not seem like real life. I have been expecting this day for many months now but now it is here, and I am afraid. I will do my duty to Ukraine, but I am so scared. Please keep my frightened words anonymous. I am with other soldiers now too and we are keeping each other brave. Over our heads we can hear missiles and artillery fly over. We do not know what is coming when the truck stops. But we will do it together.

Mychajlo
Ukrainian Civilian
February 24th

The Russians are riding tanks and moving through my town. Missiles were flying overhead followed by planes and then helicopters. No one fired a shot here. No one was hurt. Tanks, at least 20, moved right past my house. I waved at one to test if they are harmful and one waved back. They are young. They all look my brother's age who is in the army. (19) I have never heard noise like this. The planes flying are very loud. I am just glad our area was not targeted for bombs. I hope my brother is not hurt. I hope he is alive.

Alina
Ukrainian Civilian
February 24th

Last night my brother was very drunk and needed to be driven home. I live an hour away with our grandmother who is very old. When I picked my brother up from the night out, he was extremely drunk. On the drive to our grandmother's house in the village missiles started to fly over. I started to scream but my brother was unconscious and had no idea. Behind us missiles were hitting in the forest and buildings. I got him home and ran inside. I had forgotten my brother was unconscious and dragged him to the door my grandmother was woken by the noise and hit my brother in the face with a rod.

'Wake up useless boy the Russians are here!'

Helicopter and planes flew over the house shaking windows. We got him inside and my grandmother told us to stay calm and we were not a military target for missiles. She is 96 and the bravest woman I know. Russian planes passed our house later and my grandmother said again, 'I have seen this once.' My brother is awake now and didn't believe the Russians attacked until he saw them. He said he will never drink again.

"Bumblebee"
Russian Soldier
Kharkov Area
February 24th

I am a Russian army officer with the rank of captain. I joined the army on my own, of my own free will. I studied at the intelligence facility, then served in Special Forces for a long time. I performed combat missions on the territory of the North Caucasus before entering Ukraine.

Let's be clear. This is not an invasion. An Example, it's like when America went into Iraq...two times...1991 and 2004...is that an invasion to conquer? Exactly! We do not believe that we have invaded a foreign country! Yes, it was, of course, reckless on our part and unexpected for us as soldiers. We did not believe until we were given a combat order.

The first days were really very difficult and sad. Here I will speak carefully, because there is a certain amount of non-disclosure...we went to Kharkov. It all started on February 5th for us. We went to the training exercises on the border. For five days we were traveling in a convoy from the Caucasus to the Belgorod region and we did not know that we would enter Ukraine!

When we arrived, we began to practice combat training in the village, on my own; I personally added training for reconnaissance in forests and in the villages, medical training, first aid for injuries, evacuation and loading! In battle, the commander is responsible for all this! And the commander organizes all this too.

After 2.5 weeks of intensive preparation, we were transferred closer to the border...we did not believe that something would happen or something would start, we hoped that everything would be negotiated. On the night of February 24, we were given a combat order and we plunged and moved into the starting area for the change of borders...stood almost all night! Only in the morning with the first artillery shots, we set off and at eight in the morning crossed the border.

According to our orders and intelligence, we were supposed to be met at the border by people who would lead our columns to Kharkov itself, but these people were not there. Maybe they were, but I did not see them. Almost immediately, small skirmishes began with small groups of nationalists. I may be wrong of course. Maybe they were worthy soldiers of the Armed Forces of Ukraine...there were also such in the area. Or maybe they were Polish mercenaries?

When we entered the first settlement abroad, people greeted us with tears of joy in their eyes! They were very happy to see us! Especially children! After all, children are people who do not know how to deceive and hide their true emotions. Then we thought that nothing very serious or dangerous would happen here, and we drove on.

In the next settlement, we were met more sparingly...no one went out to meet us. No one talked to us. Everyone turned away from us. People seemed to pass through us. They looked at us as enemies or something, but they did not show any hostility! We gifted to them dry rations, tea, and gave flags. We did not come to conquer Ukraine, but only to give people freedom from the rotten Kyiv regime!

The fact that Zelensky the comedian and actor, is absolutely not a political person became president is not an accident! This is the man on whom the West made bets in order to expand NATO in the region. He just did what he was told, otherwise why didn't he stop the war in the Donbass and Lugansk? He lived half his life in Russia, and became noticeable in Russia, why didn't he begin to improve relations with Russia? Why are the borders closed? Why was the fraternal people banned from visa-free entry, why was it forbidden to celebrate Victory Day over the Nazis in their own country? Why did he allow Bandera to be elected a national hero, who massacred the same Ukrainians with entire villages?

Russia in '91 asked to join NATO. Then, in 2010, she also asked for something...but Russia was not taken into NATO. And you know why? Because NATO is an anti-Russian block!

And when Zelensky said that Ukraine was joining NATO, thereby allowing the countries of the alliance against Russia to come close to the border of Russia, this is where the patience of the Russian bear ended! We didn't want this war! We are peaceful! We are kind, but it was precisely the enemy that we wanted to join two times that crept up to our doorstep, and they didn't take us when olive branches were extended! And then Putin said the right things: "It was not we who came to the borders of NATO, but NATO came to our borders! Just think about it and draw an analogy with your country...but what would you do? When the safety of your family and your entire life is at stake? That's exactly why I'm here!

Let's continue...In the second village we stood for about 8 - 10 hours. The organization of interaction was practically none! Different branches of the military came together. The Ministry of Defense and the National Guard.

I serve in the National Guard. These are former internal troops! In our country, too, not everything is super good, and there is also an indicative component of corruption. There was practically no connection between the columns. The first to enter the village were units of the Ministry of Defense with tanks, artillery, infantry, then units of the National Guard riding on armored personnel carriers and simple unarmored Urals (Urals) brand of an army cargo truck.

We stood almost until the night, when we were given the command to move forward about 20 km. To the forest belt near the settlement "D" and spend the night there! The column was about 200 vehicles all together!

We drove at night without light at such a great speed that we would not fall behind and not get lost! Our units of the National Guard cannot carry out the tasks of conducting combat operations against another army, because we have inferior weapons! And at one of the crossroads, far ahead of me, one of our APC's (Armored Personnel Carrier) flew off the road and our convoy stretched because of the crash. We start to slow down the convoy.

I stopped the entire column, which saved us, because an ambush of armored vehicles was waiting for us ahead! The tanks of the Ministry of

Defense quickly finished them, and set fire to the station building, where enemy soldiers were sitting while we were evacuating the crashed APC.

As the APC returned to service, and the convoy gathered, we moved further down the road. Suddenly one Kamaz (A brand of military truck) in my convoy stopped running because an explosion, and we lost the entire convoy. They drove ahead of us because we could not leave the car with the personnel alone to the mercy of fate.

I advanced a little further on three armored personnel carriers, about 700 meters, and stopped near a burning car in the road. There was no body inside and it burned very strangely, starting from the trunk...as if it was set on fire on purpose! To our right, we detected the movement of someone, so we deployed machine guns looking there, but did not shoot. We were afraid to hurt civilians or confuse that they were civilians.

I ordered my soldiers to give a burst from a small machine gun to over the top of their heads! This saved us, because at the same moment a flurry of enemy fire fell upon us from small arms. There were a lot of tracers, a lot of sounds like bullets hitting metal. But three KPVT 14.5 calibers were able to calm this group of enemies. We drove off the road and got up behind a small forest belt and deathly silence stood all around and only heard our breathing and the beating of our hearts.

I don't know how many people we put there, but we survived and did not allow ourselves and the people in the crashed armored personnel carrier to be burned. The remaining column began to move in our direction, and before reaching us, 300 meters away...was ambushed. It was right behind us. My guys quickly dismounted and took up the defense!

We repulsed the attack, but we lost one fighter. Four bullets flew into him. They hit his clavicle, shoulder, hand, and stomach. As it turned out later, he was shot in the liver. He died after five or ten minutes. In addition to him, four of my soldiers were injured in the legs.

The evacuation of the wounded took a long time...because they deceived me and said that there was a medical Kamaz in the convoy of the Ministry of Defense (Resuscitation on wheels), I then thought that it would be best to load all the wounded there so that they would provide assistance on the go. But only after 40 minutes it turned out that this was not an intensive care unit, but a dressing station on wheels, and in addition it was packed with all sorts of junk. The evacuation took place only an hour after the battle!

Meanwhile, the column that had gone ahead began to return because they got lost and went to the swamp! As I understand it, they left a couple of tanks there that they could not pull out and as soon as a large amount of equipment gathered near that very burned-out car I spoke of earlier, the Ukrainians opened furious fire from mortars!

I dare to remind you that we were in the center of the village...and they were not embarrassed by the presence of civilians in houses along the roadsides! As a result: Out of 200 cars and armored vehicles, less than 100 of them left the village. Everything else was burned. The radio connection was completely lost, because they burned the KShM, and much more. We were lucky on the first night and we left Hell with one dead and five wounded!

This all happened on the 24th.
When retreating back to the border, we ran into two more ambushes! But we were lucky, and we were able to get ahead of them, and destroyed them first!

As a participant in hostilities and actively participated in the elimination of terrorists in the Caucasus, I have been in skirmishes! But only with small arms and not on such a scale! What I saw that night impressed and shocked me. I never got hit by mortars before! And I did not fall under the fire of a whole platoon. It was that night a Bear woke up in me, who had been sleeping all this time.

*This interview was conducted in late July 2022

Art by João "J-Dot" Alves

Ukrainian Soldier
Donbas Frontline
February 24th
(Message passed from brother to sister via text message)

We worked in combat this morning. Gunfire like you have never heard. Rifles and machine guns. Rockets, planes. Aircraft of all types and bombs of all kinds. It's quieter now for a moment so I am taking time to update you. Do not be afraid. I am not. I think I shot one. I cannot be sure. So many bullets flying it is difficult to see who gets who. We are holding. Pray for me. For Ukraine. I love you.

Pavel Filatyev
Russian Soldier
VDV Paratrooper
February 24th

In January troops started amassing in Crimea and Belarus, and on the border with Ukraine. We were training of January, doing fuck-all in reality. 20th of February we were at a range in Crimea we got the order to prepare for a column movement to an unknown destination. We kept moving daily, and on the 24th we went in.

Some boys were bullshitting about going into Ukraine, but thoughts were varying. Barely anyone thought that the invasion would actually happen. No one really believed that we would invade. I personally understood that Crimea would have terrible circumstances. Putin had a shit rating and he needed to raise it. I thought that we would be used as peacekeepers in DNR LNR during a referendum, that was my theory. That was my logical thinking. No one fucking knew.

February 24 was a surprise for the whole world, Russian troops as well. We couldn't even really tell where we were, the column vehicles headlights were off. We were on the border. During the night we had the order to paint the cars with Z. And to put white bands on left arm and right leg. We were sleeping in cars, and then 4 AM we woke up to an artillery barrage. I woke up to other military branches firing grads and other artillery into Ukraine.

*Documented via phone call in August 2022

Lyaksandro
Ukrainian Veteran
February 25th

I was in bed sleeping when the bombs started falling. I was in the army for 6 years before this and medically discharged for wounds sustained near Donbas. I cannot walk well, so I am sitting in my house watching the street with a rifle. I am waiting for the Russians. When they get here, I will defend this country.

Ukrainian civilian and her soldier brother (Text Messages)
February 25th

Vlad (brother): "These may be my last messages, know that I love you ❤"
Nastya (sister): "Don't say such things!"
Vlad: "And everyone else"
Nastya: "I love you too brother
Everything will be okay
You'll come back"

Second screenshot (10:02):
Nastya: "Vlad, what's happening?"

Vlad: "Our unit has been shelled."

Third screenshot (10:05):
Vlad: "Listen, our side is having an offensive, if I don't write for a while, I'm food for worms.

Ukrainian Civilian
North of Kyiv
February 25th

The fighting was just outside the front door. Machine guns and bombs were exploding all over. Our soldiers and Russians were fighting, and our dog won't be quiet. It is just myself and my wife here, and neither are fit for service. There is nothing to do but hide in our home and pray to God bullets do not come through the walls or much worse.

Petruso
Ukrainian Civilian – Militia
February 25th

They handed guns out of trucks and distribution points today. So many rifles were given away. My older brother took my younger brother and me (three brothers, aged 17, 19, and 25) to get them. I do not know if we will use these, but it is scary to be given a gun! I have only fired one in games before so not even real life. My older brother is a policeman, so he is showing us how to load them and shoot them.

Everyone here is really scared but the people with guns seem less scared. I am scared, and my little brother is scared too. I hope no Russians come I don't want to get anyone hurt. This is such a strange time. I was supposed to go back to university soon, but I don't think that outcome is likely.

Ukrainian Civilian
February 25th

Soldiers told us to stay inside (Ukrainian soldiers), and we can see them down the road with machine guns. It is so loud here I am afraid if they are pushed back the dog will reveal us to the enemy. I cannot believe how loud it has become. It's also so bright. The night seems like day outside because of the fires. This will be worse than last night.

Western Volunteer
February 25th

Was in combat all day. Must have loaded 20 magazines and fired that same number. High spirits but exhausted. We all are. It's dark and mostly quiet so we don't think the unit in front of us has got night vision. Not taking chances though. We are staying put and keeping our heads down. Can't say where.

Heard Chechens are near or in the area. Might be rumors but got some guys spooked about pissing in the dark because of that. I'm not leaving this spot. Pissed in a water bottle. Any Chechen shows up here I'll ventilate his skull. All for now. Will message more tomorrow if I'm not dead.

Western Volunteer
February 25th

I am with the other guy. (Volunteer from story above) Today was fucking insane, man. Combat like I'd never even thought possible. All. Day. Long. Bro, it's like World War Two over here. At one point there must have been 300 guys right in front of us. Like storming the beaches of Normandy type shit. I'm chain-smoking now under my parka in the dark, so I don't get my head smacked off.

I'm shaking bro. That was not like anything I've experienced. They stand and fight. It's not even over bro. They're still RIGHT there. At one point a rocket went like 2 feet over my head, and it felt like it was gonna suck my eyes out of my head. Thanks for asking about us. I don't care how much combat you got under your belt everyone a boot new guy in this. Everyone.

Ukrainian Civilian
Living Abroad
February 25th

My mother is dead. I found out this morning. I have cried and cried all day. I'm not in the country. (Ukraine) My sister called me crying. 'Mom is gone. She is gone.' I didn't believe it. I couldn't go on the news. I couldn't watch my hometown burn. My mother is gone. And I hate them. I hate every last one of them.

I want the world to know what they've done here. How our enemies have treated helpless people. My family is broken for absolutely NO REASON! WHY have they done this?? I hope our soldier's fight. Fight harder than any army us ever fought before. I hope they finish this. I love you, mama.

Ukrainian Soldier
Donbas Frontline
February 25th

Yesterday a man was blown to pieces. Can't stop thinking about it. Sun is coming up soon. Haven't slept at all. Gunfire all through the night, but mostly quiet in terms of danger and to keep us awake. No one in our squad got hurt in the night. Which is great. Thinking about yesterday makes me want to vomit. It was terrible.

A man was blown completely into pieces. We think a tank shell hit him directly. Or an RPG. Don't think it matters much. Most of the night was spent chain smoking and trying to load magazines as quietly as I can. Phone is gonna die soon. Don't know when or if I can get it charged. With the sunlight comes more fighting and death. Wish us luck.

Ukrainian Civilian
Draftee – Kyiv
February 25th

All men 18-60 are expected to fight. I never thought this could happen! I have sent my wife and two boys away to Poland. I held them so tight! Tighter than I could ever held them before. I hope I see them again. My boys, too young to understand why I cannot go with them. They are small boy, but brave boys. They will take care of mama.

I wept when they left. The other fathers, some much older than me, almost 60, we all cried together when the vehicles with our families left us behind. I am lucky. I was in the army once. Years ago. I know what I am supposed to do. I worry for the others. I worry for us all. I hope to see my boys again.

Ukrainian Civilian
Kyiv Suburbs
February 25th

Very early in the invasion I saw two jets fight each other. One Ukrainian jet and one Russian jet. I am an aviation (military aviation) fan and seeing this was a dream for me. I'm saying to you that I wish none of this happened. I believe war is bad, but I am fascinated by military aircraft and what they can do. Witnessing this was for me, a mix of being happy and sad.

They were very far from me and fast moving because they are jets, so I could not see who was who, but I saw them fight. One (A) tried to maneuver behind the other (B) but B was anticipating this and climbed sharply and turned to switch the roles of hunter and prey.

I saw flares come from "A", and then they both disappeared from my view because of the distance. For me this was exciting. Aviation fans are always talking about who (what kind of aircraft) would win in dog fights, but we have almost no examples of modern jets fighting and here a fight was happening in front of me.

Another jet, C, came from behind me and right over my head. It was incredible. It was a Russian SU-25, flying low to the ground and the noise was so loud it made me shake. They are my enemy, but the excitement of my interest couldn't be helped. It was a once in a lifetime thing for me to see. C flew straight over me in the direction of where A and B had flown.

I do not know how the fight unfolded after that or who won. But I personally hope that all three pilots, no matter who they are, made their way back to their homes and have a good story to tell. I hate war. I want no one to die. I hope these pilots are all still safe to this day.

Art by João "J-Dot" Alves

Ukrainian Civilian
Donetsk Oblast Frontline
February 25th

Hundreds of rockets hit near our home. Those kinds that come in large numbers one after the other. They shook my entire house. I don't know how anyone survives such things. What terrible humans are we for inventing weapons like that? The rockets killed my dog, and my neighbor's house is completely destroyed. We cannot find him, and we fear he may be in the rubble, but his house is flattened. I don't know why this happened. We are not soldiers. I just want this all to be over. I am so exhausted and tired of crying. I cannot handle the noise any longer. I feel I am going mad.

Western Volunteer
Lviv Oblast
February 25th

A few of us going into Ukraine now. Former soldiers. Weapons and gear waiting for us at rendezvous. Traveling non-stop since this mess started. We are on our way. Not doing this for any government or cause. Just got to protect as many civilians as we can. None of us expect to get home. This is a one-way ticket, I think. Doesn't matter. God is watching. Will send updates as time and security allows. 'Here am I. Send me.' Out.

Western Volunteer
Chernihiv Oblast Frontline
February 25th

I was hurt on the first day by a Russian helicopter. Not a bad one but bad enough to have it cared for by doctors for a week. Our position in the field was next to a road next to a forest. We heard the helicopters (two) coming over the trees. I ran from the vehicle into the trees, and it shot a rocket at the vehicle and missed.

They turned around and started shooting into the trees where we were. A piece of wood was blown up off the tree and it hit me in the arm. It hurt badly and I told my friend I needed a doctor. He said no doctors would be coming with those helicopters over us so I should stop being a child. He was upset we were helpless not at me, so I am not angry with him for his comment.

Jason Haigh
Western Volunteer
Hostomel Airport
February 25th

I was involved in the Hostomel airport battle early in the invasion. We encountered heavy air bombardments. We had several attack helicopters strafing us with guns and rockets, followed by Russian airborne troops landing. It was pretty much all one sided.

We got smashed by multiple attack helicopters and fast air. We were completely pinned down. Only having a few minutes rest despite being able to retreat into buildings and eventually out of the area because Ukrainian forces started engaging the air with stingers.

It was extremely intense with gun strafing runs extremely close between us. Rockets landing 50-60 meters from us at times. Some of us had bits of frag to the legs but nothing serious. We briefly saw some Russian VDV soldiers landing, the encounter was hair-raising after what we'd just been through so we broke away as quick as we could.

I served 3 tours in Iraq and Syria prior to the war in Ukraine and none of those tours come close to the ferocity of the fighting I witnessed in Ukraine.

Art by João "J-Dot" Alves

Ukrainian Civilian
Kyiv
February 26th

I saw Ukrainian soldiers for the first time today since this started. They walked past me in a long line along the road, walking toward smoke and explosions further down the road. They were smoking, and silent. I don't think anyone said anything. Citizen or soldier. A woman ran up to one of them and kissed him on the lips. And ran back to the side of the road. I asked if that was her husband. She said she had no idea who the boy was but looked like he needed to be kissed.

Ukrainian Soldier
Donetsk Oblast Frontline
February 26th

Surrounded. Front is behind us now. Love you. Bye.

*Transcribed from a phone call from one cousin to another.

Russian Soldier
Kyiv Oblast Frontline
February 26th

Heavy fighting today. Ukrainian soldiers have a deep defense which is difficult to penetrate. Aircraft superiority helps and morale is still high. The noise is terrible. So loud! I may go deaf before the evening. I am well and not injured yet. Many dangerous things can happen here. I miss home and hope to see you soon. Give the children hugs from me. I will be home when this is over. Love you to the moon.

*Phone call between a Russian soldier and his wife. Transcribed and sent anonymously.

Ukrainian Soldier
Eastern Frontline
February 26th

Tonight, they say an assault is coming. Big one bigger than the first day. We are exhausted. I have not slept more than 20 minutes since they crossed the border. All civilians in our area have been moved. It has been chaos. We stand, fight, allow civilians to leave, pull back a bit and repeat. Holding the defense now but just so exhausted.

Good news though. Today Javelins destroyed 4 armored vehicles in our sector. The burning piles are keeping some of us warm, but the bodies have been moved out and placed away from us. No one wants to stare at bodies. It is a good thing these weapons are well made. We have shot thousands of bullets in two days each man has. One man had a plastic grip melt to his rifle it was so hot. Never seen that before.

I think a sniper was sniping at us. He got someone so we have been staying down after that mostly. I want a night at the cinema with a large and huge beer. I do not care about benefits I just want a drink. I would very much like to never repeat this experience ever.

Ukrainian Soldier
Kharkiv Oblast Frontline
February 26th

Our marksman has gotten four of them today. Most effective in the company. He said he wants five tomorrow. He has earned a beer and a break tonight. All day long he has stalked the Russians keeping them worried and scared ha-ha! Half of us are sleeping now and other half are watching or cleaning weapons. Some have gone behind the line to fetch food.

Ukrainian Nurse
February 26th

Russian soldiers are in our hospital. Not to fight but hurt ones. I am a low-level nurse, so my duties are not very important. I clean wounds and change bandages. These are boys. Young boys 18 or 19. They cry for mama like ours do. I do not have soft feelings for our enemies, but I do for poor boys in pain. They are brought here, and their friends are concerned for them. This is such a waste. Why must this happen? Such waste of young lives.

Ukrainian Civilian
Sumy Oblast
February 26th

My friend and I are not afraid. We live together in a tall building. The building is empty. We have been playing loud music all day and night to annoy Russian soldiers outside. Here is a few American songs you might know.

•Russia's gay' by Rucka Ali
•Wrecking Ball
•Photograph by Nickelback
•Stroke Me
•I will survive by whoever that lady that sings it is
•Lion King Circle of life
•Team America song
•Many many more

They tell us to be quiet and we tell back 'Sorry we will make a quieter war since you are trying to sleep.' Fuck those guys.

Lithuanian Civilian
Lithuania
February 26th

I'm currently in Lithuania. A state of emergency has been imposed here since yesterday morning. People are a little bit panicked here, but everything is under control, there is tension. ATMs are short of cash as people prepare for the worst-case scenario.

There's currently a stuck family of 4 in Ukraine, Kyiv and we are looking for help on how to get them out of there. Yesterday, some Ukrainians left Lithuania and went home to their families to fight for their country.

Ukrainian Civilian
Kyiv Suburb
February 26th

I can see the fighting from my window. It is dark out and the noise is huge. Bullets are flying through the air like water from a hose. A wounded soldier walked past our house holding his arm. He looked hurt badly and my father went to help him. The soldier yelled to my father to go away and get behind something. We are not very close to the fighting, but I can see shapes move because of the light made of the battle.

In a way this is a beautiful vision to see from far away. The lights. But it is not beautiful to experience up close. I see these lights hanging in the air must have parachutes attached to them. They hang still in the sky for a while and make the ground look white. Maybe I am unwell for thinking this is a pretty sight? It is daylight now and the smoke from the event has reached my house. I will call again later.

*Phone call transcribed by a relative and sent to Battles and Beers for documentation

Ukrainian Soldier
Eastern Frontline
February 26th

I shot a tank with a missile today. We hit them good and have them halted. I am okay just some bruises and my ears are ringing. We are getting volunteers from civilians who are helping to pass ammunition and medical supplies. Do not worry. I am fine. Love you. I will call again when I can. Love you. Love you.

*Transcribed from phone call to mother from son, then sent to Battles and Beers for documentation.

Ukrainian Soldier
Kyiv Oblast
February 26th

Two soldiers captured here. Spoken with them briefly. Not bad men. Just forced into a bad situation like so many others have been in the past. I have spoken with the younger of the two and he said his grandmother is in Kyiv. I don't know if I believe him, but he seemed sincere. I told him he was here to hurt his grandmother. He began to cry and said he doesn't want this to continue. I gave him a cigarette and told him I hope he sees his home again. My kindness is not representative of other soldiers. Enough of the suffering.

*Phone call transcribed by a family member.

Western Volunteer
February 26th

Day three of combat and still alive, man. This is intense stuff. An ambush earlier destroyed several vehicles, tanks, and other materials they have been using. Progress is being made, as well as losses. To any volunteers coming, probably a one-way ticket, dude. This isn't Iraq or Afghanistan. The next 5 minutes isn't even guaranteed. Don't come here thinking you'll stack bodies because you won't.

These aren't dirt farmers with 50-year-old AK's. You'll get humbled to real, REAL combat and violence really quick. This isn't a game. I fired more rounds here in 2 days than 2 deployments to Iraq and Afghanistan. This is not a game, and this is not fun. Choose carefully before you decide to be a hero.

Ukrainian Civilian
February 26th

I saw a helicopter get shot down. I do not know whose it was because I am not a soldier. People are saying it was a Russian one. It seemed to get hit by something and then went straight to the ground. I screamed when it happened. Russian or not what a horrible way to die for someone.

Those poor boys will never have good funerals and their families will never be able to see their sons again. I do not like the invaders, but the slaughter must be stopped by the leaders! Why is the world not doing its best to stop this? This is senseless. Senseless.

Ukrainian Civilian
Sumy Oblast
February 27th

They're bombing us! I can't stand it. I'm in a basement praying to God. The whole building shakes and part of it has come apart. Please, help get us out of here! We will be dead by morning. If we don't live, please take care of the animals. I love them more than I love anything. I love you.

Ukrainian Soldier
February 27th

More fighting today. Seen so many tanks and armored vehicles that they are not so scary anymore. We have the weapons to destroy them but still very dangerous. It's aircraft that I can't stand. Constantly looking at the sky. Passenger planes will never be the same for me again. Bodies are inside of destroyed vehicles all over. The longer this goes on the worse it gets.

Ukrainian Soldier
February 27th

Best way to kill tanks. Create the distraction. Have troops visible to an enemy while you move the opposite direction. Once the tank is looking toward the distraction, whether it be rifle fire, smoke, or troops in contact, move to the fire position. You have moments to fire when you reveal yourself. The turret is not fast moving but you must be quick. Tanks always have infantry near or supporting vehicles. Fire the rocket at weak points, move away from fire position and reattempt if the attack was not a success.

Former Russian Soldier
US Citizen
February 27th

So, no one wants to fight. It's the truth. About half the forces had no idea what they were doing. They were supposed to go to a training site like JRTC. On the way to the site phones were confiscated and live ammo was passed out (that's relatively normal for large training exercises) A few hours later they are suddenly getting shot at and pretty much are just defending themselves (as invaders, I know how that seems ridiculous)

Really, only the officers know what's going on in most regular units. And the officers started stationing themselves further and further away from the fight as the days go by, to the point where they are out of radio range at this point, and no one can contact them.

The exception to this was some paratrooper and Special Forces units. Some VDV companies were briefed on airfields they were going to seize, but even then, only a couple were. Even the Spetsnaz was kept out of the loop. It seems like somewhere in between Putin and his generals, there was a miscommunication or a lie. All of the supply vehicles are still outside of Ukraine, and the ones that went with the troops into Ukraine have already been destroyed or exhausted.

The Spetsnaz teams were told it was a three-day excursion, now anyone who is surviving has to commit war crimes by literally raiding petrol stations and food stores of civilians. A lot of regular soldiers refuse to fight and are just abandoning equipment and vehicles and walking away. Most of the ones you see fighting now are those who have a hard charger officer.

Almost no one can get a hold of central command, it's not even a matter of jamming, there's just no long-range commo equipment or relays that went with the troops there. Originally, the units were supposed to blitz from day 1-2, regroup on day 3, and form Army groups so that they could become balanced forces. As you can see, this is not the case.

Because there's no link up with central, it's mostly just battalions on their own. You see in these videos tank columns, helicopter wings, and motorized rifle columns all by themselves with no inter-cooperation. That's because they have no way to talk to each other and are tens of miles apart.

Ukrainian Soldier
Mariupol
February 27th

While our front was under heavy grad bombardment and tank shelling, I stood hidden away in a door frame as if it would help protect me if I was hit. I looked down the street to see a family that didn't evacuate as the front once again came back to them. As I sat staring at them, their life continued as normal despite the heavy bombing and vibrations.

Western Volunteer
Abroad
February 28th

Headed over to Ukraine now. Honestly, I'm terrified. Everyone I've chatted with said it's probably a one-way trip. That's okay. Sometimes you've got to put your money where your mouth is. Found out another guy on the plane has the same end destination. I feel horrible. I should have done this weeks ago. My girlfriend didn't want me to go. I'm single now. Maybe this is the dumbest thing I've ever done? Maybe it's the best thing? All I know is it feels right, and it feels necessary.

Russian Civilian
February 28th

My boy is missing. I am a mother (Russian), and I cannot locate my boy. He is 19. He is involved in this illegal occupation (her son is a soldier) and he did not want to go! Our boys are being sent for no good reason! Why? I cannot find my boy, and no one can tell me where he is. I am torn inside and want to die. I cannot lose him.

Ukrainian Civilian
Kyiv
February 28th

Today it is quieter than yesterday, which is joyful as it is. We hope this tendency keeps up. The voenkomati (military recruiting offices) aren't expecting new volunteers, they are over flooded. I went to three today and everywhere was told they are full.

Sashka
Ukrainian Civilian
Kherson
February 28th

It is quiet here (Kherson area), little bursts of firearms here and there. I think we will be annexed into Russia as the water has already been redirected to Crimea, the water transfer station has the Russian flag on it already. The situation is normal, driving to work right now, the city is quiet.

Today saw a lot of Russian military vehicles otherwise it is pretty quiet, disperse gunfire here and there. They (Russians) are finishing off the small resistance. They are not firing onto the cities and are not killing civilians at all. They're only firing at armed resistance and tanks. They are not touching the cities. We have water, we have service, and we have light (electricity).

The route to Poland is perfectly safe, a lot of what you're seeing back home is western propaganda. Even the rocket that hit the high-rise in Kiev by accident (that everyone has been reposting) was not of Russian caliber. All the Ukrainian regulars are surrendering and only the Nazi nationalists are not giving up, there are not that many of them. The Russian troops are not mass surrendering, have you not read our history bro? Russians never surrender.

*American immigrant that migrated back to Ukraine.

Ukrainian Civilian
February 28th

My little brother is a soldier fighting on the front. We don't talk at all except for one time a day. I am going to school in the United States, and he's fighting. He texts me once a day. 'Still alive.' And my heart just explodes with happiness. All day long I worry for him. I wait by my phone every second just wishing to see his name pop up.

I don't know what I would do if I didn't get that message. Still alive…still alive…to me, the fate of Ukraine is as much attached to the fate of my brother. If he falls, for me, Ukraine falls too. The world will be gone. My whole world. My brother. My hero. Slava Ukraini.

Western Volunteer
Kyiv Suburbs
February 28th

During the second day of fighting in Kyiv, a mother with her two sons were looking for shelter. They got caught in the crossfire, two of my friends sprinted towards them as the rest of us provided suppressive fire. Each one picked up a kid and brought them to a safer place whilst the mother waited in cover. One of them came back to bring the mother to safety, he got shot in the leg. He stood back up and brought the mother to her kids. When he returned, just right in front of us he got shot again this time fatally.

After the fighting was over, we went looking to see if the mother and kids were still there and they were. Sitting in a corner of a room holding each other, the mother started crying and blamed herself that one of ours got killed. We comfort her and told her it wasn't her fault. The kids gave all of us a hug and then I started crying. As I'm becoming a father it was a very hard moment for me.

The fighting was hard, brutal and terrifying. When other units took prisoners, we learned that most of them were very poorly equipped, not well trained and most of the younger soldiers were reservists who thought they went on military exercises. Once they got shot at, they defended themselves they said. They told they were ordered by their senior officers to advance to Kyiv. All they wanted was to go back home. A few were allowed to call their parents, when they told what happened their parents were in shock and surprised. They had no idea their sons were fighting in the invasion.

We are afraid, of what might happen in the upcoming days, we are afraid of what might happen to us, our friends. I felt I had to do this; I arrived a day before the invasion started. Personally, I didn't think a full invasion would happen but then the night came of Wednesday February 23rd. In all honesty I've never been that scared in my life. All sorts of weapons were fired at us. Bombs of all kinds were dropped, cruise missiles flying over.

Everyone from back home was begging me not to go but, I do believe I made the right decision. It's not about being a hero or just to kill. For me this is about defending the Ukrainian people and the rest of Europe. Doing the right thing, that's why I came here.

If I don't survive at least, I know what I died for. We're all willing to give our lives. To Ukrainian soldiers: Stay strong, have faith. We all have to do this together. Nothing is as strong as the power of the people willing to die for their country, sacrifice everything they worked for. It will be a long battle but, in the end, the Ukrainian flag will wave everywhere as the people of Ukraine shall be victorious.

No matter the cost we will never surrender, we will fight until the very end. People from all over the world showing their support which only makes us stronger. The Ukrainian people are the bravest people I've ever met and it's an honor to fight alongside them. Their courage, bravery, the will to fight and with a true fighting leader like Zelensky, they inspire millions of people around the world.

Ukrainian Civilian
February 28th

Russian saboteurs at night drain fuel from people's cars! Their army is full of poorly equipped soldiers. Russia suffers heavy losses, more than 3,000. I saw with my own eyes columns of destroyed Russian equipment, killed soldiers. Most of them don't even have a bulletproof vest, only tactical vests. Enemy equipment is outdated, with poor walkie-talkies, incomplete ammunition.

In most cases, Russian prisoners did not even know where they were going, many surrendered, because they know that Ukrainians are good, and the prisoners are treated with dignity, although this is unnecessary! Ukraine is a strange nation, we have problems, but in difficult times, when they want to scare or break us, we immediately coordinate, self-organize! We are ready and meet the occupier. Our spirit is strong, we know that in any case we are a victory for us!

We do not agree with the Putin regime, even if Russia achieves its goals, people will not lose heart! Let's guerrillas, kill the invader by all available methods! Russian troops are trying to make their Blitzkrieg, they are pressing the number! Not strategically to win but to break through. The enemy bears heavy losses! Their fighting spirit is falling, and we feel it, and we fight with greater fury! I myself am forced to sit at home, the territorial defense lacks weapons and equipment for all comers

37,000 people came to the territorial defense, and 90,000 people are waiting in line to get weapons, in my city of Bucha, near Kyiv, it is 20 miles away, at this very time there is a fierce battle! The Russian army is trying to break through to Kyiv, they are not doing very well, they are pressing, and the Ukrainian Army is courageously defending itself, holding positions!

I can't go to the tanks without weapons at the moment. I feel a public obligation to disseminate information about this situation! I promise, as soon as I get a weapon, I will go to defend my dear Ukraine! Glory to Ukraine!

Western Civilian
Abroad
February 28th

On the first day of the invasion of Ukraine it was a day like every other for me I went to log on to go speak with my online friends but today was different. A lot of the server was filled with people from Ukraine and surrounding countries. In that time people in the server set up what was essentially an improvised battle net. It did start as nothing serious just a couple hundred people watching the war live. But then it progressed.

People from Ukraine were offering to support our movement and offer us support to get as much of the war documented as possible. Freedom fighters from Russia who detest the Putin regime were asking us how they can get tickets to Ukraine to fight against this hatred. We soon started to realize we needed to organize better and monitor what info we were giving out to which people. One of the most significant moments for us was watching local partisans during the night evacuating families while they stay to fight, we have seen Russian tank columns destroyed. As well as many bombings through the cities of Ukraine.

Eventually many of us started to map out troop movements and send them to Ukrainian people on the ground. Later that day we watched the same unit we reported about was destroyed by Ukrainian soldiers and partisans. Now I'm not saying we were directly responsible, but we definitely had some part in helping out with this attack. We do not know how many people or who we have helped but I'm sure at least someone has gotten out of something horrible because of what we had transmitted through this brave group of people online.

Gregori
Russian Soldier
Eastern Front
February 28th

I am a Sergeant in the Russian Armed Forces of the Russian Federation. I will not name myself. If you must make me, call me Gregori. On the 24th we have crossed into Ukraine. The enemy is sometimes fierce, sometimes they meet us surrendering. Often, we get soldiers that surrender to us hand us their weapons and ask to go home, which we are letting some do this I am told.

We fight from convoys to villages, and see the Ukrainians take positions often in schools, nurseries, and abandoned hotels. We attack them, though I don't like it. It's cowardly to me to hide where children should play, but I think it speaks to the desperation and their hatred of us. The first day for my guys was hard. We lost two men to heavy machine gun fire from far away, but we hit the enemy positions with the BTR's Main cannon, and the position was destroyed. God keep their souls for they were good men.

Ukrainian Soldier
February 28th

Three kinds of invading soldiers here. You can tell who they are fast. The first kind are conscripts who don't want to be here. They want to go home. Hungry. Poorly armed and trained. Poorly supplied. They surrender without much provoking. They are children to us, and I feel bad for them.

The second kind of Russian is harder inside. They are sóldiers. Real soldiers. They have officers with them who aren't so stupid, and they will stand and fight, sometimes push us away from them. You need to be careful with them. They are professional soldiers who don't just have 3 reloads for their rifles like the first group.

The third kind is Chechens. These we view as the same as Mongols. Dangerous and violent. They came here for fun it seems and do not get captured alive by them. They carry knives.

Western Civilian / Volunteer
February 29th

I remember the first time it was being broadcasted of Russian forces sending troops close to the Ukrainian border. Each day more troops were sent. I and a few others were following the developments closely. A week prior to the invasion one of my friends told me we should go to Ukraine in case an invasion would happen. I told him and I was sure of it, "There won't be an invasion, Putin would be crazy to launch an all-out attack." In the end, he and 3 others convinced me to go.

My family tried talking me out of it, my pregnant girlfriend begging me to stay home. I told them if an invasion would happen, I can't and don't want to watch it from a sideline. We arrived early afternoon of February 20th, everyone seemed to be calm, no concerns of an invasion. Sure, there were people who were afraid. Children were still happily playing outside, life seemed normal.

February 21st, Putin announced the recognition of Luhansk and Donetsk. Fear was slowly starting to rise amongst the people. "Is it going to happen, an invasion?" People asked each other. When Putin gave his speech announcing he was launching a special military operation, we were watching it at a local shop. Tensions began to rise even more, not even 30 minutes later all hell broke loose.

Heavy artillery shelling, a barrage of all kinds of bombs, cruise missiles, fighter jets conducting air strikes. Russian troops advancing with tanks, armored personnel carriers came from every direction. We grabbed as much weapons as we could and went out. Fierce firefights throughout the whole night and day. The most intense combat I've ever seen, I've never been that scared in my life. It was hell.

There are people out there on the internet sitting safely behind a screen who are saying that we're just warmongering junkies, finding joy in killing etc. Every volunteer I know and have met over here, hates war. We don't want war; we don't want to kill. We want peace, we went to defend the people of Ukraine, the innocent people. We didn't go with the hopes of an invasion and to kill Russians.

War is terrible. Once this war is over, after we've won. We will stay to rebuild the country, rebuild the homes of the people. Give them their life back in peace and freedom. That's why we're here, for them.

Western Volunteer
Polish – Ukrainian Border
February 28th

Night all this shit started I had a bad feeling, I was covering for CG and watching all these OSINT feeds reporting cyberattacks and the huge stepping up of rhetoric from Putin.
Somewhere somebody posted a still image of the last footage from the Crimea border post, a soldier running. I was kind of stunned for a second and went to wake up my wife so we could get ready to bug out. My

paranoid ass planned for all this. We got out with her brother and a couple of friends.

Driving West I was raging, feeling fucking useless and wanting to strangle any Russian I could find. At one point when we stopped for water, we watched a cruise missile fly over us. It was surreal for me. Today I got into a position to help a volunteer force with their cross-border logistics and finally feel like I can contribute. It means spending most of my day hunched over smartphones and my laptop, but I have it fucking easy compared to the fighters.

Ukrainian Soldier
February 28th

I say this to Russian soldiers: Surrender. Give yourselves up and you will see your homes. Do not resist the will of the Ukrainian people or you will not leave this place. You will feed crows. Russian soldiers. I know many of you did not even know you were ordered to come here, and your officers are cowards who hide miles behind where you are. Give up, and you will be treated like a grown man and allowed to go home when this end. Your mothers call for you to return.

Do not obey your orders. Russian soldiers. Each day we destroy your tanks. We destroy your soldiers. More and more Ukrainians join the battle against you. Give up. You will find no glory or victory here. Only piles of your dead comrades. Give up.

Western Volunteer
Eastern Front
March 1st

Day 4 of combat for us. To say we are exhausted is the fucking understatement of the century. I think we've slept 15 hours if that. Finally got a bit of a break. Sitting here looking at my hands and just now realized how burned and cut up they are. Everyone is chain-smoking and taking it all in. Everyone who survived that is. Constant, unrelenting combat of this magnitude is a nightmare of which I don't think anyone who isn't 95 years old or here can comprehend. I'd suck a dick for a flight out of here tomorrow. No, I'd suck 50.

Former Russian Soldier
Communication with former comrade
March 1st

'My dearest brother, as of now the kettle is boiling. I yearn for fresh air and think I'm going to the beach to maybe have a bard sing for me. Might even skate to Vlad's dick. Be a while till I come to mama's house. Keep in touch.'

This is a code.
Kettle is boiling = compromised
The beach = he's gonna hitch a ride somewhere East, likely Kazakhstan
Bard = an informant or someone who will help him, because they sing (service) for money
Skate = take a train
Vlad's dick = Peschany, a town south of Vladivostok
Mama's house = Mother Russia
My former VDV comrade is telling me he's been made for attempting desertion.

*A former Russian soldier exchanges a message in code with his former comrade. This was sent to Battles and Beers for documentation

Ukrainian Nurse
March 1st

Treating wounded Ukrainian civilians and Russian soldiers in this hospital. I have spoken with a boy (Russian) who is wounded in the leg. He is a nice boy. I hope my country does not be upset with me for saying this. We spoke about his home in Russia, and he is excited to go home. He has three sisters. I hope one day he can see his home again. These are just boys!

Eastern Volunteer
March 1st

I am 27 years old have a 3-year-old daughter just started the first leg of my journey to Ukraine. Currently flying to my hometown to say goodbye to my daughter fly to London at 9.45pm tomorrow night and get a connecting flight to Krakow where I'm meeting a group of Europeans to travel into Lviv and join the Georgian foreign legion. To say I'm shitting myself is an understatement.

I'm terrified and it's not of dying it's of the unknown. I don't know where I'll be in a weeks' time and that's what scares me. I know in my heart this needs to be done I know it's right it's selfish to my family and friends and my daughter but in my opinion in every other aspect it's completely selfless and the right thing to do. I've never seen combat or served but I have a long history of military service in my family, and I know my ancestors would be proud of what I'm doing.

Russian Soldier
Northern Front
March 1st

Though we seem hatred filled and hardcore militarists, we are good and honorable people. What we do now, we do because we must. War isn't fair unfortunately. I hope it ends soon for all our sakes. I don't want to kill more good people that may just be defending their home. I think of it the same way if it were backwards. We would also fight to the very last man if our nation was invaded.

Western Volunteer
Donbas Front
March 1st

Advice to volunteers: This isn't a game. What we are witnessing is a scale of combat that's unprecedented in modern times. I'm an infantry veteran of the battles of Fallujah and Ramadi and even I'm questioning my qualifications for this. If you aren't a professional soldier, don't get involved. Watching YouTube videos and receiving civilian level training just isn't good enough. I'm sorry, I know you want to help, but it's not good enough. You can help more by staying out of it.

Your ignorance of conventional warfare will get yourself, or those around you killed. Light discipline. Crossing danger areas. Treating sucking chest wounds. Self-aid, buddy aid. Max effective ranges. How to dig a fighting position and not get your head shot off. I saw this in a comment on here and I'll repeat it. I don't walk into a bank robbery and pretend I'm a police officer. I don't walk into a plane and pretend I'm a pilot. I don't walk into a fire and pretend I'm a firefighter. To be a GOOD, USEFUL soldier takes at least two full years of active military training.

Leave this to the professional soldiers and medics. You will seriously help MORE by staying HOME. Don't get killed or get someone else killed because you want to brag about how you "Were in the big one". You had your chance to volunteer and receive professional training for the last 8 years. You missed it. Oh well. You wouldn't hop in a fighter jet and try to fly it, why would you hop in a trench and try to be a soldier?

Aiden Aslin, @CossackGundi
Western Volunteer - Ukrainian Marine
Siege of Mariupol
March 1st

This is Cossack. We are surrounded in Mariupol. No way out. My request you continue your support for Ukraine and its people. If you're ex-military, look at the resources already up and get to Ukraine ASAP and help the Ukrainian people in whatever way you can.

*Message sent to Battles and Beers from Aiden Aslin to disseminate among other Instagram pages

Western Volunteer – Ukrainian Soldier
March 1st

I'm a Foreigner who has been serving in the Ukrainian Armed Forces since the start of 2020, 6 months after leaving the Marine Corps. When I first came, they even denied me from joining due to the language barrier and returned home but flew back a few weeks later to try my shot again which this time they approved but said "this is up to the commander of the Armed Forces" and so I was told to wait but wanted to prove that I was not just some "war tourist".

So, from then on, I was serving in a hand me down Ukrainian Army uniform as well as my old USMC cammies without pay...for close to about 5 months. Some of the most stressful times we're not knowing if I'd still be denied and just stranded in Ukraine broke. Finally, time passes and given the okay to take the Oath of Enlistment, this would definitely be one of the proudest moments of my life.

My job is Reconnaissance, we are constantly studying in the class about weapons and sabotage techniques then in the field we go over patrols, combat drills, parachuting, etc.

Even though I've been here awhile my purpose isn't to sit in a trench as glorious as that sounds, we will conduct missions along the border, detain and search people, security work, plain clothes missions, more parachuting and just about anything else. It's a pain but at the same thing I've been able to travel all over Ukraine in about every major city so far because of it so I don't have many complaints except for the food. My feelings just like many others are of uncertainty in this conflict and what is to happen after to the families and innocent.

Many soldiers when they found out Russia had invaded and attacked, they immediately called their mothers and wives to make sure they're okay. It's something I'm glad I don't have to stress for here even though my family has no idea I'm here. If Ukraine's government does collapses people will continue to fight and just become insurgents like their grandfathers. No Ukrainian will ever lay down their rifle. Peacefully and let some puppet government especially Russian tell them how to live.

Something extra...which will be unpopular, but I say shame on all you other foreigners trying to come now. Where were you before this when they called for help? Yes, there were and are a few but the ones coming now do not care about Ukraine at all you are after self-glory, clout, fame, money, etc. I've received hundreds of messages over the years and when I did help out of the hundreds only a handful came, and the ones who did came have already all left before joining.

Within the last few months some have come and signed (in a different unit) but even they have run away in the middle of the night back to their homes in USA/UK. Ukraine doesn't need foreign fighters.... it needs more drones anti-armor weapons. If the modern American service member cries about burnt chicken from the chow hall, moldy walls in the barracks, freaks out about being sent to Japan/Germany, or gives themselves PTSD Over made up situations in their head where they kill themselves in a VA parking lot because they have to wait for a Doctor appointment....what makes you think you'll be able to handle something like Ukraine?

My old commander was a Chechen. One of the best guys I've ever served with. He's actually the only reason I was able to serve and gave me the chance. It's just strange though to see how quickly public opinion has changed for Russia in Chechnya. Their fathers fought and died against Russia and now their sons are Russians pets.

To be honest when I saw the video of Chechens getting ready to come, I was nervous only because of the stories you hear during the first Chechen war where Russians were beheaded for fun or had ears, nose, lips cut off. Now they mean nothing to me. They are no different from a Russian, or Belarusian soldier who decides to come to Ukraine and fight against us because they will all suffer the same fate. Most of them are already dead by our drones not even a day into entering Ukraine so their reputation has definitely suffered a HARD BLOW.

Russian Soldier
Northern Front
March 1st

The situation is good here for now. Morale is very high after we got reinforcements. We have enough to eat, and enough rounds to shoot. I am thankful we have the guys though. Without my friends and soldiers here, I don't know if I could be able to do this. I often doubt my ability to lead here, when will be the day I catch the fatal bullet, I ask myself? I can't think about that though. I have to be tough for the guys. I try to write every day for that reason, I can't tell the guys I'm worried, they need me to remain strong for them and be the dependable shield of a brother.

So here it has to go, my thoughts, feelings and worries. The Ukrainians can't hold on for too many more months, we may have even taken Kiev if we didn't keep negotiating everyday like we do. I don't get the point anymore. They don't want to talk with us, they never have. Someday soon, I pray, the war will be over.

Jordan
Western Volunteer - Canada
March 2nd

Today's the day, sounds like a line out of band of brothers but it's the day I leave for Europe, yesterday was a joyous and yet bitterly cold day, my mother helped me finish my preparations for my kit, in all honesty I think she just wanted to spend the day with me.

We spent the day from store to store gathering my essentials, we joked with an underlying sense of I may never see her again after the airport, perhaps. But in any case, I know that this is the right thing to do, not any part of me feels this is a mistake or I'm going for the wrong reasons.

Today we leave in less than 30 minutes to take me to the airport, my dad left for work already. That goodbye was miserable as he's the man who first taught me to shoot, ride a motorcycle, build cars, and now, I'm left with my mother, she's in high spirits so am I, but you can tell they are both scared as much as I am.

But this isn't a fight for just the Ukrainian people this is a fight for the sovereignty of Europe and all that choose freedom and democracy over a tyrannical government.

Ukrainian Civilian
Mariupol
March 2nd

I am on the second floor of my building, what can I say? To all the people that I've already written about our 'noble defenders' of the AZOV regiment that is shooting Russians, heroic fucks! You understand they're sitting here after coming into our homes and shoot from our homes and then we receive a Russian response. Here are the defenders we have, hiding in the civilian fucking population.

Russian Civilian
Russia
March 2nd

My friend wrote me he is serving near Mariupol, in the regiment. Oh, what horror. He said 70 percent. 70 percent are dead. Their unit has three and a half thousand. 70 percent is already dead. Fuck, do you understand how many corpses there are fuck.

This is fucked boys, they're about to check (kill) our whole army, these fucking Ukrainians. Can you imagine what's going to fucking happen? Fuck. They're not gonna conscript us pensioners but the kids and young ones will, you cannot imagine what is happening.

He (Putin) is talking mighty about our army, what fucking army fuck. Army is not ready at all; these boys have never fought before. It is complete ass, do not watch the (Russian State) news, its complete bullshit. Complete bullshit.

Felix
German Civilian
Berlin
March 2nd

I am a volunteer at the central station in Berlin. Since I speak a bit of Russian, I can give the people some orientation. We help arriving Ukrainian people if they want to stay or continue their journey. Someone they want to go directly somewhere else. Some people even wanted to go to Spain and even further away. I was warned before that it might be very tuff, because it can be heartbreaking, but I didn't care.

Yesterday I helped with another volunteer carrying luggage of a family (A mother with two small children). Suddenly the small girl started crying and said to her mom: I want to go home, I want to go home, I want to go home mom. It literally killed me in this moment and also the other volunteer. I have the highest respect for the mother, who calmed her down. Earlier we had a family who came with 12 children and just two mothers. They managed all the way to Berlin. Those mothers and grandmas are so strong. I have the highest respect for them.

Week Two: March 3 - 9

Ukrainian Soldier
March 3rd

I will confirm. I was not in danger. I did see rockets. Hundreds of them fly through the sky in such big numbers it was frightening. It makes me wonder what else they will use. In the moment I feared for my life, but the rockets went right over us to positions behind. The noise of them was huge. It was like someone crushing metal in your ears. Men from behind came to join us that evening who were in the middle of it. One of them told me so many rockets hit the ground that all he could see was nothing because his eyes shook inside his head.

Russian Soldier
Crimea
March 3rd

I should have listened to my father and not go that day. (Recruiting Office) I was driving back with the corpse of a friend who was lying under my feet in an armored vehicle, who had no half of his face, and his blood flooded my face. That is what I'm dreaming of. I can't and don't want to fall asleep.

*Russian soldier who was wounded and sent back to Crimea. Sent via text to a Russian friend, then translated and sent to Battles and Beers for documentation

Ukrainian Civilian
Kyiv
March 3rd

I am alive. Ukraine is fighting the enemy. They shoot bombs at civilians; a vacuum bomb was dropped on the city of Ohktryrka. Shot residential areas of Kharkov Kyiv and other cities. Samubu Nuclear Power Plant was bombed today. The large nuclear power plant of Europe in the city of Energodar near the city of Zaporozhye.

Ukraine needs help my children need your help Already More than 25 children of Ukraine died at the hands of Russians, sorry if my text is bad, I cry and write to you. Our president asks to close the sky and asks to give us airplanes. Why it is necessary, it is necessary to protect the children from attacks from the sky they drop bombs on us.

Our men are fighting, I am alone with my children, he is crying and all the time asking, "Where is dad?" I don't know where my husband is, I don't know if he is alive or not. Thank you for writing to me, I don't know if I survive or not and when I can write next time.

Ukrainian Civilian
Kyiv Oblast
March 3rd

I had not seen any Russian soldiers until yesterday. I saw a dead Russian yesterday. His face was pale color and his skin seemed like rubber. I've never seen a dead person before. There was a small hole in his head and blood all over the side of his face and clothes. He was sitting in the seat of a car. Soldiers shot it. He looked young. 20. I went into his pockets and didn't find anything. I thought maybe I would find a family photo or a phone. Nothing. Maybe it means he has no one at home.

Russian Soldier
Kyiv Oblast
March 3rd

I could not write yesterday, hard battle. The enemy was well entrenched and had heavy weapons. We lost three men, unfortunately. We took their position and captured the rest of their gear. About 7 captives, all either foreigners or Ukrainian army members. The foreigners are Canadians. Because of their role as volunteers, they're being handed over to GRU back at base.

Not sure what happens with them, not my business either. The Ukrainians we took back are being processed and then will be prisoners until this is all over. They weren't exactly bad guys either. Just normal guys, in my opinion. I even had a smoke with one of them. His name is Vasily. God grant them safety and their souls be saved, as our guys we lost are in heaven I pray.

When we took the position, we also found radio equipment, ammo, PKM's in various shapes of disrepair and some in good condition, and a single RPG-7 that was broken when we secured it.

*From the journal of a Russian soldier. Given to Battles and Beers for documentation by the soldier

Art by João "J-Dot" Alves

Western Volunteer
March 7th

The first day of the invasion. Artillery was raining down on us, heavy machine gun fire from multiple directions. It didn't stop, it was terrifying. The first dead body I saw in this conflict was a Ukrainian soldier, I found peace with it in a way. I knew why he gave his life. Civilians on the other hand, innocent lives, how can you kill civilians? Especially children, they had a whole life ahead of them and just like that they're gone.

My first enemy kill, he was 20/21 years old, I guess. I went through his pockets; he had a family photo. I was wondering if he wanted to fight or if he was against the war. I'll never get the answer. In a different time, we might've been good friends. After all the civilian deaths I have no remorse for them, no mercy, let us kill them all.

(To Russian soldiers) Do you want to live? Lay down your weapons and surrender. You'll be sent home, back to your family. If you stay you will die a brutal death. One by one, we will kill you all.

Polish Civilian
Poland
March 7th

I keep seeing flocks of Ukrainian refugees passing the border. Most of them seem to have come by personal cars and there are also full families. The thing is however that many of them that I've seen when it comes to male refugees are not just kids and elderly. You have many males in their 20s, 30s, and 40s who look healthy by their movement who have not been drafted.

Since the law there requires anyone from 18-60 male to be drafted, I think this is a corruption case, which is typical whenever a draft happens. As a man from the Balkans myself I fully support Ukrainian freedom fighters and pity those who have fled their country when their homeland needed them most.

Ukrainian Firefighter
Kyiv Oblast
March 7th

I am not a soldier, but I have seen more dead people than most soldiers. Burning people are horrible smelling. More than once I have pulled fingers or skin off pulling burnt people from bombed buildings. I fight fires as a volunteer. I was a paid member, but I left three years ago to go to university. Now I am back fighting fires.

These fucking Russians shoot their rockets and missiles at buildings and our work never stops. Some (firefighters) wear bulletproof vests because they need to. We put out one fire and another building is struck and another fire starts. We are lucky. Most people are in shelters now and the buildings are empty. Still, we must fight them.

Ukrainian Soldier
Azov Regiment
Letter to his wife
Siege of Mariupol
March 7th

My beloved, I am very worried about you and miss you very much. I regret that I was not with you for a long time, spent little time with you. I so want to see you, hug you very tightly.

You are very important to me; you are my everything. Every day I look at our photos, I remember how our baby crawled for the first time, I'm very worried about you. I love you very much.
Everything will be fine, and we will be together again, and raise our Timofeychik.

Ukrainian Soldier
Kharkiv Oblast
March 8th

War is not real in your head before it happens. Does that make sense? It does not be real until it happens. I was wounded on day 5, moved to hospital, and now am going back to duty for light wounds. It is not real? It is not real to the moment when guns are shooting.

Your soldiers are wounded and killed near you. Or civilians get blown up. When the war began (2014) I was too young. I could not understand what war really is. Now I am a soldier and I know. I know I hate this (the war and the killing), but we must defend Ukraine.

Jason Haigh
Western Volunteer
Kyiv
March 8th

This had to be the worst experience of my life so far. The invasion had started, war had been declared. Everyone's tenseness went up (naturally). No chances were being taken. Russian saboteurs, Special Forces and Chechen mercenaries were operating in the city under the disguise as civilians!

I was moving through the city in civilian clothing with a friend. We had a concealed weapon (For obvious reasons) and two radios in case tele comms (Communication) went down and we got split up. We were arrested and searched. Once those items were found, that was it. We were seen as spies!

The next few hours were hell. Hooded, hands cable-tied behind a chair and beaten. Couldn't see my interrogator but his hands were like fucking shovels, and he bashed my head hard, leaving me with some mild physical injuries. The beatings were bad enough but it's only pain. Pain is temporary and at least it tells you you're still alive! The worst part is the mental turmoil. Constantly questioning yourself how long before they kill you, how long before they fuck you up and you die slowly, how long will I be here. When will they realize we are the good guys?

Then they question your photos...they question people in your messages, nothing more than loved ones back home. But for them it's a tool, it's an emotional weakness that anybody will have. And they had it to work with.

The things they said about people were fucking unimaginable. Were they taking pictures of me and sending it to those people? Were they messaging them and saying things? And yes, it made me want to fly into a rage and kill every fucking one of them. I was completely vulnerable and at their mercy. And it was scary! Eventually, we were released.

They found out we were the good guys. I always had it in my mind in the Middle East that capture was a possibility, but not once did I expect it in Ukraine. However, this is war, and nothing can be unexpected, really. It doesn't make me regret my time there, I just couldn't stay after that. War is Hell.

Western Civilian
Russia
March 9th

I'm in Russia, I'm not Russian, just an international student, last year of university. Couple of days back we went to a bar and restaurant with some friends, just to distract us for a bit from everything. It was kind of late, place was getting empty quickly. After eating we were getting ready to leave when a guy that we thought was a waiter approached us and said, (In Russian)

"Hey guys, how are you? So, here's the deal you can order anything from the menu, anything and I'll pay for it, don't worry it's not a scam I'm telling the truth."

The guy went on for like 5 minutes trying to convince us. We noticed he was a bit tipsy, so we sort of agreed just to not make him mad, and he took our orders. Then he sat with us and started rambling. Well, turns out this guy was a freaking Spetsnaz.

At first, we didn't believe him but then his friend came by and sat with us too, this guy looked a bit older. Way older, and he was also Spetsnaz and had served in Chechnya and Syria. He confirmed it. They were both Spetsnaz and they were being sent to Ukraine this week. Our stomachs and heart sank. Like we knew, they knew what was going on, and we got really silent.

The younger guy: let's call him "A", he was barely 23 years old and the older one, "B", he was entering his 30s. "B" was silent and started telling us that they'll go over there, and by their looks, they didn't want to but also couldn't refuse. And they knew they may not come back, "A" wanted to give me his phone for free, pay for all our food or drinks, because he knew money was not anymore a need for him.

He was in like a happy or euphoric state (Drunk basically) "B" was more somber. With us being international students, I think it took a bit of weight off of them because…well, being a Russian soldier, everyone hates you right now.

We weren't going to give them shit, not because we were afraid of them but because we knew and we could see, they didn't want this. No one in Russia wants this, the only ones that do are the retards that buy the state media's bullshit.

Western Volunteer
International Legion
Battle of Kyiv, Moschun
March 9th

North of Kyiv in the second week of March the fight there was bloody. We fought in villages and the woods against Russian VDV and Spetsnaz soldiers. Some regulars and conscripts also. It was my first experience in battle ever and my 5th time firing a gun. A Russian BTR came from the road to the edge of our village next to trenches we had dug. The bravest thing I had seen in my life happened. Two soldiers ran from the village into the trench. They carried rockets. The BTR shot our buildings. (Buildings in this part of Ukraine are easily destroyed. Constructed of wood)

The two soldiers in the trench went as close as they could and fired a rocket which hit the side of the BTR. The BTR stopped firing and for a few minutes did not move. It was smoking and Russian soldiers began to leave the area because our defense was too strong to overtake. A Russian tried to leave the BTR, and he was shot by the soldiers in the trench. The whole fight those soldiers stayed in that trench by themselves on the front almost next to the Russians in front of us.

Art by João "J-Dot" Alves

Ukrainian Soldier
March 9th

Combat is scary and very loud. I was nearly killed on February 28. A line of Russian tanks stopped not far from us and began firing. The machine gun from one felt like time slowed. Zip! Right past my head. We left the area since we had no weapons to fight tanks and waited for help. The time we ran away they kept shooting at us. Russian bullets going right past us, and one destroyed the rifle while a man held it. He dropped the destroyed rifle and ran even faster past me. This is humorous now to think about. We are all running and then this soldier runs past all us even faster running like an Olympic runner.

Western Volunteer
Poland
March 9th

The worst thing for me to see is the children. These poor, homeless, tortured children. I am an aid worker working on the Polish border helping refugees get where they need to go. All day long there's an endless stream of mothers, sons, daughters and elderly coming across. The look on their faces is always the same: Sadness.

I grew up listening to stories about my Opa and their time as refugees during World War Two. The struggles they endured and the horrors they faced. It never seemed real to me. Now here I am witnessing it first-hand. If I took a black and white picture of these poor people and showed you, you'd almost think it was from the 40's.

How is any political dispute worth this? The children don't understand what's going on. How is any of this still happening today? It just breaks my heart.

Polish Civilian
Poland
March 9th

Mothers here are the best in the world. They have been leaving infant strollers at the train station for Ukrainian mothers to use who are fleeing the war. They get off the trains and are greeted by their Polish neighbors. I live in a border town in Poland. In 14 days almost 300,000 people have come here or passed through here. Can you imagine that? 300,000 in a town built for 1/8th of that. I think many people still remember the suffering from the last big war. They don't want to repeat it and are doing whatever they can to ease the suffering of other people.

Anton Kyryk
Ukrainian Civilian
Bucha
March 9th

Why do Russians torture civilians in Ukraine? It seems just yesterday being a pilot of Gulfstream G200 (A civilian aircraft) I was looking down at the serene and beautiful coast of Tivat from the altitude of 12000m (7.5 miles). Yet, a couple of days since I am on my knees in a house in the suburbs of Kyiv, hands tied with a wire behind my back, cloth over my head, and gasoline over my body…listening to ruminations whether to set me on fire inside the building or outside.

On Feb 24, 2022, the war entered our country. We learned about this at 5:55am when my godfather rang us. Over the first day, we couldn't understand how this was a possibility in the middle of Europe in the 21st century. We lived in the town of Bucha which is about 2km from the runway of the Hostomel airport.

From the very first day of war on, the bombings never ceased in our area, soon converting into shelling and active combat on the streets of our town…We, Ukrainians, lost "Mria" (A famous Ukrainian aircraft) the shed of which I saw being obliterated just peeking around the corner. I took pictures of this atrocity…The first three days were very scary because of the bombing, and a lot of aircrafts were flying just 20-30 meters overhead. We spent these days in the basement of the house we were renting at that moment.

My wife hunts, and we had some hunting paraphernalia which came handy: sleeping bags, flashlights, canned food, and other stuff we needed in order to survive...In the very first hours of war, we realized that we had two main problems to face: we did not have cash in hryvnias (Local currency), and we were running out of food for our dog, a member of our family.

We decided to drive around and try to find out where we could exchange money (euros) to buy drinking water and dog food. First, I thought that we were in a traffic jam exiting Bucha towards Irpin on the Vokzalna Street. Turns out it was just a 750 - meter line for the gas station. I realized that when I left the car leaving my wife to make sure we were advancing in the line. We managed to pass these cars through the oncoming lane and – after some management on my part – enter the neighboring town of Irpin. After a few visits to the local currency exchange units, it became obvious that there was no cash to be found.

In the third unit we visited I was visibly distraught and having said that my dog will be left to hunger, the staff were kind to give me all the 20-hryvnia bills they had. I was really glad to have exchanged €200 for three wads of "green Frankos" (Franko is a national poet depicted on the 20-hryvnia bills which are of green color). Looking to spend the money we secured, we saw the most enormous lines, the longest of which led to ATMs and vets.

We decided to go to the local hospital where we knew there was dog food. We bought a big pack, but even that pack was already opened. The food was being sold piecemeal.

We were really glad to have found the little one some food, deciding then to return home. On our way we saw an open store and stopped nearby. When we left the car, we saw an enormous smoke plume coming from about where our home was. We bought some cereal, some ramen, and 2 bottles of liquor to disinfect wounds if need be.

We then moved towards home, exactly towards that very plume of black smoke…The entirety of the trip was accompanied by explosions, but they were rather far. Having retuned, and bought drinking water on our way, we started preparations to the war that had already started.

We spent a couple of days in the basement. Then the Orcs Ukrainian slang for Russian soldiers and their Belarusian or Chechen colleagues) destroyed the local powerline. We were trying to find water, food, and a place to charge our cellphones and power banks.

On the seventh day, a friend of mine asked me to carry a little girl called Polia whose mother was trying to evacuate to the city of Irpin. I met them at the local Bethany church and set out with the 1.5-year-old Polia to Irpin on foot. We passed by a lot of destroyed and burnt military vehicles of Rascists (Russian fascists) on Vokzalna street. I carried the girl through all of the security checkpoints, then our soldier drove them to the train carrying evacuees, and everything was fine.

On my way back I filmed all of what happened on Vokzalna Street on my phone. I went to the building of the city council – they needed help delivering medicine around the city. Me and my friend Stas decided to help and used bikes to deliver the medicine to basements and houses. After about ten tours of the city, teroborona (Units of civilians who volunteers for defense) nicknamed us "field postmen".

We needed to deliver two packages of pills and baby food to Jablunska Street. The city council had information that orcs had a camp in the town of Vorzel – and two packages we needed to deliver were going to the house at the very end of Jablunska Street, which borders on Vorzel. We decided to leave the packages at 177 Jablunska Street; the local people could handle the rest.

We turned right from Haharina to Jablunska, and about 100m in we found ourselves under a flurry of automatic rifles firing at us. I jumped to the left and was lucky to fall into a ditch. Stas jumped to the right, under a fence. I called the city council and asked who it was that fired. Larisa, the woman from the city council who was overseeing our delivery efforts burst into tears and told us that there were no Ukrainian soldiers in that area.

We discovered a new firing point, it appeared. Stas ran across the street to me and carried the bike with him. He was still being fired at, automatic rifles again. We weren't hurt and decided to get back to Haharina through private property and then run. We walked to 300 Jablunska and found a small wicket. Stas opened it, peaked outside, but I dragged him back – that very instant we were fired at by a sniper, but he was using a different gun, not an automatic rifle. There were two shots.

We knocked on the doors of the house at that address and begged to let us in. All the people there are scared, they see death. And the press tells everyone that orcs dress up as civilians and knock on the doors asking for shelter. The owners first said they wouldn't let us in. We were standing in front of the house, and we heard shots right next to us – it was the automatic rifle again. We now think they meant to finish us off in that ditch. The man who came out of the house to talk to us ran back inside and closed the doors.

We ran down to the cellar and hid there for about an hour and a half. It was freezing. We called Larisa and she asked us to let her speak to the residents of the house. I knocked on the window, which they opened a bit, and the city council implored them to take two volunteers in. They said house owners could call 102 (Police emergency number) and officials from Rada (Parliament of Ukraine) would talk to them. After 5-7 minutes we were let into the hallway where we spent the next five days. The residents gave us a bowl of broth each and offered hot tea.

There we learnt that the owner of the house, his wife and kids decided to go to their relatives to take a shower and stayed there because of the shooting on the street. We were also given a baby mattress on which we slept.

The following day the house owner came back with his family. His name is Artem, he's a very nice and kind person who found us a comforter and fed us. It was freezing cold, the temperature in that small hallway was at about 7 degrees Celsius or so…But we had access to a toilet.

In a day, on March 5th, the house next to the one we were sheltering in was taken by Russian soldiers who chose it as their base, having come in on a BMD. They came to search us, and their leader didn't believe his eyes when he saw the videos, I took of burnt Russian military vehicles (Vokzalna Street). When I told him it was just 500 meters away from us, he paled in his face. They let us use the potbelly stove and we could cook hot food, because prior to that all we had was buckwheat softened in cold water.

Soldiers of the Russian army even came to fry dumplings on the stove once; they soon left. The active combat, shelling, and bombing never ceased. The other house next to us was destroyed by a bomb. 92-year-old women who lived there was dragged out of debris, but she was not at all glad to have been saved. Her face was badly wounded. On March 6 the orcs didn't come back to us – they found a stove at their place.

March 7th. Their leader came around and told us that a green corridor towards Irpin was active. We hesitated, because there hadn't been cell connection for two days by then, and we didn't know anything. The last text from Larisa from the city council was not to go to Novator (A local area) because Russian soldiers were there. We hesitated more still, because we had no knowledge of what happened to our families which live next to Novator.

Our decision was to go. (Evacuate) Perhaps it was a mistake. We came out on Jablonska Street and saw that some people were already walking toward Irpin. We grabbed our bikes which we left around the house and decided to walk with the bikes so that if teroborona sees us they know we're the "field postmen". (Volunteers who brought medicine to civilians)

We walked through the Vodoprovidna Street along the shelled cars with other civilians. Soldiers of Russian army who were at 217 Vodoprovidna aimed at us and ordered to lie face down. We did as told, saying that the green corridor was active.

They told us to approach one by one, still aiming at us. I was upfront and approached first. There were about twenty of them around the building and there were some military vehicles and some equipment. They searched me aggressively and took away the phone. Then they threw me into a cellar and locked the door. In a few minutes they threw Stas in as well. We were captured as prisoners of war.

They opened the door, asked the passcode for my phone, and then closed the door. In about ten minutes, I was called out to be interrogated. They led me into a shed while aiming a gun at me. Then threw me to my knees in front of their leader, still aiming a handgun from the front and a rifle from the back at me. They asked where the Nazis were, where Aidar and Azov were. They asked where the captured soldiers were and where our guns were.

Then they hit me on the head with a handle of a handgun, to scare. I bled a lot. The interrogation continued for several more minutes. Having looked through my phone, they realized I'm a (civilian) pilot and asked about that and battered more. After that they led me back to the cellar and locked the door. In a few minutes, they brought some napkins and a clean towel.

They said there was water down in the cellar, to which I said it was too dark to see where it was. I had a flashlight in my backpack which they took away. They then brought the flashlight and locked us once again. Stas poured some water on my hands, and I washed the blood off my hands and my face. We waited. In about thirty minutes, the doors opened, and the voice said "льотчик на выход" (Ordering me out of the cellar)

This was the last time I saw Stas. When I came out of the cellar, I was blindfolded with a piece of cloth that was then coiled around my neck. Then they tied my hands with a wire and started poking me with a rifle, threatening to hang, lynch, and shoot me. Having bent me, they led me somewhere – all the way telling these are my last minutes. We arrived at some space where there were a lot of this scum and with a blow (which hurt my leg) I was thrown down to the floor.

All of this was accompanied by heavy battering. When I was lying on the floor, they started pouring gasoline over me shouting they'll roast me. At this point, some official entered the room and ordered not to make the room dirty and take me outside. I was led outside the building and thrown to my knees; my head leaned on the wall. When I was standing so, they hit me with a butt of a rifle on my ribs; the ribs cracked. The battering continued. Then I was led somewhere else again.

I was standing there and asked for a smoke (I haven't had a cigarette in 16 years, but still I did smoke because I couldn't smell gasoline because of stress – I thought it was water, to scare me in some way). I stood there smoking through a piece of cloth soaked in gasoline, gasoline dripping off of me…Then someone said to, "Cut his eyes.", and someone else wanted to clarify whether he understood correctly that the intention was to cut out his (mine) eyes.

They decided to take off the cloth off of my head, untied my hands, and nearly strangled me while taking the cloth off the head because it was coiled around my neck. They put cotton pants of a Russian soldier on me, then an empty bulletproof vest and a potato-beetle-striped helmet (same as those of ribbon of St. George) then they tied white bags to my sleeves, same as they had. They brought a chair and sat me down; told me I might have a chance to survive.

I was gradually realizing what will happen. They pointed to a human mannequin lying nearby, a model of a human, and said that it doesn't fit and doesn't work. Then they asked if I understood what I had to do. I said I wasn't stupid.

They promised to let me go after I come back from the tank. I asked to bring Stas, they told me they would bring him after the jobs complete. It was the time to get out on the turret of that tank. I was told to fiddle with the gun mantle at the top. I climbed up and was behaving as brainlessly as I could. I patted the gun, lifted the backpack which was lying on the tank. Then our sniper shot, who they wanted to detect using me.

I think the sniper understood it was a costumed person and shot at the tank, not at me. My arm was wounded by a shatter of something – a part of the tank or a bullet – I grabbed a pack of dry food which was lying on the tank as well and ran behind the shed where the Russians were waiting. I told them I brought food and asked for something to wipe the blood which was streaming down my hand.

Having sopped some blood off, I saw a black shatter and asked for a knife to get it out. They were very surprised that I wanted to take it out myself and I told them they could do it themselves instead. Wide-eyed, they found some pliers which I used to get the splinter out.

They gave me some light beverage, then beer. I refused, asking for alcohol which surprised them again. They managed to find a bottle of whiskey stolen from a destroyed store. I rinsed the wound and drank some.

They said I'll need to go again, to which I told them they promised to let me go. They couldn't detect the Ukrainian sniper the first time around. I was sitting in the same chair and waiting. Meanwhile, they were regrouping to see where the shots were coming from. While we were sitting, they decided to put the armor in the bulletproof vest after all.

One of the ceramic plates was shot at that very same day, when the vest was worn by a 19-year-old Russian soldier. You can't imagine how dumb they are. Their tank mechanic can't even insert armor plates into a bulletproof vest – they all laughed at him.

They put the plates in and put the vest on me again. Then it was the time to go again. I asked to bring Stas out. He has a 4-year-old daughter. They said after you climb up the tank, count to 20 and come back. Having climbed up, I started doing the same as the last time – patting the gun, touching the backpack which was still there. I forgot to count – but they shouted for me to come back. I came back and they said it was "Utter bullshit".

They told me to wait and that I'll need to climb another tank, the one further away in the yard. I was called by a different group of soldiers who were explaining what'd happen to me. They said there will be a soldier with an automatic rifle behind the house which was in the yard. If I think of running, they'll shoot me.

I asked them again to bring Stas, to which they said they'll bring him after the job's done and then we'll be able to go. I sat and waited again. They were regrouping. Then I needed to go for the third time. I was told to bring a 20-liter barrel which was atop the tank. My head ducked in; I ran. When I reached the tank, there were a lot of soldiers behind it – they were hiding there. I climbed the tank, grabbed the barrel and ran back. There was no shot the third time.

They started undressing me -- they took off the helmet, the vest, and the cotton pants. One of the soldiers took off his red sweater from under his pea coat, and they put it on me.

Art by João "J-Dot" Alves

Their leader came and spoke to me. "Слушай меня. Тебя отправили в мою бригаду что-бы расстрелять. Я принял решение использовать тебя по другому и дать тебе шанс. Ты трижды ушёл из под снайпера, наверное ты святой". 'Look, you were sent to my group to be shot. I decided to use you in a different way and give you a chance. You escaped the sniper thrice -- you must be a saint.'

I said they promised to let Stas go, to which he said it was not within his power. He ordered the soldier to accompany me around the corner and let go. There, the soldier showed me a neighboring piece of property and told me to pass through a wicket and go. I asked him to try to help Stas and reminded again of Dasha who's four years old and is waiting for her dad at home. I also asked what I need to do if I meet other soldiers on my way. He said to tell them "я работал на углу с "Успехом" ("that I was working at the corner with the Uspech group").

I exited Vokzana Street and walked along the street, hands above my head. I passed the very same burnt vehicles which I saw carrying the girl, Polia, to evacuation not five days ago. There were more burnt vehicles there now, and a burnt refueller as well. Having reached Bucha's railways station, I was afraid to cross such a vast open space. I was moving slowly, careful not to step on a mine.

Around the corner, I saw two Russian soldiers who were aiming at me. They also had automatic rifles. I said I was working at the corner with Uspech, and they let me come back to my wife who hasn't heard from me in a few days, and who does not know what happened to me and whether I'm alive. They lowered their rifles and said only that they weren't sure I'd make it.

So, I walked with my hands over my head all the time, and running across the crossings with my head ducked in. I made it. My wife, Yana, almost fainted when she saw me. When she hugged me, she asked, through tears, why I reeked of gasoline. It was only then that I realized that they weren't intending to scare me, but to really burn me alive instead.

Yana tore the clothes of me and washed me in a basin in the middle of the room. I was scared to go outside the next day. I am still scared of the sound of a started car and slamming door. At home I learned that on Mar 5, five armed soldiers searched our house while my wife was there. They took away her hunting gun and all of the equipment, demanding to know her connection to the shootings on the street...They thought our reflex camera was a night-vision device, and they thought camera lenses to be optical enhancement for the gun.

The scariest of all is that while living in Bucha, we have gotten used to seeing corpses. Corpses around the street, corpses in shopping carts, parts of people around... When asked for directions, we were told once to "take a left behind the corpse". There just wasn't anyone around to clean up the bodies of our civilians killed by Russian "Zaviours" (The rhetoric of Russian government is that they are "saving" Ukraine form Nazi's.)

It is abhorrent to see the cars with 'CHILDREN' written on and were destroyed by gunfire. (Cars that are used for evaluating children and are fired at) It's unimaginable that 67 unidentified Ukrainians were buried in a mass grave next to the church...And a mother with a toddler was buried right in the yard in front of their house.

You cannot even fathom my dread at the thought of what happened to Stas, whose kid is four years old. But I kindle the hope, very very desperately! He was just helping people, and it was for this that we were locked in a cellar. We, civil volunteers, who had pills in our backpack, phone numbers and addresses of people whose survival depended on those pills. On March 9th we managed to evacuate to Kyiv.

A family of ten people with a toddler who was ten months old, and their dog evacuated with us. So, we travelled, our dog at front at the feet of my wife. For the other family to be able to leave with us, we had to give up all of our clothes. It took 9 hours to get to Kyiv. The last car in our fleet was fired at and it couldn't move. We were asked to help to drag it. We were driven to the bus station at Borschahivka (a district in Kyiv) there were food and medics.

The girls brought us a little boy to change his diaper into a warm tent for kids. Meanwhile, I approached a guy from the rescue forces, asked to hug him, and burst into tears. Russians are not people to me anymore.

Week Three: March 10 - 16

Polish Civilian
Poland
March 10th

I live in a border town in Poland. In 14 days almost 300,000 people have come here or passed through here. Can you imagine that? 300,000 in a town built for 1/8th of that. I think many people still remember the suffering from the last big war. They don't want to repeat it and are doing whatever they can to ease the suffering of other people.

"Hiroshima"
Ukrainian Soldier/Medic
Battle of Kyiv, Moschun
March 11th

We defended a village near Kyiv for 5 days. There were 21 of us in the beginning. Every day we were shelled by 'Grad' mines etc. Nothing serious. On the 3rd day, a Russian KA-52 helicopter found us and attacked. But his partner (other KA-52) was put down so that one flew away.

On the fourth- and fifth-day Russian aviation found us and bombed us. Being bombed by aviation feels like…you see a flash somewhere near you, you close your eyes and when you open them, you find yourself somehow in the other part of the room covered with plaster.

On the 5th day (It was evening) the plane started to bomb us with cassette bombs (Like carpet bombing). I was running into the cellar and a blast wave knocked me off my feet and I flew down the stairs. Next blast wave knocked my brother in arms (Call sign Chief) off his feet and he also flew down the stairs next to me. But he was not that lucky like me because a heavy metallic door to the cellar (which was also hit by a blast wave) hit him in his back - so he got a spinal injury and a traumatic brain injury.

So, we are in the cellar. I immobilized him with my special litters, put a Sam Pelvic Sling, which didn't work because it was not his size (because it so stupid to produce pelvic sling of different sizes). I made an improvised pelvic sling from two "SICH" tourniquets (which was a fucking great thing to do, because they immobilized his pelvic better than anything else) and put a Shanz's Collar on his neck.

During that time, we were hardly shelled. The cellar inside felt like an aquarium. After that, when it became calm, we realized that our radio was destroyed (Because of shelling) and we were out of connection with other units, so we needed to evacuate him by our means, nobody was coming to take him.

We went out of the cellar and took Chief immobilized out as well. There were only seven of us left or eight including Chief. We transported him on foot. Walked about 2 km from the village. The guys transported Chief, and I was walking behind them to provide a rearguard.

After that we needed to hide with Chief in a village house so a Russian drone and plane could not find us (they were trying to find us). We spent in that house all night long. I wasn't sleeping and were controlling/stabilizing his condition (Giving him all possible medical care so as hypothermia would not kill him) all night long while commander of my unit and other guys were not sleeping at all to check and to guard our hideout.

We heard the fucking drones and a fucking plane flying around and over us; we heard war machines (Tanks, BMP, BTR) moving very close to us (and we couldn't confirm if those were our guys or Russians, because we were out of touch with our guys completely). But not one of those 7 guys ever left the house that night. We just had one AK-74 and nothing more.

Mines (also "Grad") were falling not far from our hideout all night long. But nobody left the hideout, nobody slept. Even I felt so strongly that it had not been possible for us to survive, we were thinking only about one thing: "How tactically can we evaluate Chief in this situation". We waited till the morning. Only in the morning we could confirm that our guys were close to us, and we could finally evacuate him to our guys and then I personally evacuated him to the hospital. Chief is alive now and feels fine.

That evacuation was the longest in my experience, it took 12 hours. After I passed Chief to doctors at a hospital, adrenaline rush left me and I became deaf for a week. I am very grateful to God because on that night I met seven very beautiful souls, whom I can trust my life.

"Doc Snickers"
Ukrainian Soldier/Medic
Battle of Kyiv, Moschun
March 11th

I'm a combat medic, was attached with a company to go retake a town of Moschun just outside Horenka. As soon as 80 of us got off the buses we got bombarded by Russian artillery with the aid of an observation drone flying a kilometer or so above us. In the break between bombardments, we retreated from this absolutely exposed position in the woods outside the town.

Unfortunately, we had a few wounded, and, by whatever miracle, none dead. One of the wounded was a section commander, young guy of 22, about 6'6 and 235 pounds of muscle. He caught a big piece of shrapnel in his upper left arm which broke the bone and tore a large part of his bicep/triceps away. He did well and handled it like a man but soon from the loss of blood he couldn't walk.

So, the 4 of us had to carry the guy on a cloth litter in his gear and with our gear for about 1.5-2 km, thru woods by rushing from cover to cover while dodging artillery. Some landing within 15 meters of the hole we currently were praying into which ever God was listening.

After about a kilometer, the barrage lifted, and we could finish our trip to the road in relative peace and commandeered an abandoned vehicle to transport the wounded to the unit ambulance. The guy survived and was able to keep his arm, though after the extensive surgeries he will be recuperating for a long time. As for us, we had to walk 3 more km back to Horenka, just in time to catch the bus going back for the same assault on the same town in the same place…well shit, orders are orders, what else could we do? Ate a snickers and loaded back up on the bus.

After getting on the bus for the assault we got stopped halfway before reaching the town because the point where we were going to unload got hit again with artillery. So, we took positions inside the forest and waited for orders. After an hour or so we were told we would be going back to Horenka and try again for Moschun tomorrow.

There was one more thing we had to do, they needed volunteers to take a few little minibuses to go to the places that we got hit with artillery earlier and take any and all ammunition, backpacks and stragglers back with us. I volunteered. Not because I'm a heroic individual with a vision of glory and triumph, no, my backpack had to be left behind while were carrying the wounded and it had my dry socks, underwear, and my much-needed supply of candy. So yes, in essence, I volunteered to go rescue my candy and I would do it again. We loaded on the minibus, three in each.

We kept the doors open since we have been hearing small arms fire from that general area. As we sped in, it was hard to recognize it, trees have fallen everywhere, and there were two still smoldering vehicles and burning grass and wreckage everywhere. But an angel in a form of an old man! It was an old volunteer soldier who stayed behind and, between bombardments, collected all our bags and ammo in a neat pile which he was sitting on top and eating a can of spaghetti. George Clooney never looked as great as this old man with missing teeth filled with spaghetti.

We took him and all our things and headed back to Horenka. There, we were told to split into groups and find a safe place to sleep on the last row of houses of the town. My unit found a three-meter-deep cellar and all 12 slept in (since no food was brought, we scrounged for food and we're able to get really delicious canned tomatoes and pickles). Most people had left the area and the houses were showing various degrees of damage.

During the evening we thought about sleeping in one of the houses instead of the cellar, which was cold, damp and cramped, but decided not to. And thank goodness. At around 11:30 pm for an hour straight our line was hit with howitzers. It was hitting close and the whole cellar would shake, and we get covered in dust. We awaited the new day with sleep deprived humor of hungry men.

In the morning, we climbed out of the cellar and viewed the destruction and received our orders. The unit I was with and my other friend/medic get rotated out, while we had to stay and get attached to a different unit, since medics usually were few and thus floated between units. But we wouldn't get linked up till the afternoon so what progressed was just a weird day.

We dug trenches, hung out with Georgian snipers, found Nutella in a bombed out kitchen, unwittingly became part of a tractor heist (I was asked to drive it to a different location, I didn't know the guys didn't own that tractor or had permission to take it from this unit), and occasionally hid from artillery, one such shell destroying a beautiful old tree 15 meters away that we were just admiring.

At around 3pm we gathered with our new unit and were told to board a white van. Me and my buddy were the last ones to about to get into it when I happened to look down the road at another vehicle approximately 50 meters away, when an artillery shell hit just on the other side of it. We ran for the closest cover and layer down on the south side of a building since the Russians were shelling us from the north and this put something in between us. The whole village got bombarded with our ears ringing from one that landed very close, close enough to shower us with dirt and send fragmentation into the wall above our heads.

Once the shelling stopped, we were told to get back into the white van, which, by some miracle was still able to run, regardless of the fact that all the windows were cracked or broken and that the walls of the van had enough holes in it for it to earn the nickname "Pasta Strainer". After a short drive back to the town of Moschun we disembarked and, hiked thru the woods on the outskirts to the building that would be our forward observation post.

We had to carry all the ammo, food, water and, in my case, 4 shots of rpg-7 or what we call "Plushki" or "Piggies". En-route, we had to sneak towards our building since the idea was the enemy couldn't see us, but that is hard to do with 15 people. So, we incurred the wrath of an AGS grenade launcher, mortar fire and three strafing runs by a single chopper. We hid in unfinished buildings, to minimize their accuracy, since they knew our general area but not exact location. But still they managed to lightly wound 2 of ours that were evacuated back.

At dusk we managed to get to our designated building and after establishing a perimeter and hissing from prying eyes we began our forward observation duties. That was to be our home for the next 3 days.

Dakota
Western Volunteer – International Legion
Battle of Kyiv, Moschun
March 5th - 11th

I felt a moral obligation if anything to go. An indescribable tug on my heart, kind of thing. Indescribable. It was strange because I had just started college on the 22nd and I was very excited to do normal people shit. Cyber security or something. Russia invaded on the 24th and I was alone at my girlfriend's house, and I thought, man oh man. I gotta go.

I messaged this guy, an Australian reporter. He had lived in Ukraine for a few years. I asked him how to get over there. Once he realized I was serious he was like okay man, here's the contacts you need and how to get there. Just normal guys quitting their normal lives to get over there. I bought my ticket for March 2nd.

I got across the border in Ukraine and I meet up with Sasha, this woman I got in contact with. She takes me to the nearest military outpost in the middle of the night. We go in there, me and this other guy and we are talking to the commander. We are the first foreigners he has met. He hooks us up with a ride and we go to another base. When we get there, we go to a tent. This is where they asked us if we had combat experience. I said I had a little from Afghanistan.

I went to talk to a colonel. He had seen a lot of James Bond movies. He's sitting there with his legs crossed trying to be intimidating. He says, "I have a special mission." Basically, a bunch of SOF guys had shown up and were like, "Give us weapons. Give us rockets. We are gonna go to Kyiv and fuck up some Russians." And they wanted more dudes to help them. Meaning us, Western Volunteers.

They had the guys who had volunteered meet with the dudes assembling this team. Just normal dudes it seemed, but it seemed extra special to me because I'm a regular infantry guy. They explained that we were going to fight and if we wanted to do this we had to be down to clown. I told them I knew how to use javelins and they were like awesome.

We went to a gear issue where we got camo, Kevlar's, carriers, etc. I had brought my own carrier. They had my team go and check the Javelins. I checked one out and they had no batteries. They were useless and they sent me to a warehoused to find them. I went to three diff buildings and the number of weapons they had was huge. I found a bunch of javelins, but no batteries, so I eventually went back and yeah, they ain't got shit.

We rolled out on March 5th in the middle of the night in two big buses full of LAWS and other kinds of rockets. Stacks of ammo. We eventually get to Kyiv. The whole trip you're just brooding at the thought like, oh man this is gonna be like Stalingrad because all we had heard was the city was surrounded. I honestly started praying which was new to me. Eventually we got to this safe house. A very large building. Nice accommodations.

We came into contact with Ukrainian SOF. GUR guys. Two hours after we arrived and had showers, we signed contracts, had our pictures taken, and guys were wigged out about signing a contract because the war had JUST started. I was wigged out too, so I wrote down the wrong phone number and home address. I probably shouldn't have done that but oh well. The GUR guys didn't really tell us shit other than we were going on mission, and they were taking 20 guys with. So, two hours after we get there we get in some military vehicles, and they start throwing in cartons of cigarettes. They came in very handy not even 1 day later.

We loaded up, drove to wherever because they didn't tell us anything at all. I thought this was pretty fair because we were the first westerners they had seen. The organization wasn't there yet. We arrived in Horenska. We got off the trucks. It's like 20 or so westerners and at least 200 Ukrainians. They made us the lead element to push down the northern road. We are looking at Horenska and it's been shelled to shit. We can hear mortars firing off in the distance. The city was embers, walking by destroyed buildings. There were zero Russians here.

We eventually get to the end of the road. A Ukrainian says, "Okay guys put your bags down we are going to patrol through the tree line. Be back in three hours." We put our bags down and he points in front of us. "Everything this way is Russians."

We start patrolling through the tree line maybe 5km. We are in along wedge formation, and we are pushing through the woods. Moschun village up ahead. I'm on the right most corner. We come to the outskirts of the village, and we can see the edge. We hear machine gun fire, snaps, and mortars. It reminded me of band of brothers. We are just lying in the dirt and once there was a lull, we push up to the outskirts of the village to a massive trench line. The Russians had taken it, but while we were assaulting, they had run away.

They had left behind a bunch of blankets and rugs. My buddy Kevin comes up, Former Ranger, he's like "Hey we need another dude to assault this house in the village." So, we push up from the trench and maybe 50 meters ahead of the trench is this big shed and we clear it. Then we push into a courtyard of a villa type home, and we get to the house

103

itself and there's rounds going through the building. I didn't realize this until Kevin said the rounds were impacting behind my head.

I fired into the building, and we push in. There really wasn't anyone in there. Whoever was in there ran away. So, I, our Doc, a Canadian dude, and a Ukrainian guy named Lu are in the house with a few others. Lu is on top floor; Doc and I are bottom floor holding security. We are just waiting and its maybe 6am. We are there for hours. Until nightfall. Its pitch black and the only thing we can see is fires burning in houses. 12 of us total in the house.

I call up to Lu "Lu where is everyone?" Lu says, "Fucking hell guys, remain tension." So, another hour passes. I ask him again, "You're the one with the radio, where is everyone?" Another hour passes and I ask him again. He comes down, and says "Guys, I don't think anyone is in the trenches behind us. We may be surrounded. Remain tension." Big fat L there, Lu.

So, I'm looking at the only door coming into the house. Doc is looking into the courtyard. As I'm looking at the door, I hear a dude coming. I'm ready to shoot him. A guy steps in and says, "Friendly, friendly, friendly." It's our friend Ryan. He comes in with a PKM. Army vet who fought with the Kurds, knows his shit.

We ask him where the fuck everyone is. He said they placed him in a field with a PKM and they just left. So, we just light cigarettes, and we start smoking. We are blocking the light with our hands and shit. Then we are looking at this house burning, and we hear this guy (Russian) screaming behind Russian lines. We said they must really hate that guy they fucking left him.

Then we hear a squad coming up to the house, don't know if they are friendly. We are about to light up the whole wall. They end up being friendly and it's literally the rest of our Western friends. They kept saying "That was fucking crazy!" We have no idea what they're talking about, so we ask what was so crazy.

I guess they ran 900 yards down the road behind the Russian lines into a house and didn't realize they were behind the lines. They stopped in a house and had no idea where everyone else was. Then I guess they heard the Russians outside trying to give challenge and pass. The Ukrainian commander with them racked a round into his handgun. All of a sudden, a Russian guy gave the challenge again, but the Russians left the house alone because it was dark. So, these guys just waited an hour and then ran back down the road to our house. We told them we didn't think anyone was in the trenches and we are probably surrounded. We had two or three guys on security. The Ukrainians commander just told us to go to sleep, but we kept a 50% watch.

There was a weird gentlemen's agreement between us and the Russians. No one had night vision. No one would shoot at each other. They would play battleship with artillery and mortars. Nothing really happened. No one knew where anyone was so if you went into a house, it could be a platoon or squad of friendlies or enemies. So, everyone just stayed put and tried not to die or piss off the other side. We had a single thermal handheld. That's it.

The second day, morning time. Chris goes up on the long gun. Its 7am and he's aiming down the road, and he sees like three Russian guys having coffee or tea. He yells down and asks, "Can I fucking kill them?" The commander goes, "Ehh, hold off." But Chris says he can see them. So, the commander says okay. So, Chris shoots one and hits one in the pelvis. And no shit right after that we start taking all the artillery. So, it clicked there again. Another gentleman's agreement. You let guys have their morning coffee and then the war starts after.

So, we started taking a fuck ton of artillery. When you take artillery, you first hear the firing, and then you wait for the impacts. It was hitting all around. In the trenches, buildings, everywhere. So that's how we started the day.

We got intel from a drone saying a convoy of 13 vehicles. BMP's and tanks crossing a pontoon bridge the Russians had built. So, Tim (former Ranger) and I go out and prep LAWs. We took like 12 LAWS and a few AT4's and got them all ready to rapid fire these fucking things. We are sitting by the gate of the house waiting, then we take another barrage. This time mortars. So, we sprawl out on the ground. They get closer to the house and so we creep closer to the house. Two 82mm mortars land right next to Tim and me in this very soft garden earth. I look at it, he looks and me, and I say, "I think it's time to go back inside the house, man."

A couple of barrages later, a Russian BMP arrives, and Jesse myself, and our Ukrainian commander go to kill that BMP. We run outside and run toward the trenches. At this point we have two friendly Ukrainian tanks. One tank is going down the road toward the west alongside the trenches. We get behind the tank. We start taking small arms fire and. Our commander shot a Russian about 75 yards down the road from us. Through a window in a shed. Jesse and I run off to the right of a tank and run behind a destroyed brick house. The commander comes with us. Some other guys join us.

I'm looking over at the tank and all of a sudden, we hear the BMP in the distance. We can't see it, but we can see the fire it's laying down. It was firing 30mm at the tank and it was the feeblest attempt I have ever seen to kill a tank. The Ukrainian tank commander ducks into the tank, waited for the BMP to stop firing. When he peeked back out, he pointed at the BMP, and it felt like I evaporated. The main gun of the tank fired and fucked that BMP up in an awe-inspiring display of fire.

I see in the distance this massive plume of smoke and the BMP is just fucked. That by itself basically halted whatever advance the Russians were trying to do at the time. It just stopped. Jesse and I are like, fuck there's nothing for us to do now, so we go back to the house we were originally in.

Apparently while we were gone a company of Russians were coming down the road and that road is only like 800 meters from the house. Chris, while they were doing this had killed like 10 guys with the long rifle. This is a fine example of the Soviet mentality they have. Chris told me they literally could have low crawled across the road, and he wouldn't be able to see them, but they just kept running across 3-8 at a time. The Russians ran into a big yellow building like 800 meters down the road and scattered.

A couple guys fired LAWs into the buildings. Ryan fired into a building and definitely killed a bunch of dudes. At that point it was mostly artillery barrages. Later Kevin, Jesse, and Tim, who were gonna go up the road and I volunteered to go with them. Just the four of us, the stupidest fucking thing, just us four ran down the road towards Russian lines, and we get to a point where we take a left behind a fence next to a broken-down shack.

We hear snaps and pops of gunfire around us. I see a Russian dude in a window. He fires overhead of us; he didn't know we were there. So, I fire like 10-15 rounds into the window. The guy either got killed or went away from the window. After that Kevin and Jesse were like, we should jump the fence and storm that house! And I'm like guys there's just four of us. We had no knowledge of what was behind the fence, so we turned around.

We run back down the road and the whole way back the Russians are shooting at us. I don't know how I didn't get shot because I should have been shot in the ass. We get back to the house and grab a few LAWs and we go out 50 meters in front of the house. Ryan is like," I see a guy" and he goes into a shack that is kind of small. So small you have to crouch in it, and he fired a law. The back blast of the LAW blew the door of the shack open, and it fucked up the shack.

We decided not to do another suicide charge down the road and go back to our house. There were a few moments when someone would take a LAW off the kitchen table and just fire a LAW at a random house with Russians in it. The houses are matchboxes, so every LAW just fucked the houses up. Night comes, we understand the gentleman's agreement. We have 50% security and it's very uneventful.

Day arrives on the third day. A tank round comes through the back of the house and woke us all up. It came from behind us, so our commander calls the tanks and says, "Don't worry friendly tank." The tank round almost killed us. More barrages, glass shattering, it becomes normal. We decided we would move all the couches up against the windows to protect ourselves from the shrapnel a little bit. At this point the Russians have some more armor but they are keeping them on the other side of the village. A BMP and a tank, maybe more.

It's like 9 or 10 in the morning now. Mind you, we had left our bags in Horenska. So, we had been subsisting on random shit in the house like cookies and pickles. I hate pickles but I was so hungry and that was the best pickle I've ever had in my life. For the most part we are relaxing. Chris is the only one working He's on the sniper rifle for hours at a time. At one point we take another heavy barrage. They happened often with lulls between them. Around noon, Lu wants me to go with him to the trenches to check up on the guys back there. There are quite a few guys still there this whole time. So, we go back and check on them. By the end of the battle, 5-7 dudes who had come with us had fled the battle. They had just run away. It was the most infuriating thing.

Western Volunteer
International Legion
Battle of Kyiv, Moschun
March 11th

I was present for some of the fighting in Moschun very early in the war. I've seen some other guys both Ukrainian and western share their stories so here is mine and what I remember. I remember cowardice, bravery, the smell of cut trees and lots and lots of artillery.

Moschun is a medium/small size village on the outskirts of Kyiv. The Russians were trying to take it and we were sent to stop them. A little after arriving we start taking an artillery barrage. Being a veteran of the GWOT, I thought I knew what IDF was like, but this is prolonged, accurate IDF that isn't fired by amateurs with no formal training. (Thinking ahead about the butt hurt GWOT guys who want to compare the 7 mortars they took to a whole 30-minute barrage with hundreds of rounds fired)

During one of said barrages, I was occupying a house and I turn around to see a trench we had taken that had friendlies in it. I see around 5 guys literally throwing their rifles and just run away. I started yelling at them to at least wait until the barrage was over and then take off like a pussy, but they didn't hear me and kept going.

This was not something I was expecting to see, and I still think about it a lot. Seeing your friendlies just take off and leave your already small force smaller than it was. Disgusting.

With all that being said, the Ukrainians and westerners who sacked up and stayed are men I can count on. They stood tall and held firm and we didn't let the Russians have that village. The herd would be thinned even more after the battle, and later on we even came across some of the guys who deserted us. But that's another story for another day.

Viktor
Ukrainian Soldier
Battle of Kyiv, Moschun
March 11th

I am a T-84 crew member and participated in the defense of Kyiv early March. North of Kyiv was heavy fighting, and our group was to support infantry working on the Russians in villages. Our greatest fear is drone warfare and enemy tanks.

In Moschun, we were told enemy tanks and BMPs were in the area. We drove to our positions and waited for orders from the commander. On our left, some buildings. On the right, fewer buildings. We were on a road. The commander told us to be awake and ready to work on enemy vehicles.

A BMP (Russian) was more than 200 meters from us. Their auto cannon fired on us. We fired back and destroyed them. We were very excited about this because we had done our job as soldiers in our specific military task.

This was a realization for me. That was an expensive vehicle to produce. Their crew needed months to train, and it cost money to bring it all the way here. All that money and time was for nothing once we saw it. We destroyed a vehicle worth more money than I will make in my life in 10 seconds.

After that, we saw no more enemy vehicles that day. We heard their auto cannons, but our assigned task was to block that area and so we did not leave to find them.

"Viking"
Georgian Volunteer – International Legion
Battle of Kyiv, Moschun
March 11th

We were brought in a nearby settlement on trucks, about 5 kilometers from Moschun. There was a large mass of forest between us and the Frontline. I'll never forget the artillery sounds getting closer as we got near the front from Kiev. It was funny when "Adomas", more elderly and very experienced operator barked at us to "Put on your helmets, tourists!" He was one of those men you follow instinctively.

We marched through the forest on foot, in a very disorganized, disorderly manner. Not everyone is on the level of physical fitness required, there were many who fell behind. It got dark, units were separated.

It was cold. I've never felt this cold in my life. In s trench, -12 degrees Celsius, constant artillery barrages. I didn't even have any winter equipment, this is March 5th I think, so logistics were shaky, and they didn't have anything my size. Luckily, I brought PPE with me from home. Others had to make do with what was issued, sub-par equipment.

I thought cold was gonna take me, but we lived through and rejoined the larger element. Spread out on the trench and dig in. We were constantly under artillery, but IDF really doesn't do it for me after Afghanistan. This was the day I filmed that viral "Missed me Dickhead" video.

Soon after that the commander came by my trench and singled me out to reinforce the "kill house". There were some men there, mostly American, holding a forward position where two snipers of ours were not giving the Russians ability to advance. The rest of us were rotating security, making sure nothing got a drop on us. We were alone in the settlement, allies behind us in the trenches.

It was cold. We had very little in terms of food and we were constantly bombed.

Most of the boys were pros. They knew what they were doing. Everyone kept their cool even under such stressful and downright suicidal situation. Commander decided to get some shut eye and handed me the radio, told me I was in charge while he slept, since I was the only one with both English and Russian skills and could bridge between Americans in the house with me and the Ukrainian command.

Third day one of our guys made Pasta. No kidding the most disgusting and at the same times most delicious pasta I've ever had. With tomato sauce and all. Only an American would find the nerve to cook pasta in that situation.

Snipers were doing most of the work. Really giving them hell. Killing all their artillery spotters making their artillery very inaccurate. In contrast, we could visually walk in our artillery, so ours was effective at some degree. One of the scariest moments was when our tank shot us. He didn't know we were there I suppose. But in the house, we thought either we're surrounded or it's friendly fire... None of those options is appealing. We got lucky. Very lucky that it didn't bring down the whole place on us.

I think it was the 4th day SU25 dropped a bomb on us. I slept through it I was so exhausted. Malnourished, in caffeine deficit (I usually take 8 cups of coffee a day and I had none for 4 days). I was going on cigarettes and anger at this point. Mood changed. Everyone was tired. But everyone kept their game face on. Word was we were going to get reinforcements and move in to clear the settlement. Finally! We all thought, we can take the fight to them. CQB is my bread and butter, and I was excited for some breaching and clearing. That order never came.

Fifth and final day, I believe, was when it got really heavy. Commander was in the back trying to sort out the reinforcements situation and had the only Radio we had with him, meaning we had absolutely no communication in the house. Russians were throwing everything at this tiny house. Artillery, mortars, everything.

At some point I heard Russian voices, barking orders. They were close. I shouted, "Battle stations!" So everyone who was resting to get sharp real fast. We were on sectors, expecting to get rushed and repel an assault on the house. It never came. What did come was an ungodly amount of artillery that was getting more and more accurate.

House took a very close hit and panic set it. Commander wasn't present to make a call, we had no comms and next hit like that would bring the house on us. I decided to take the responsibility and told everyone to grab our stuff and retreat to the trenches. Luckily nobody argued, if we started bickering about who had the biggest dick there, we'd die.

I wasn't in charge of course, there were guys in that house 3 times more experienced than me, but someone had to call it and I accepted that responsibility. We got out. I was the last man. House was destroyed soon after. The commander, we found in the trench, he was unable to get to us due to artillery working our position. Turns out getting out was the right call. That position was compromised and indefensible at that point.

We were rotated out soon after. Replaced by fresh troops. These were the most horrible 5 days of my life. It's a miracle we survived. We got lucky so many times...So many things went right...Russian incompetence was legendary. Even their Spetsnaz that was sent after us were wiped out in 15 minutes. But mostly it was the men in that house who stood like giants in face of impossible odds. I didn't even know their names while in there. We didn't have time to even ask about it. But that battle for the tiny house at the edge of Moschun created bonds that ironclad.

So, I think it was the 4th night in Moschun, not sure. We had to temporarily bug out of the house back into the trench. I was about to go to sleep, and one American is yelling, 'Holy shit there's a bear here!'

111

Now I don't know how Ukraine fauna and wildlife works, if they even have bears. But I had an AKM on me. And I hear like…grunting and snorting. Like a bear sniffing around for food. It's dark, so not much visible; and this American claims he has a thermal and sees a mass like a bear near a tree behind the trench line. Like right on us. So, I'm like, "Fuck...I gotta fight a bear now?" The whole trench is up, guns pointing in the darkness. We just wait to get mauled, man.

Turns out some fucker is sleeping under a tree covering himself with like 15 blankets because it's so cold, so he looks like a fucking massive bear. While snoring. Like a motherfucker. Thinking it's a bear sniffing. Man, if it actually was a bear I would just give up and let it eat me. Artillery, SU25, Spetsnaz, Snipers, and now a FUCKING BEAR? Bears where I draw the line.

"Mexico"
Western Volunteer – International Legion
Battle of Kyiv, Moschun
March 11th

I fought in Moschun in a trench line. The trench was immediately located on the south side of the town. It essentially bordered the town with the tree line aft of us. I fought there for a total of six days, five nights. The timeline of events is hazy to me. It is difficult for me to explain, but one is so exhausted and overwhelmed that keeping a mental track of when exactly every notable event occurred is more difficult than one would think.

I arrived in Poland on March 3rd, 2022. I stayed in Poland for exactly one day before securing a ride to the Ukrainian border. Once I arrived at the border, the Polish authorities helped me hitch a ride with a group of other Ukrainians entering the country. I was taken to a recruiting depot and then immediately taken to the Foreign Legion (5-6th of March)

I was greeted by interviewers and Ukrainian military personnel. They interviewed me to check for combat experience and special skills and qualifications. Evidently, they were incredibly pleased because I was immediately placed on a "special team" that would be commanded by Ukrainian SF officers but fully composed of foreign fighters. It was a mixed bag of experienced, highly skilled and experienced and highly unskilled (I realize just how many liars and show boaters there were). Most of the other volunteers had zero combat experience and therefore, were placed in the regular battalion.

I stayed in the staging area for about three days and two nights. We were given FLNs and lots of other heavy equipment. However, most of the heavy equipment we were issued either didn't have batteries nor firing pins. You can imagine how upset we were. Other weapons included medium MGs and sniper rifles, AT4s. We were also given some basic uniform items, vests and armor of varying quality and terrible mag pouches that had way more straps than necessary.

After 3 days we were bussed to Kyiv. It was a long and very cold ride and completely packed. I was increasingly nervous about the checkpoints which were on high alert and manned by very nervous young Ukrainian troops. Keep in mind that the threat of saboteurs was very high. The bus ride took us all night and much of the following day (maybe the 10th?). There were a total of about 25 of us (the exact number escapes me.)

We arrived at a staging area that was once a hotel. Quickly signed contracts and took ID pictures. Then we were given exactly one hour to prepare. I remember thinking that that was ridiculous given that none of us had slept. I guess I was not totally aware of the dire situation Kyiv was in at the time.

After about an hour we were loaded onto trucks with all of the weapons and equipment. In my naive mind, I thought they would take us to a low-intensity area just to acclimatize to the situation. I was wrong. The closer we got to the front, the more it was evident that they were taking us to a hot area. We drove passed artillery and mortar positions -- could see burning buildings and hear shelling very close. I began to get increasingly nervous.

We arrived at a small village, north-south axis. The village looked like it had received shelling and perhaps some fighting. There our commander ordered us to file into formation and patrol an unknown distance. Again, in my naive mind, I thought we were going to another staging area. I had not seen a single map and had not been given any type of situation briefing. I thought it ridiculous to have us patrol to a front without some sort of situation briefing.

As we advanced, we could hear the shelling getting closer and closer. I got more nervous but maintained that the shelling was too far away to be lethal. The patrol was lengthy (I am guessing 4 clicks). When we were about 200 meters away from a trench line, the shelling got very close. Very close. We crawled the rest of the way to the trench.

I was struck by how...rudimentary the trench was. It was not very deep nor well-constructed. It was manned by *about* 20-30 Ukrainians though I can never be sure of the exact number. (I didn't do a count).

Our team was divided into two groups: An advanced group that would push inside the town immediately to our direct front and occupy a house. The idea was that this team would set up a sniper and observation position. The other team would remain in the trench. The shelling at this point was light and the enemy was only taking distant pop-shots from the town. Being new to the situation (and trench warfare in general), I simply unloaded an entire magazine into the town. Not wise, but again, I had no idea what we were facing.

The first night was relatively calm but freezing. In fact, the entire time was very, very cold. We tried to organize ourselves into a team. We elected (without my approval) a boot Marine by the name of Gonzo that had ZERO combat experience. He was to oversee us absent the forward advanced team.

The following day the shelling was getting much more intense. Rounds were falling very close, and individuals were getting incredibly nervous. I admit, I was too but I figured that I was safe in the trench. By the evening, some people had already run. We had a Welsh guy, and an American Corpsmen simply leave the battlespace. The Corpsmen took his medical gear with him. Awesome morale moment. The Welshmen simply disappeared. Later we would find out that he would tell a Colonel that we were all dead. It is important to note that no one was even shooting at us besides the occasional pop-shot from the town. It was *just* heavy shelling.

The third day is when things got ugly. The enemy was directly shooting at our trench with sustained and accurate fire. I encountered a sniper that was very much invested in my future. He was in an elevated position and was firing into the trench. Thankfully, he did not hit anyone. The drones also started making an appearance at this time. I never actually saw the drones, but boy, I could hear them. They would hover over our positions all day and all night just buzzing about. One Ukrainian however was killed in an assault having been shot through the neck. I only saw his body. On the same day I was ordered with six other men (three deserted) to dig foxholes slightly to the rear of the trench but with the objective of plugging in a gap between our trench and adjacent trench. This adjacent trench was manned by Georgian and Ukrainian troops and were receiving pure hell.

While digging my foxhole, we spotted three Russians run into a building *about* 300-400 meters away. We took shots at them, but virtually *all* of our rifles stopped working. They were one shot weapons (We had to take them about to earn an additional shot). We tried to clean them, but it was simply impossible to live in a trench with a clean rifle. I wish I had had an AK74. One of my English friends (Who didn't run) claimed to have dropped one. I cannot verify that, and I am skeptical. Just seems awfully lucky to do so with one shot weapon and while the Georgians were also shooting at them.

I know for sure that the Russians knew exactly where we were because while digging, they were shooting and hitting my berm. I learned to never assume you are hidden or too distant. It was late afternoon on the third day before I finished completing my foxhole before I heard a drone hovering over our heads. I knew what was going to come. I quickly curled up in a ball at the bottom of my hole. The shelling that would follow was incredibly intense, accurate and terrifying. Easily the most scared I had ever been.

The shelling would come in waves of six rounds. It would shake the ground a little, make your ears ring and chop down trees and branches. Then it would stop for about ten minutes. I would use those ten minutes to continue digging. I wanted to dig to China as a means of escape. The shelling would begin anew, and I would just be a ball. I remember being very scared but also purely exhausted. I even slept a little between rounds and would have trippy dreams beyond what I can describe. When I was awake, I passed the time praying. I remember feeling something very very hot next to my cheek while curled in a ball. I panicked and thought that I was bleeding/hit by something.

It was already getting very dark so I couldn't see anything, nor did I feel hurt. I fumbled around and picked up a piece of shrapnel that had landed right next to my face. The metal must have shot high into the air and come back down in my hole. I am a very, *very* lucky individual. To highlight how close the shelling was: my friends saw a round land about three meters from my hole.

115

In between shelling I did grow very concerned for some Ukrainians that were located in a shallow pit about 50 meters from me. I stood up briefly and yelled to another group of Ukrainians about 25 meters from my hole and asked about the far Ukrainians. They motioned the neck cutting gesture. They had been hit and completely blown up. I have a friend that has footage of us talking to them the day prior. Spooky shit. I also saw a Ukrainian walk by our foxhole while shot in the shoulder. We tried to help him, but he was *extremely* aggressive and just wanted to continue walking to the rear staging area. Honestly...we just kind of let him go.

Night had fallen (still third day but well into the evening) when we were finally ordered to leave our holes and return to the trench. Stupid me thought that somehow everything would be better there, and I gladly left my hole to the main trench. I was wrong. The shelling just followed us and a BTR (or BMP not sure) was firing over our heads. A tank had shown up earlier that day and was firing at targets inside the town. I imagine the BTR was targeting the tank. It was incredibly scary seeing a ball of fire fly over your head.

A Ukrainian that knew English asked for two volunteers to either destroy the BTR or get a rocket to a closer unit. I and a British fellow decided to go. We both insisted that the Ukrainian come with us because we feared being shot by other trench lines. We had to traverse the whole town with trenches to our left and the enemy to our right. It was scary but surreal at the same time. We passed half burnt-out houses.... some still occupied by civilians. Thankfully, the tank destroyed the BTR before we had to. We handed our rocket off to two random Ukrainians that had set up an observation post. I remember thinking how insane they were...just two dudes.

When we returned to our main trench there wasn't much left for me to do but try and get some sleep, on the ground in the freezing while ignoring the incessant shelling. Needless to say, it was a futile exercise.

The fourth day was arguably the most interesting. The Russians had gotten much closer to our trench and were spraying the trench line. The squad leading Marine was in a state of full panic and decided to not only run, but also to destroy two light machine guns on his way out. He also took our only pair of NVGs. He claimed that the Russians had broken our right flank and that we were going to be surrounded. While it is true

116

that our right flank was receiving total hell, it was not true that they had broken.

That day, the fourth day, the Russians were laying heavy fire on the trench but were *not* advancing to it. The closest bodies to our trench were about 100 meters away and there were a lot of buddies. They littered the place. But it is absolutely not true that bodies were right up on our trench. Not true. Anyone who tells you otherwise is lying. The closest the enemy got was about 30-40 meters in a building on the second floor. There were two of them and they were spraying the entire trench line. A Ukrainian (the one that spoke English whom everyone called "Maniac" owing to his total lack of self-preservation) grabbed an AT4...climbed up on the berm...ignoring the fire...took a well-aimed shot and vaporized the enemy in the house.

He jumped back into the trench and said, "I hope I didn't kill them. I just want them to go away." What an odd thing to say. I joked and said "Well, you didn't give them a headache!" The rest of the fourth day was shooting and shelling. I would shoot my one-shot rifle. A Ukrainian civilian had his back blown off. They gave him a blanket, a corner of the trench and simply let him expire.

Fifth day nothing of note. Fired some Gustovs at enemy armor, but all I did was watch. Just more shelling, a little more small arms fire. However, that night was ugly, but for different reasons:

1. We were told the Russians had massed hundreds to attack us and had various types of armor. I basically didn't have a rifle, so I just picked up a rocket and prepared myself for my one-shot glory. The attitude (though it wasn't said out loud) was that the enemy was probably going to overrun us. Maybe I was the only one thinking that, but that night in the trench was cold and quiet. We made a watch schedule but without NVGs it was pretty useless. I was so tired and exhausted I ended up sleeping on top of a good friend of mine. Woke up to snow on me. The attack never happened.

2. The enemy was probing our lines with drones and small teams and did launch flares into the night which would wake me up.

117

3. I could hear a Russian dying. I don't know where, but I have a friend that could corroborate that.

Day six was eventful. I was ordered to go to an advance position and join team one for an assault. I went to the house and found about 15 guys in there at once which I thought was a horrible idea. I was given an MG seeing as to how my rifle simply didn't work. We waited and waited to be ordered to move out and attack. Meanwhile, we kept getting shelled. The rounds would land incredibly close to the house and shake everything.

Everyone would drop to the ground, though I felt that that was a ridiculous endeavor because if a shell hit the house...we would all die anyway. I remember saying "Should there be this many people in here?" and another foreigner got mad at me and asked, "Why are you nervous?" I didn't answer but I thought the question was ridiculous. Why shouldn't I be nervous? I just had half of my friends run from me, been shelled for days and nights and haven't slept.

The attack never materialized, and the shelling was getting closer, so we were ordered back to the trench. There, a gunship showed up on station but never engaged us. I asked a Ukrainian "What do we do? Should we shoot at it?" He said, "Dig and hide."

We stayed in the trench before finally being ordered to leave. Like an idiot I actually thought that the game was put on pause and that I could just walk home unmolested...I was wrong. The moment I stepped out of the trench and started walking rearward I heard a drone above. I realized in that instant that the Russian is going to see a fucking platoon leave the trench at the same time and that artillery was going to get us. I began running as fast as I could. The artillery did come, and it chased us the whole 4 clicks back to the staging area. I was exhausted and terrified. I had no idea what to do but kept on running. I thought maybe I should hit the deck, but I decided against it. I was so far outrunning the arty and if I get hit now...well that's just God's will.

I stopped running about 200 meters from a truck that was to pick us up. I was too exhausted, sleep deprived and hungry. About 50 meters away I realized that I was endangering my friends by not running more. I ran the last 50 meters and was hoisted up onto the truck to a group of very angry individuals. The truck sped away.

Art by João "J-Dot" Alves

Ryan
Western Volunteer – International Legion
Battle of Kyiv, Moschun
March 11th

My name is Ryan, I am the dude everyone from Moschun & Irpin that everyone calls the White Hajj. I ended up in Ukraine at the very beginning of the 2022 invasion by Russia. Like most already in Ukraine when Zelensky put out a call to arms I and others in country ended up having to go to the main base and register with the international legion.

Luckily, I got put with ex-veteran foreign fighters. We were the first to leave the base. We had spent maybe one or two days together figuring each other out before going to Kyiv. By the time we reached Kyiv on the 4th or 5th I believe with our truckloads of weapons and ammo we were ready to fuck shit up. We got to our new base and our commander showed up. Originally, we were not going to go out, but our incessant arguing over a period of two or three hours of "let's go we don't have time to wait", either annoyed him enough or got him to realize we wanted in the shit regardless of the brutality of the current fighting.

He ended up relenting and called us a few transport vehicles to get the 20 or so of us to the front. At this point I was rocking a PKM so I dropped my body armor and kevlar to save weight so I could pick up a backpack full of ammo instead. (I didn't start wearing body armor until the end of April after I got caught in a helicopter attack in the far north doing drone recon with aerorozvidka, which is a whole other story.) We loaded the shit out of the two transport trucks with ammunition and rockets. (M72, AT4 etc) We all jumped on top of our weapon stash in the back of the transport trucks or into pickups hell-bent on smashing whatever area we got too. We ended up in an area SE of the town of Moschun. We all dismount grab our packs, rockets, ammo and gear. We are told through a young Ukrainian who spoke English that we are going to do a movement along the woods down a road and clear the area.

We get into a staggered column and start moving forward. The young Ukrainian at one point tells everyone to drop everything but ammunition so we can move through the forests quicker. We all drop our gear and get ready to move and engaged the Russian forces in the woods.

As it turned out, there were no Russian forces in the woods at that point and as we were walking through the woods, we started taking artillery fire.

Everyone starts moving for the nearest cover, I'm towards the rear with a guy we called Canadian Doc, at this point we both are smoking and joking as we move half assed (basically walking and just dropping when we could hear the arty come in) through the artillery fire towards the Ukrainian trenches up ahead. That changed when we had an airburst round shred a bunch of treetops within meters of us and we both looked at each other and we ended up hopping into an abandoned position that had got hit sometime earlier.

We all end up getting to the trenches and there's small arms fire and artillery coming in, we find out there's enemy forces to the front in the village. So, I rush forward with a PKM towards a garage type building nearby. (There was a road directly to our front that you could see all the way down through the village.) I post up at the edge of this building and our commander is yelling for me to get back in the trench.

So, I get up and move back towards the trench. After about five minutes, our commander chooses around 10 of us to assault into the village in front of the front line and the rest would hold down the trenches. He points to the same building, so I ran forward and posted up at and we basically buddy moved towards it, clear it and setup shop.

At this point we still didn't know the village name, what all we were up against and where the friendly forces all were. Once we got into the house there were some Ukrainians that joined us there and our commander sat down with the Ukrainians, got information and relayed it to the one person in our team that spoke Ukrainian and English. The information we got was basically everyone to our front was Russian, there were no friendlies to our front the only friendly forces we had was to the rear of us directly behind us and then directly to our left rear and right rear, so we were basically the cannon fodder in front of the frontline. We were basically the "Fuck You Russia come and take it/hold at all costs."

Once we got the information from the commander, we decided to set-up a sniper position in the second story. That was done by one of the commanding guys for the westerners we'll just call him K, so K and the sniper went up to the second floor they started observing and immediately they found a dipshit Russian that was probably 800 meters out just standing in the middle of the road in front of cover without a care in the world. At which point they asked to schwack him.

Our commander said, "No do not do work, wait, wait for my command." So, we waited for a little bit, the commander came upstairs and then he looked through the sniper scope and he saw that the guy was still standing out in the middle of the road and a little bit later he finally said, "OK, do work." At which point the sniper took the shot and hit the guy in the lower abdomen.

After he took that shot, we figured we were going to get engaged so everyone got down and we just waited, the sniper was observing the whole time and K was in the next room looking for targets, but the Russians never fired a single shot back, they didn't do anything. That Russian soldier just laid there in the road, they didn't try to help him, they didn't try to do buddy aid. He basically just plopped down like a sack of potatoes and just bled out.

So, during this whole time from the point that the sniper took that shot to after we're still receiving artillery nonstop, there's rounds landing to the left of us, to the right of us, to our rear where the trenches are, (The trenches were getting absolutely fucking pounded), to our front. So, we got guys running up and down the stairs the whole day, taking cover wherever we could find it in the building and moving back up to firing positions after the arty hits.

Our commander ended up making a catch phrase that we still say to him to this day, which is, "This is normal." as every time we'd drop to the floor, he'd be sitting there laughing at us or standing there with a "What the fuck are you doing?" look on his face. Looking back up until the last two days he never got down on the floor like we did. And only did once our house started taking artillery and rockets within meters.

The first night there we decided to push out a nighttime recon. So, I moved forward to a machine gun position around 75 meters further up from the house, the commander basically said to hold this area and myself and two Ukrainians stay there. The rest of the recon element moved forward. So, the team moves up to my front left, we have no night vision, or anything. So, I'm sitting there for maybe 10 minutes, and I realize my rear security guys just disappeared.

About 40 minutes or so, I'm still probed in this shed and I finally say fuck it and rolled back. I got back to the house and found our rear element on guard. No one had heard from the recon unit, so I setup the PKM at the front door and the other two go upstairs to see if they can spot the team with thermals. Around 15 minutes or so later the recon team rolls back in. Apparently when our doing recon, they ran into Russians right on the other side of a fence and waited for them to leave before moving back. The rest of the night was pretty uneventful outside of flares and artillery from the Russian side every once in a while.

We also fucking froze our asses off because at the start we dropped all our gear but ammunition including our cold weather shit as we were told it was a quick mission, so we all huddled together wherever we could find room to lay down when not on guard.

So, the second day we all woke up to very little artillery going off and we're just basically waiting, smoking a lot of cigarettes and joking around. I don't think any of us at the time really realized or thought about how big of an absolute clusterfuck of a situation we were in. We weren't in a really well built solid structure, if we had gotten a direct hit by artillery, or mortars, we all would have been fucking slaughtered, there was more Russians up in front of us than we had ammunition to handle, and we were in front of the frontline by around 150-200 meters, so it was a situation where when you look back on it, we should have probably all gotten schwacked.

So, on the second day our commander had to go to the trench line to our rear to talk with the Ukrainian forces there. When he left, he said, "Guys I will be gone for 10 minutes do not do work. Just wait, don't shoot." So that lasted all of a good five fucking minutes. K ended upstairs with the sniper and me and another guy J followed behind them.

We ended up watching the Russians move around and we all basically looked at each other yelled down to our guys on the first floor and said fuck it let's do it. I'm not sure if the sniper or K who let off the first shot, but once we broke the silence that morning, it was off to the fucking races.

We immediately started taking a massive amount of artillery and Russian troops started moving into buildings towards our front. I was in the room next to our sniper hide. I threw the PKM up on the window frame and sprayed the upper floor of a building that the Russian's had ran into

123

with a quick 50 round burst or so before ducking and moving out of the room in case of an RPG or return fire.

After that K started engaging from the sniper room. He pulled back and next thing I hear is, "Get a rocket! Get a fucking rocket!" I run halfway down the stairs and one of the guys chucks me a M72 LAW. There's a few minutes of arguing. (The day prior there was talks on what you can shoot out of a small room. I basically said you can shoot anything at least once from a room, just keep the door open, ha ha). After the argument I unlocked the LAW and I run in the room with the rocket prepped, aim at the building about 350-400 meters away that K and the others said the Russians were in and let it fly.

The room I was in was a baby's room, maybe 8ft x 8ft, so a pretty small room. When I fired the law off, it blew all the glass inward and down onto where I was at and kicked up dust everywhere. I hit the house but hit around a foot above the window into the rooftop overhang. Almost immediately a fire started and engulfed the roof and upper floor. I ran out of the room and K and another guy came in and started shooting at the Russians who were running in and out of buildings.

At this point there was small arms fire, but none of it was coming directly at us. After a few moments, I ran back upstairs with two rockets, I prepped one and waited for the guys to give me details on the next target to hit and move out of the room. They said something like red building on the left 600 meters, so I run in shoot another LAW, but there was one problem, my dumbass had swung the door shut instinctively behind myself. I fired the rocket and things just went blank for a few seconds.

I turned around and it had ripped the door completely off its frame and pushed it over, and the ceiling in the room had fallen down. I had a scorch mark on one of my hands as well. By shutting the door, my dumbass created a situation where the back blast pressure, fire, gas had nowhere to go.

After a few seconds I walked down the steps coughing up my lungs and was nauseated. The guys got a good laugh out of it once they realized I was okay.

At some point our commander came running back thinking we were all dead. I'm assuming due to the massive artillery barrage that we were taking and for the fact that there were now buildings on fire and non-stop small arms fire. So, he gets back and basically yelled a bunch of

Ukrainian words. The only thing we really knew at that point was Suka blyat pisdietz.

After a few minutes of yelling, K manages to get our commander to see the chaos and damage we inflicted from the upstairs windows. The commander comes back down and basically says, "Ok do work". The rest of the second day is pretty uneventful. More artillery, some GRAD and mortar fire. We pop shots at the Russians who have yet to engage us directly.

They still haven't hit our house, we all still are freezing, and we have no food, so guys are eating whatever was edible in the building at that point. So that night, I'm on guard duty watching the entrance to the building and I start hearing something that sounds like a cat or something. I pop my head out the door (Our area had a fence around it.) and listen more closely.

It's screaming and moaning coming from the Russian side directly where hours earlier we had engaged the Russian forces. So, another guy D was up as well and I yell at him to come here, come and listen. D is basically like, "What the fuck do you want?" I say come on get the fuck over here and listen. So, he comes over and you can still hear them in the distance. He looks at me and says,
 "Is that a fucking cat?"
I laughed my ass off while trying to explain to him that it was the Russians we had fucked up earlier in the day, their guys had left them bleeding out in our killing field. Some of them were likely less than 200 meters from Russian friendlies. They continued to scream and moan until the early morning hours.

That day we were able to build trust and respect with him by annihilating the Russians and from that point on we no longer needed permission to engage enemy troops.

"Goodie"
Western Volunteer – International Legion
Battle of Kyiv, Moschun
March 11th

I was in the kill house in Kyiv in the very beginning weeks of this war against Russia, we managed to survive in this house against the artillery, Spetsnaz and everything the Russians sent at us for 5 days and nights! Americans, English, Mexicans and many more fighting for Ukraine and its people until the dying breath of us all! They fired GRAD at us, sniper fire, artillery, machine guns and much more and we all still came out of this place alive!

I will never forget the night where our commander told us all to lay down and don't talk or say a word and point our rifles to the front door as the Spetsnaz unit was just outside ready to come in and kill every one of us, we could hear them shuffling and moving outside saying words in Russian just in arms reach of us all outside in the garden!

But we called in close IDF onto our position and it killed all of them! The whole house shook, and the ceiling collapsed, and the windows smashed and I've never been so scared in my entire life! Not a single one of us said anything as the bombs landed on us killing the Russians outside, not one of us expected to survive, I think!

I don't fight with these guys anymore but if you're reading this you know who you are, and I love each and every single one of you! We survived the most brutal times in this war and managed to move on and fight furthermore against the Russians and continue protecting and documenting our stories against the enemy! Moschun will forever be imbedded in my memory for as long as I live!

The bombs that fell on us every single day and night, the sniper kills, the PKM kills, the sniper bullets coming at us in the trenches and the top floor of the kill house! The tank firing his cannon just outside the house and every single one of us ducked because we thought we'd been hit by a HE, sleeping on the floor wherever we found time and room to get away from all the noise and everything going on, Seeing the houses burning in the distance and hearing people screaming for hours upon hours and eventually the screaming stops!

These are the memories I will remember and never forget for as long as I live. Every single person here fighting in Ukraine is a hero and rest in peace to all who have died and will die protecting this incredible place against the Russian enemy.

Art by João "J-Dot" Alves

Kevin
Western Volunteer - International Legion
Battle of Kyiv, Moschun
March 11th

Most of us came into Ukraine on March 2nd or 3rd. We came in on the western side. I had already been in Ukraine for five or six hours. They were asking everybody, "Do you have combat experience? Where do you come from? Any experience in the military? Are you ready for combat right now?" That type of stuff.

I met up with some other guys who were pretty cool. Prior military experience. The Ukrainians said we couldn't leave for combat until we had 20 guys. But we didn't want 20, we only wanted the most experienced. We ended up with Jesse, Chris, Dakota, and some other guys. All prior service. Then we get approached by this big light-skinned guy named "Texas", a big corn-fed dude. He had no military experience at all. Everyone said no, he shouldn't come. He has no experience. Then Texas said, "I will carry all the weight." And Jesse was like, "Fine, you're in. He is a big boy.

So, we take off, go to Kyiv. Get off the bus and arrive at a hotel. I was given the phone number of a Ukrainian Special Forces soldier, and I was told to let him know when we arrived. So, I text him, "Hey we are here." And he tells me to meet him in the lobby. I meet him, and he says, "Okay, are you guys ready to fight right now?" and we tell him yeah, we are. So, he tells us to drop off our gear in our rooms, only bring cold weather jackets and stuff like that because we will be back.

We drop our shit off, and there's a big meeting out front. There are two Five-Ton trucks outside. They get into one Five-Ton, we get into the other. So, like 25 people in each truck roughly. Then we head out to Moschun. I think we got there around 2 or 3 in the afternoon. As we are driving in, mortars are dropping near the trucks. You can hear the small arms. We are starting to hear the war sounds. At first, we arrive at a trench. The trench is in the wood line behind the village, and going there as crazy as it was, we were patrolling like we were trained to in the US military. And this dude, (the commander) is like, "No, don't do it that way. Just walk slow and stroll the road. There are landmines out here."

A car comes flying past us. 90 miles per hour down the road. We are still walking and ten minutes later that car comes flying back, but now it's full of bullet holes, its leaking fluid and has got two flat tires. The driver has been shot in the shoulder. The commander stops him and is talking to him, and I'm like, what the fuck? The commander says, "He drove down there to see if the Russians are down there still. And I was like, so they're down there? The commander goes, "Uh, yeah." So, we just kept walking that direction.

We get into the trench and get everyone into position on the outskirts of the town. The commander says, "Give me six guys. Your best. We are going to run up into the village. The rest of you guys are going to support by fire and cover us as we move down this road."

We captured one house, which ended up being the position we stayed in for five days. And then we move down like five or six houses down the road. We are moving fast. At this point, a lot of buildings are on fire. You can hear the tanks and the artillery, and we were basically moving toward the sound of the guns.

We were bounding up this road, and it got dark pretty quickly. We stop at this house, four houses ahead of the forward line of troops. We are the closest guys toward the enemy. It was me, Tim, Jesse, Chris, our commander Vadyim, a Ukrainian guy called Knife, and I think that was it.

We huddle up inside of this house. It's dark. We don't have a radio, so we can't tell the guys that we are coming back to them. So, we are trying to figure out how to get back to the trench, because we have to go carefully. Vadyim, his English was not that great. He is trying to explain to us what the plan is, and we are taking a knee inside the house. It's already been hit by a tank before we arrived, so it is already destroyed. I remember it was so cold. I could feel our uniforms crunching from the cold.

All of a sudden, while we are having this conversation, we start hearing this noise. You could see that someone was leaning on the aluminum fence on the front half of the yard. Then in Russian, someone started yelling. We are still so new to this war, and we are like, "What the fuck is that?" and Vadyim was like, "Shut the fuck up. Don't move." So, we all froze. He said, "It's the Russians. They are calling out for us because they can hear us, so they are asking for the password to figure out if we are friendly or not."

By now it is pitch black. The only way we can see is from the illumination from the fires in the village. Vadyim told us to point our rifles at the gate, and if anyone walks through there to kill them. I take position in a window. We are completely surrounded now. We can see them in spots around us through a chain-link fence. We can hear them stepping on the broken glass around the house and just talking amongst themselves. At one point, one of them cocked his weapon. It sounded like a pistol. When he did that, he said something. The commander said, "They don't know where we are at. Stay still."

The guy Knife, he peeked through a hole in the fence. I asked him how many are out there. He told us about 20, maybe more. It was at this moment I just couldn't believe we were in this situation. It had only been four hours since we got here.

So, the Russians are moving around. We are still in our positions. Being as still as we can. Guns up just waiting. After the third hour, we realized we were not going to be able to stay here like this all night. So, we decided to go one by one to the house mentioned earlier. The plan was to go through the back fence and move one by one. So, we bound one by one, back toward the direction of the trench. Its late at night when we get back to the trench. So, we get reorganized, decide to clear the house closest to us (The Killhouse).

We clear it. We get set up in it. Put a sniper in the window, a PKM in another window, and setup other guys in other windows. All night long we sat and watched the Russians. The Russians weren't doing a lot of moving at night at this point.

We waited until morning, and as soon as morning came, all hell broke loose. We were in a gunfight from that point on basically. So, day one we set up defensive positions at the house. Earlier in the day we went back up the street a little bit, fired a couple rounds, and hit some dudes who were kind of just wandering around. They were mostly hitting us with artillery and tanks. At about one in the afternoon, the commander says, "There is a Russian tank coming this way. I am going to leave the house, go two streets over with this Ukrainian tank, and we are going to try to destroy it. When I leave, no shooting. Don't draw attention to the house."

So, then he left. A little while later, I was in my position upstairs in the window, I see two houses down on the left on a little balcony, the window opened. I was on my guard shift and I'm on the 338 long rifle. I looked at Ryan who was up there with me and I asked what we should do. Ryan said, "Well, Vadyim is not here. So, shoot that dude."

The guy is looking out the window, trying to see if he can see the tanks that we are also looking for. I shoot this guy. I hit him, and he falls out the window. The next guy comes up and he's looking down where the first guy fell. I shot him too. And now I can see a whole bunch of activity on the entire floor of that house. Before I can say anything, Ryan runs up and grabs an M72. He fired the round right through the window with all these people in there. So now the building is on fire. Ryan shoots another one and hits the downstairs. It just kicks off after that. They're shooting at us; we are shooting at them. It went on like that for 30 or 40 minutes. Just as quickly as it started, it stopped.

Vadyim runs back in, the house is covered in debris, it's all smokey and there's bullet casings all over the floor. The windows are all blown out too. He says, "Is everyone okay? I said no shooting!" He looks out the window and half the village is on fire! There are piles of rubble everywhere. There's a Russian guy out in the street, dragging himself across the road. We start laughing, he starts laughing, and Vadyim says, "I left you alone for just a little bit!"

That night after our huge gunfight in the daylight hours, we only had one thermal optic. At one point, someone woke me up and said, "I think there's an animal dying out there." And Dakota says, "No, that's a Russian." And out the window was a Russian soldier just lying in the road, screaming. Screaming the entire night until he bled out and died.

At some point in the night, some other Russian soldiers came and took his boots, took his gear and his rifle, but left his body there. He screamed the entire night. I'll never forget sitting in the window in the dark. It was dead quiet, except for the occasional explosions from the artillery. But I could hear this dude screaming. Echoing in the dark for both sides to hear. I just sat there and listened to him.

After that, we roll into the next few days. Those days were pretty much the exact same thing as day one. On the last day and a half, which basically ran straight for 18 hours, the Russians started pushing us hard. We exchanged rifle fire at multiple points. I think it was the middle of the day, and Chris is on the sniper rifle. We had been watching the Russians periodically. We shot a whole bunch of them throughout the days that were just hanging out in the houses or wandering around. Chris got a bunch of them too.

In this moment, Chris is pointing over his sniper rifle to the end of the street near a big pile of rubble. He says, "The Russians are crossing the street right there!" So, I run into the other room with the PKM machine gun. I see the first guy cross, and Chris drops him. Then all of these Russians just start running across the road. Chris and I just keep hitting them. Hitting them with the machine gun, hitting them with the sniper rifle.

We were just tearing them apart. It got to the point where we could see them stacking up getting ready to run across. We were visibly watching them get hit in the legs, chest, in the face. I hear Chris laughing, and I start laughing. I was like, "Is this real? Is this actually happening?" Vadyim comes up to our floor and asks what is going on. As this happens, the Russians try again. A group of 10 or more tries to cross. Chris is already dropping some and Vadyim is yelling, "Shoot them down! Shoot them faster!" It was an insane moment. Insanity. So that was that.

They hit us with a bunch of rifle fire and hand grenades. At one-point, Russian spetsnaz came. I remember being in the living room, and I remember thinking this is it. This is how we are going to die. The Russians dropped 1,000 lb. bombs near us. Tons of artillery. If they decided to use thermobaric missiles we were done. We didn't really know what was going on outside of that. That night we fell back to the trench because we were certain the house was going to get destroyed or overran. We were so exhausted and so cold.

On the last day there was a Russian drone just hovering right above us, calling in really direct fire. We were like, okay, we've got to leave right now. So, we bounce. We had to run really far to these trucks that came and picked us up. It was kind of insane. It was just suddenly over. It's hard to verbalize just exactly how fucking crazy it was.

"Viking"
Georgian Volunteer – International Legion
Battle of Kyiv, Moschun
March 11th

I met Nightcrawler in an elevator and I thought he was African. Turns out he didn't have a centimeter of skin left without tattoos. Also, he had a soft armor sewn into his skin on his stomach. He's Romanian by ethnicity but British. About 5'10-6'. Kind of chubby dude. Face covered in tattoos that you would see on one of those American shows about death row criminals. From a glance you knew this guy was absolutely mad.

So, first night in Moschun. It was freezing cold. And he stood next to me in a trench and made weird sounds. Like exhaling 'Haaaaaaaaaaa' That kinda sound. And I asked him 'What the fuck?' And he said it was a Japanese technique. That in his mind he was breathing fire. And melting the ice around. Warming himself. I physically moved like a meter away from him man.

At some point during excessive shelling, he disappeared for like an hour and then came back. When asked where he was. He replied that he was doing Tai Chi in the back

Sending good vibes to us or some shit. Like in MMORPG games, there's like a Bard or something that gives buffs to the party. Doing tai chi katas in the middle of bombardment. Claiming to be working on teleportation so he could assassinate Putin.

I distinctly remember that for some reason this guy almost never had a rifle. I've never seen him with a rifle. What he had was like 7 knives Not even tactical. Like fucking kitchen knives. With blades taped and he had them in his pants.

He was always calm. Menacingly calm. Like silence of the lamb's maniacal calm. I've never seen him eat or sleep. He told me his name, but I have forgotten. Everyone called him Nightcrawler. After Moschun he disappeared. Maybe he did learn how to teleport.

"Nightcrawler"
Western Volunteer – International Legion
Battle of Kyiv, Moschun
March 11th

I am Nightcrawler. I just did my bit. The battle was just a nightmare. It was nonstop day and night, but the internal unit struggle was very draining. I made some great connections out there. It wasn't properly organized, and no one trained together. The guys who had no experience weren't listening to the guys with experience.

Regarding the breathing, it was so cold that people were freezing. They wouldn't get out of their blankets, and they weren't doing their shifts and I was on my own a lot. I didn't sleep the whole time. I was trying to help them by teaching them how to breathe and create heat inside their body. I was just trying to help.

To me the main drain was people within our own group I just didn't trust. This guy didn't like me. He thought I was part of a cartel because of my tattoos, and he was really rude. He was horrible to me. I took it like a test because I pride myself on my level of restraint. He was just pushing me, pushing me, and he was supposed to be on our side, so I didn't push back. Out there, no one knew who anyone was. We didn't have any training together and we were thrown in the deep end.

I spent my two weeks there. I helped some people. Every second I was fighting off Russians or helping the group fight off Russians, we were saving lives. Giving people a chance to get to safety. I went out there just to save lives. I didn't go out there for any other reason than to help save lives. If people have got a problem with that, that's sad. It was a fight for humanity.

When that tank drove over that woman in the car and reversed over her on the TV; I saw that and came straight out. I came out to help people. I had a bit of time off and thought I'd do some good. We saved a lot of lives. I'm not down with Putin's regime. I love Russia. I love Russian people. I do not love Putin's regime and his brainwashing. That is not okay. I had to come back because I had a court case. A guy tried to shoot me in England with a shotgun.

Ukrainian Soldier
Battle of Kyiv, Moschun
March 11th

First, I felt very excited. I got one. They came here to take us over and destroy our country and I killed one. Second, I felt sick. The body began to be hard when we approached. My whole life 'Do not kill do not kill' and now I'm being told 'kill kill kill' and my heart and mind are arguing about who is right. I do not want to kill but I do. I have to. I do not want to hurt anyone.

I was driving a taxi a year ago and now I am killing Russians on the streets and in fields. The mind and heart cannot heal from these things. To bury a man who died of normal things is normal. To blow men up and try to kill as many as you can is not normal. No life will not be the same for me. Not me or the Russians who live. I want them to go home and leave us.

Western Volunteer
Yavoriv Training Base
March 13th

I arrived in Ukraine on March 4th. Our four-man group entering from Poland consisted of myself (former Canadian Army), Doc (Canadian Private Security), Fresh (Polish kid with no experience at all), and Nims (American Private Security).

We originally were stationed in Lviv, we spent about a week in that beautiful city before we were sent to the IPSC (International Peacekeeping and Security Center). I was working as a sniper. We were supposed to conduct more specialist training at this military base in western Ukraine.

It was my first night. I heard rumors about an air raid drill during the night, so I remained clothed with my boots on, and my kit staged for quick access. Around 0430 I came to the conclusion there would be no drill and I needed a few hours good sleep before my 0700 formation. I awoke to glass on my face and my building shaking at 0600.

I grabbed my rucksack (leaving my duffel bag containing my combat uniform and all my identification) and ran out. We ran to a trench we recently had dug. Could do nothing but pray. Our ammunition deposit was hit first. We had no anti air weapons. I was able to find a rifle amid the chaos. So, there I stood, posting security for over 30 men, while two jets bent us over and fucked us.

I sustained shrapnel wounds to my right hand and decided to return home to my family. This war took a lot from me during the short time I was there. The most fucked up part is the one barracks that got hit was Bravo Company. I was just assigned to that company. 1st Platoon.

I'm just glad I made it out. Pretty much all the lads in bravo barracks were killed immediately or burned to death.

Michael St John
Western Volunteer
Yavoriv Training Base
March 13th

My name is Michael St John, I'm an infantry mortar man and spent some time in Afghanistan...I arrived to Lviv on March 11th sometime around nightfall. I spent that night in Lviv. The next day March 12th I was picked up along with some Georgians and a Finnish gentleman. We arrived at Yavoriv Training Base at maybe around 1500. The Georgians and I were placed in a group totaling of about 20 people. We all walked over to our military tent and chose our cots and introduced ourselves. After we had our gear belongings down and were finished with our introductions a man came over and told us if the air raid sirens go off that we can run across this makeshift bridge and into the woods. Right after that I spoke to our group about bettering our defensive position just in case... A few guys said nothing had ever happened there so it shouldn't be a big deal. I told them that complacency is one of the biggest killers and that nothing happens until it does.

They all agreed with the decision. I reasoned with them that we could cut down some small trees and brush directly across from our tent to the stream. We all began to cut down the brush and placed some cardboard on the mud at the entrance to the stream. We then grabbed about a dozen pallets and lined the stream with them, that way we would be right above water level and wouldn't freeze to death if we had to jump in. We then took a spool of Ethernet cable and tied it across the stream on both sides for something to grab onto as you slid down into the stream about 6 feet down. After our work was done, I took a walk around the base just to get a lay of the land. I was told there was a gym so I wanted to figure out where it was so I could utilize it in the morning. I then returned to the tent and met with some of my new friends, and we proceeded to the chow hall to get some dinner. There we ran into maybe a few hundred people eating dinner. Ukrainian regular forces and foreigners alike.

Most of the Ukrainian forces were in training and were female and males alike, just people volunteering to save their nation from the invading forces. I didn't expect this to be the last time I'd see most of their faces... After chow we just went back to our tent to relax for the night till the next morning. Maybe around 8PM we had the air raid sirens go off... Just a false alarm. We go back to our cots, and I lay awake most the night just listening to music. 330 rolls around and I decide to take my boots off to let my feet air out finally, I also took my pants and my combat shirt off.

Not more than 30 minutes after undressing into my skivvies and undershirt and socks an endless night would unfold. All I heard was the afterburners of a fighter jet kick on above us... I'd never seen 20 people wake up and run so quickly out of a tent before in my life. I ran out in what I had on, that just being my shorts t-shirt and socks. My warming layers were of no use to me if I was dead. We hauled it directly across from our tent and began sliding into our trench in the stream.

As man by man gets into the stream and on the pallets, rockets begin raining down over us. We all are laying with our faces buried into the pallets, with just the overwhelming smell of the pine wood. It didn't seem to matter how far down in the ground we were each blast shook your insides. I thought daylight would never come. I was pissed that I was going to die on my first actual night in Ukraine. An all I wanted to do was run to help those being blown up. But I was helpless...We were all helpless.

Laying there as the fighter jets circled around again and again... Each time with devastating effects. The sky began to glow orange and red. Little did we know the Russians still had a surprise for all of us. In came the cruise missile, leaving behind a 20ft deep crater by about 75ft. All the windows blew out of all the buildings. Door frames ripped right off. While all this happened, I was beginning to shake from being so cold laying on the pallets right above the water. It must have been about 20 degrees Fahrenheit. Thanks to the guys I was with for covering my exposed body parts with theirs to keep me warm.

Anyways so we finally came out of hole in the ground, and it was complete chaos. People were running into the woods to leave and some untrained and trained alike were on edge and some freaking out. Some of the trained combat veterans started getting rifles from the Ukraine regulars. We were all getting ready for alleged paratroopers to come in and fight.

The Ukrainian officers told anyone who didn't want to stay to go to the side and they would be brought back to Lviv to go home. No one from our group left at that moment. The Georgians were ready to die on that ground against the Russians. We managed to get ahold of a German MG42, Russian Scorpions and some beat up Belgian FN-Cs. We took cases and cases of ammo and ran to the corner of the airfield close by and set in a machine gun position.

As people were leaving, we dug in. Ukrainian emergency services showed up and out the fires out and collected the dead. The situation was such chaos at this moment because there were people here with no training. Some thought it was call of duty... Till they finally saw the death and destruction it caused. The doc was going around in the woods making sure everyone was okay. Somehow this middle-aged man managed to wonder over by us. He just couldn't speak or really do much of anything. He was in complete shell shock. He'd been blown off his feet standing outside one of the buildings not even close to the ones hit.

With all the death and destruction caused it was crazy just how quiet it was throughout the whole air assault. This was one of those events where either you were alive or dead. There really wasn't an in between. There was no hiding from the force caused by the rockets let alone the cruise missile that hit.

So, throughout the next few days hundreds of people left, and rightfully so. After what happened most of us agreed that we were most likely a bit nuts to be staying. So, our group stayed.

As for those leaving like I said previously, a lot thought it would be like a video game. Most people on that base were untrained civilians looking to go fight. And the Ukrainians entertained their idea and provided them with training. Only at this point most finally realized what war actually was and decided enough was enough. I watched as the Ukrainian officers were cordial and polite offering these people transportation out. An honestly it was good to see them leave. We agreed it was better they leave now than when they make it out to the front.

Of all the combat ready teams we would be the only ones who stayed. I managed to grab an Artic Warfare Magnum chambered in 338 Lapua from a soldier leaving to go join a private military group. I stood there as the Major told him he wasn't taking the rifle with him as it belonged to Ukrainian Armed Forces. Thankfully I'd packed my Leupold optic to bring with me to Ukraine. Even then my 14x scope wasn't even worthy of being on the rails of one of the world's best rifles.

Once the pandemonium settled down after a few days' things began to fall into place. We received what armaments we needed and other gear. Finally, we boarded our vehicles, and the colonel shook each and every one of our hands and thanked us for answering his Countries call for help. As the vehicles started up and began pulling away, the Colonel stood there at attention and rendered a hand salute.

US Military Serviceman
United States
March 13th

I was in Ukraine in 2019. I spent my time in the Training Center in Yavoriv that was destroyed. That was sacred ground for peace. Ukraine wasn't like all the countries I've been to in my 8 years of military service. It was an amazing country with incredible people. I made many good friends there - civilians and soldiers alike.

Ever since the attack began, I've been reaching out to all. Six of them never responded or have even been seen online. I'm assuming the worst has happened. Being in America watching this happen to good people is unbearable. I cannot sit idly and watch as this injustice happens. Not when there has been a call for help, people with all kinds of skills have answered but my skill for the past 8 years have been nothing but violence. If that's what Ukraine needs, I will give it to them. God will see this through.

"Viking"
Georgian Volunteer – International Legion
Battle of Irpin
March 13th

Irpin was...Different. Moschun was positional, hold the line deal...Irpin was all offense. Urban, very urban. Long, straight roads with houses on each side, literal ambush valleys. It was a horrible place to maneuver.

We loaded on trucks, went to a nearby forest and from there on foot. We had to go over a red bridge, really narrow one at that. Definition of a chokepoint. We marched a lot into the heart of the city, one of the guys had a step counting fitness watch thingy and said that whole infill exfil was about 15 miles. Tactical movement that long is exhausting.

We came to some building and a sniper among us decided to find a nest on the top floor, asked for us to breach and clear the building. I almost lost my eye when we shattered the glass door, a piece of it flew right into my eye, cut my eyeball. Luckily, Allfather gave me two.

I took point, clearing the floors, only to find there was no sector for our sniper. Waste of effort and time. So, we rejoined the others. We found the central park, on the other side of it were the enemy. Ukrainian Commander ordered me to stay by his side at all times, since I spoke everybody's language in the whole operation, I could translate for him.

Seven Americans bounded ahead; I still don't know why. With no backup, no second team bounding with them, and they got into contact, under fire from BMD with a 30mm. They were pinned down, bad. I was urging the commander to let us open fire to just draw the enemy towards us so the guys could evacuate but he refused, saying our fire would be ineffective against the BMD. AT weapons were ineffective due to thick tree mass between, we couldn't fire them.

Eventually the commander decided to pull back and regroup. I told him we have to wait for our guys to fall back, but he was adamant about finding a better regroup position. So, I obeyed the command. Luckily, they all made it back, despite having no damn covering fire. Realizing that element of surprise was lost, commander decided to call it a day.

He sent me to evacuate another team few blocks down, mostly Brits. Paratroopers, a real rowdy bunch with bad attitudes and balls of solid steel. We took friendly fire from Ukrainians who didn't recognize us. Luckily their aim wasn't all that great.

We finally reached the staging area and exfilled on foot. I don't think I've ever been this tired in my life. This was our first op in Irpin. There were many that followed.

Ukrainian Soldier
Azov Regiment
Siege of Mariupol
March 13th

I took a Russian soldier prisoner. He came from a basement, and we held guns on him in case we needed to work on him. He told us there were more soldiers in the floors above him, and we sent this man back behind us.

We heard an explosion and then the radio said we needed a medic near us. I was not present to see what happened because we were working on the other Russians in the floor above. What happened was a drone or artillery had hit the road our soldier and the prisoner were on. Killing the Russian and our man.

The enemy above said they would not surrender because we would kill them. I said that we did not kill their man they did. They said this was impossible. We could not get them to move. There was a window leading to a room, and the room was the only room intact for them to hide in. We were in the hall and the stairway.

We said we would throw grenades into the room, and they said nothing. We threw one grenade and shortly after some enemies came with their hands in the air. Grenades are not as deadly as people think. They are loud and can kill you if you are close, but they hid behind furniture and survived. I was about to throw two more in when they came out and chose life.

Ukrainian Civilian
Sumy Oblast
March 14th

Rockets and missiles come down and kill. Two weeks of this. I haven't seen one Russian soldier but many dead people. Near here they are putting bodies in a big grave. My father works for the men burying the bodies. He says this is not a job for human beings. I feel sad for him. All the time there are fires and trucks trying to put out the fires. This does not seem real sometimes. This is the modern world. How can this happen? This needs to come to an end soon or no one will be left.

Western Volunteer
Kyiv
March 14th

I am going home. This is too much for me. I got caught up in the fervor of wanting to help and didn't actually think this through. I will admit it. I am running away. It's just too much for me. My prior military experience was not like this at all, and I'm glad it's not. The Taliban never bracketed me with artillery, and they never shot at us with tanks and aircraft. This is just above my level of fear management.

I feel like a coward. I came here to help, was in combat for bit and now I'm leaving because I just can't get my fear under control. I'm going to get someone killed if I stay here. I just feel so bad about this, man. I just felt like I was always on the verge of a panic attack.

Ukrainian Soldier
Kyiv Oblast
March 15th

Russian BTR vehicles I think are worse than tanks. The gun on them fires faster and they carry soldiers. If we see a BTR there are soldiers near it. If we see a tank sometimes it is alone and easier to destroy. Not long ago we were shot at by BTR main gun. It to me is the worst. A missile or rocket or artillery just shoots and hits wherever it lands. Vehicle fire from tanks and others makes me angry because they are shooting straight at you. Wounds from these are horrible. A whole leg can be removed. A shot to the body makes someone almost explode. They are easy to destroy but not good to fight directly.

German Civilian
Berlin
March 15th

I arrived In Berlin from Cologne where I go to boarding school, and over there in West Germany you don't see a lot or anything of Ukrainian refugees, but as soon as I arrived in Berlin today, I was greeted with the sight of full platforms. I am not kidding Berlin central station which is one of the largest in Europe was full to the brim with Ukrainian women and children. they were stacking the platforms with suitcases, bags of scrambled food and other things, they all looked very disoriented and looked to me and others for help while the volunteers from the city administration were struggling to gather all of the refugees to some sort of tent outside where they get documented or something I don't know.

But it really got personal when I got into the train home, it's usually an empty train but today it was full of Ukrainian women and children, honestly it stank and was loud of children screaming and mothers trying to calm their babies down, but it was manageable.

I remember, and I can't get this out of my head, a Ukrainian girl at my age (around 17-18) she was with her family and just looked completely destroyed. Her face was red like completely red, and she had this look of panic and confusion on her face. Her eyes were completely open like completely and were full of water, but she didn't cry. She looked to me several times, but I couldn't take it all, it had me sweating and shaking and just feeling like crying myself. They eventually got out of the train but afterwards I just sat down and started grabbing my head and sort of letting out tears. I can't forget that girls face, and I will probably never forget it.

It's easy watching this all on a screen and on the news but when you're actually there yourself seeing this it just hits you like a wrecking ball to the stomach

Western Volunteer
Siege of Chernihiv
March 15th

Brought my hobby drones with me. I'm not here to fight, just use my drones to help out. I have no experience in battle, but I figured these things could be of some use.

From up there you can see everything clearly while you fly around. A bird's eye view of the destruction and blown-up buildings. It's kind of crazy to see. It's scary, even though I'm safe from where I am, the sights are crazy. A few days ago, a Russian soldier spotted my little drone as I was flying over them, and he tried to shoot it. Man, my butthole puckered up so tight trying to get that drone out of there. I brought a few drones and already lost one to an accident, so I wasn't about to let another one get shot down.

It's sort of weird observing through a camera. People on the ground point at you and try to figure out what you are, then they shoot at you, sometimes they wave, and depending on which side they're in they ignore you. The craziest part is flying through a battle going on. I fly pretty high for those and have a good view of what's going on. I can spot tanks, vehicles, and sometimes soldiers if they aren't hidden very well.

"Viking"
Georgian Volunteer – Ukrainian Foreign Legion
Battle of Irpin
March 14th – 28th

One time we were moving through the city and came under heavy IDF. The only house gate we found we entered and found the basement door open, so we all piled in there to take cover.

It was a real Gucci basement, with its own gym. Everyone decided to sit down and rest, but it hit me that it was a multi-story mansion and there were floors up there we haven't even cleared so I rushed up the stairs, going door to door, kicking in every door and clearing rooms. It was a really Gucci place. I mean, every bedroom with its own bathroom with Jacuzzi in it and stocked kitchen on every floor.

Expensive furniture. This wasn't some babushka's humble abode. On third floor I breached a room and lo and behold, there's a black cat sitting there. Apparently, the owner left the cat behind with plenty of food and water. I love cats. I have 3 cats at home, strays I found on the side of the street. I immediately picked him up, gave him pets, changed his water and litter. I was furious someone would leave a cat behind like that.

Eventually I was done with clearing the top floors and reported downstairs that we're all good. Artillery stopped so we were ready to carry on with our movement.

Days later I was told that was the house of the Mayor of Irpin. I'd like to visit one day, see how the cat is doing. I hope he survived. The most eventful mission in Irpin was when I was placed in the unit led by the legendary ROKSEAL.

We drove to a staging area and accepted a mission. Move through the city, take a building, and ambush Russians. Simple, as briefings go. Unfortunately moving through these tightly packed neighborhoods proved difficult, we had to make a hole in every fence to cut through the yards.

At some point a local ran up to us and warned us where the enemy was. He helped us navigate the concrete jungle. I think guys like that are real heroes. Rest of us are professional operators, this is what we do, but this guy was some civilian in his fifties, he put his life at risk to make our op easier.

We made it to the house, real quiet like, and we could hear the engine of an armored vehicle just on the other side of the building. Boys rushed upstairs to find a vantage point from which they could fire an NLAW. It didn't go as planned. Our NLAW guy was spotted, and he took fire, dropping the NLAW he ran downstairs. At this Point the ROKSEAL had already dropped two Russians escorting the BMD.

We expected it to turn its turret and rip us to shreds but apparently driver was so confused he started making a U turn in the middle of the road. That gave us much needed time. Running downstairs, I saw that apparently one of our guys had taken a hit and was tended to by another. I gave him my shears to cut his uniform to see the damage, it looked like a shrapnel wound. No biggie we thought, just shrapnel but he was losing blood. He lost consciousness but miraculously came back to the land of the living himself. I've never seen this happen, I thought once you lose consciousness you're out until medic gives you adrenaline or something but no, this absolute mad lad just woke up.

We patched him up and began evacuation. It was like Favela from call of duty, running through houses, yards, jumping fences under fire. It was the most high-octane adrenaline packed event of my life. It also made me realize I should've gone easy on powerlifting and prioritized some cardio...To quote the great flannel daddy, "If you're not fit, you're gonna die".

We had to breach through every obstacle, make a hole everywhere while under indirect fire. Every crossing we made we had to have covering fire set up, while having a wounded man, who by some miracle of God was literally sprinting to his own Medevac.

While jumping over a fence our Ukrainian Commander nearly broke his leg. He started limping and now we had two down. Nevertheless, through all this adrenaline and action, ROKSEAL managed to be ice cool. He gave clear, straight commands in a calm manner. Commanded the whole squad with such professionalism that it was absolutely surreal.

I strongly believe that it was his skill as a commander that got us out that day. All of us alive. Seeing him being completely calm and taking charge was very reassuring. We finally made it to the staging area, our wounded man literally walked to his medevac, never becoming a burden to anyone.

Later we learnt that it wasn't shrapnel, it was a 5.45 round that key holed into his shoulder and tumbled down his ribs. He got very lucky. We all made it back. Days later our assault teams cleared the whole town, capturing the BMD that was shooting us. Alpha 1, our sister unit chased the Russians all the way out of the town. Soon after Russians abandoned both Bucha and Gostomel.

Western Volunteer – International Legion
Battle of Irpin
March 16th

My experience with war before this was in Afghanistan. There wasn't much destruction involved there in terms of whole villages being leveled, but here; it's something out of World War Two. Entire blocks are on fire and destroyed. Bodies lay about and stray animals try to feed on human remains.

It's hard for the mind to comprehend. Just weeks ago, I was home. These neighborhoods were quiet and alive. People went to work, watched TV, went shopping and played with their kids.

Now there are sandbags on the windows. Explosions are a constant part of life, and everywhere you look someone is having the worst days of their lives. Destroyed vehicles both military and civilian litter the streets. A car was blown so high by an explosive it ended up crashing through a house.

I said this is hard to comprehend, and it is. Many of these neighborhoods look and feel like home. Peace is an anomaly and this for me is the realization that destruction like this has been the norm for thousands of years. How spoiled we were the last 80 years. How fucking spoiled.

Week Four: March 17 - 23

Nadezhda
Ukrainian Civilian
Siege of Mariupol
March 17th

I go outside in between bombings. I need to walk the dog. It constantly whines, trembles and hides behind my legs. I want to sleep all the time. My yard, surrounded by high-rise buildings, is quiet and dead. I'm no longer afraid to look around.

Opposite, the entrance of the house number 105 is burning down. The flames have devoured five floors and are slowly chewing on the sixth. The fire in the rooms burns gently, as if it was a fireplace. Black charred windows stand without glass. From there, you can see curtains gnawed by flames falling out, like tongues. A feeling of impending doom and calm takes over me.

I'm sure I'll die soon. It's a matter of days. In this city, everyone is constantly waiting for death. I just wish it's not too horrible.

Three days ago, a friend of my nephew came to us and said that there was a direct hit to the fire department. The rescuers died. One woman had her arm, leg and head blown off. I wish that my body parts will remain in place, even after the explosion of an air bomb.

I don't know why, but it seems important to me. Although, on the other hand, no-one is being buried here during the war anyway. This is the answer we got from the police when we caught them on the street and asked what to do with the dead grandmother of our friend. They advised to put her on the balcony. I wonder how many balconies have dead bodies on them.

Our house on the Mir Avenue is the only one without direct hits. It was partially hit twice by shells, in some apartments, windows were blown out, but the whole building almost did not suffer and compared to other houses, looks like it got lucky.

The whole yard is covered with several layers of ash, glass, plastic and metal fragments. I try not to look at the iron atrocity that flew onto the kids' playground. I think it's a rocket, or maybe a mine. I don't care at this

147

point, but it's unpleasant. In the window of the third floor, I saw someone's face and twitched. It turns out I'm scared of living people.

My dog is starting to howl, and I understand that they will start shooting again now. I stand on the street in the afternoon, surrounded by such silence as if I was at the cemetery. There are no cars, no voices, no children, and no grandmothers on the benches. Even the wind died. However, there are still a few people here. They lie on the side of the house and in the parking lot, covered with outerwear. I don't want to look at them. I'm afraid I'll see someone I know.

All life in my city is now smoldering in the basements. Where I hide, life is so fragile, it can be compared to a candle. It won't take much effort to blow it out. Any vibration or breeze - and darkness will come. I try to cry, but I can't.

I feel sorry for myself, my family, my husband, neighbors, and friends. I go back to the basement and listen to the vile iron grind there. Two weeks have passed, and I no longer believe that there was ever another life. In Mariupol, people continue to sit in basements. It is getting harder for them to survive every day. They have no water, no food, no light, they can't even go outside because of the constant shelling. Mariupol residents must live…

Art by João "J-Dot" Alves

Ukrainian Soldier
Kyiv Oblast
March 17th

Any aircraft gives me huge anxiety. A jet flew over us and shot rockets into the trees where our vehicle was. It happened so quickly that we didn't know what was going on or happening.

Luckily, no one was near the vehicle when the explosions hit. The vehicle (van) was destroyed, and one person was wounded with a splinter from a tree, but everything was okay. I still am not liking the feeling of being hunted by jets. It's much like a mouse being hunted by an owl. We run and get under something or try to not be seen. I haven't seen any in some time, but at the start they were everywhere.

Belarusian Civilian
Belarus – Ukrainian Border Town
March 18th

The hospital is always receiving wounded (Russian) soldiers. Everyday buses and vans full of men arrive and are taken inside. Sometimes men are carried out. I can't tell but they look dead to me. Some are moved from one car to another. Some come out walking, some are carried. Some have bloody bandages already on their arms heads and legs. Just too many.

Many more enter the hospital than leave every day. More and more every day come. I do not want to get involved. I do feel sorry for these boys. No one should be without an arm or die for something as stupid as war. You are alive one time and what a waste is dying in a war.

Russian Civilian
Western Europe
March 18th

My cousin is one of the soldiers of Russia in Ukraine. (I immigrated West years ago) He was wounded and sent to Crimea. We conversed and he told me some things. He is a good man. He is artillery and said that while firing a Ukrainian truck of some kind started shooting at them. They had to run away but took the position back with the help of two tanks.

He said they had trouble with Chechen soldiers. He said they were fighting with their fists because the Chechens would take the good gear, good weapons, helmets, and stuff like that while the regular soldiers didn't get great stuff. He said the Chechens would 'pose for cameras' wearing their stuff and not fight.

They fought them during an argument with their fists because they had to do the actual fighting while others (Chechens) stood by and took pictures and only fired their guns for the cameras.

He told me the media is also not entirely truthful. Fighting is actually much worse in parts than they say. He does not desire to return to fighting but instead wants to go to Tibet to see mountains there.

Russian Soldier
Kherson Oblast
March 18th

I am a contract soldier. I enlisted at 18, I am 20 now. I made the rank of Junior Sergeant for being strict for uniforms and rules. My original base was near Moscow, the Motor Rifles that are there is my unit. I was among the first battlegroup to attack on the ground, first we pushed through the north of Novorossiya, with support of artillery, armor, air, and tactical missile groups.

Our first hours were a strange mix. Sometimes the enemy was very fierce, and sometimes they surrendered immediately. Most of the enemies we have fought so far are not Ukrainian army guys, or at least normal ones.

The most of them are foreign mercenaries, AZOV and the like. I steadily realize most of the Ukrainian army types aren't interested in this war with us. It's the AZOVites and the mercenaries fighting down here.

We have captured a lot of their gear too. Many Javelins and NLAW's that weren't even used. Painted with Ukrainian colors but not even fired or anything. Like they're just, posing with them. They probably just did not get chance to use it.

It's scary to me. The west is backing groups that demand ethnic Russians in Ukraine shouldn't be allowed to vote and should either be "cleansed out" or kicked out. A few days ago, we engaged a Ukrainian BTR that was running away from us, it ran over a civilian vehicle. Thank God nobody was inside.

I know that war is cruel. And is the most evil to civilians who wish to live in peace and happiness and live successful and safe lives. I know to Ukraine we must seem evil with green uniforms and balaclavas. But I wish to note for 8 years plus we said nothing other than, "Please talk to the Novorossiyans, please work something out, you said you would." To Ukraine. And for years they laughed and spit at our concerns. And now who will pay for it? Innocent civilians who didn't want this War.

American, Ukrainian, Russian. All suffer because of western backing to an illegal regime that promotes our deaths as cool and good. Is sad really. I have many Ukrainian friends, haven't talked to them since the start of this special operation, and I doubt many are even alive now. We are brothers, we shouldn't be fighting in my opinion, but nobody listens to us otherwise. It's terrible that's how it works now.

Apparently in western media Russians are depicted as barbarians. There are calls on social media for genocide against us. I ask those people this: "Do you think putting your Ukrainian flag up, and hiding Russian products in your store will stop us?"

Harming old women and their Russian corner store in America because of something happening in Ukraine only proves one thing: cowardice. If you have time to attack innocents, come and fight us. See what happens to foreign mercenaries that attack the Russian Army. It's a painful death by rockets and artillery and CAS.

Our first contact was heavy MG fire from a KORD position, maybe two of them. They hit our BTR, and it sounded almost like when you hit something with a hammer and it vibrated, it's similar. Luckily the BTR is a tough shield. We dismounted and returned fire, the BTR's main gun also shot at them. After a few minutes we were given the order to cease fire. It was as quiet as death, and I looked over to my left and saw two of the guys, one was wounded.

He's alive. Another one was wounded, but the blood pooled around him. He wasn't so lucky to live. We lost a good soldier that day. After this we mounted back up and loaded the wounded into the BTR, the rest of us but the medic stayed on top, and we were driven over to the enemy position, and what I saw haunts me now. 4 guys, 2 women. All dead, their legs and torsos mangled from the heavy fire we returned. They weren't even AZOV, just poor bastards. I made the sign of the cross, I pray they were granted eternal life as I pray for my own guys.

The position had a few things in there. An NLAW, a Javelin, the KORD HMG I spoke about, and ammo/rations for themselves. But not used. If they used it, I may not have been alive. To this day I do not know why they didn't. Other positions after this we found were very poorly equipped and surrendered. We have orders to let them go usually, and they go back home. We take their equipment and stuff yes, but they go home to their families. I wish for their sakes the war ends and we can go home too.

Our morale is very high, I think. They're good guys. Some are fathers, some are just normal guys that wanted to fight. Some are conscripts, but they're okay. Often, we are forced to make hard decisions, I think. Decisions the media in the west and people that are so critical of us could not make sadly. If I handed the senior team at VICE news my Kalash, what would they do? Really? If they had to be in my boots, and fight the Ukrainians, what would they do? They would happily give me my rifle back.

But back to the guys. I found them all to be good men. Many of them like me pray each and every day and evening we make it, a defending force by law of military prowess will always be in a better shape to defend unless something else happens. My message to your western viewers is this: Always consider everything that comes out of Ukraine to be a lie until proven. Even if it makes sense, be careful. I know I've seen footage from 2014-2015 being used as 2022 footage.

My message to the western fighters is this: Don't get involved in a private conflict that isn't your fight. Think of your kids, your mother, your father. Your brother and sisters. Are you willing to fight an actual army over what CBS is showing you? I know many of these same people have always been critical of the news and media for lying to them actively. Why now change that because "Evil Russians"? It doesn't go both ways here, you can't say you don't agree with the media or US Leadership, and then switch teams and say RUSSIANS MUST BE DESTROYED because it makes you feel nice and warm inside.

I wish for your western friends to enjoy long, fulfilling, and peaceful lives at their home. We have a saying at home, however. "Come to us as a guest, and we will treat you as a guest. Come to us by sword, and you will die by swords."

We aren't the Taliban western armed forces are used to. We are a modern, conventional and trained army who will complete our goals and defend our Fatherland. I think people should understand that, so they can have this chance to consider that choice and think twice about it.

It's a strange mix. Some are very determined and will not let their position fall until they do. That's rarer to me. More of them are willing to surrender rather than die. It's not worth dying for if I was in their position, but I know that is biased. The most resistance comes from AZOV, or the ones that didn't run like cowards to Poland. At one moment, the scariest part was when an entire field looked empty, was but then opened fire on us. Must have been 30 fighters all at once engaging us. An RPG flew over the BTR, luckily, we engaged them as best we could, and most of them withdrew. I think we took some wounded, but nobody was killed thankfully.

As for compassion I think the bravest was one of the guys, Dima, dragged a wounded guy, his PKM, and another guy back to us over a decent distance taking heavy fire from his back. They hit him in his armor, he's still alive.

But yes, compassion. We passed a destroyed Ukrainian tank; we heard something from it, so the BTR stopped. We dismounted, and I climbed on top of it and found the hatch was stuck closed. I beat it with my rifle stock until it opened, and I pulled out this wounded gunner. We fixed him the best we could, I tried to comfort him. He must have been 18 or so.

So many dead young guys, and I often wonder why even send them out for this. It's pointless, like sending the lambs to the slaughterhouse. They know they're going to die. I think many of us don't have this deep seeded hatred of the Ukrainians. We have our issues with their leaders, much like Americans in this. But you? Like people? No. Most people like ours wish for a peaceful happy life.

Ukrainian Soldier
March 20th

He died two weeks ago. (His friend) He died and is my friend. He was killed by a drone, and we haven't found his remains. He had a sister and a brother and two dogs and a mother. His father is dead. He died when he was a child. His family loved him very much. We (his fellow soldiers) loved him very much. He was funny and joked around.

Our favorite joke was two cigarettes he would put in his lips and pretend to be a vampire. He would crawl into people's holes with a light and say he was there for a drink. He was very funny. When the drone hit, I looked for him. I couldn't find him. I knew after an hour he was dead. His family loved him. We all loved him. He will be missed, and our country and the world are less because he is gone from the world.

My heart feels the loss heavier and heavier every day. I didn't have a brother until I had him.

Western Volunteer – International Legion
Battle of Moschun, Irpin
March 11th – 20th

I arrived in Ukraine within the first 10 days of the invasion. Being a prior infantry Marine, with years of experience working in the Emergency room, I felt I couldn't just sit and watch this go down on TV, so I booked a flight to Poland that left in two days. Nothing could have prepared me for what I was to experience. It took me two days from the time I got into Ukraine to be in my first firefight on the outskirts of Kyiv which I later found out was Irpin. I was one of the first members of the newly formed international foreign legion of Ukraine.

I can confidently say that drones are a game changer in war. When I joined the Marine Corps, we didn't even have protocols for drones. Now they were flying maybe 15–20 feet right above our heads watching our movements and likely used to bracket our positions. We were told we were fighting their VDV airborne units who were dropping in consistently and maneuvering around us. At one point, they were on our right and left flanks while they were keeping us in place with a heavy shelling.

At nighttime they were shooting up illumination rounds and moving about. There was dead bodies within feet of us, there was no way to really get them out, our injured have no choice but to stay in the fight. Being a medic, I know I had a target on my back and there was many instances where I had what I believe the snipers missing me by inches. Crazy thing about my experience is almost from one day to the next I am back in sunny Southern California. Back to my regular life, the same homeless people on the street, same people in the hospital complaining about the smallest things. It's like I never left. We don't know how good we have it here...I want to go back.

DPR Soldier - Separatist
Donetsk Oblast Frontline
March 21st

I never feel any experiences in war zone but today I did. Many Ukrainian army soldiers was killed and three surrender. I kill some of them. I can't believe I did it. But we lost one armored fighting vehicle. When we're finally arriving in a village, it was 7pm. We saw a lot of Ukrainians over there. (Civilians) They had a knife, axe. Grenade. It took us one hour to make them calm down, after one hour talking.

We told them to go away and leave this place. One pregnant woman with her husband beg me so bad because they're afraid I will shoot them. I told her that I have no reason to do bad stuff at her, her husband got some food from us. I ask her to leave this place and then give them two choices.

1. Go to Poland. We will give you supplies and ask you to leave.
2. Go to Russia. Rescue team will arrive here. We will give them new life.

Somewhat this Ukrainian woman is uncomfortable. She said she will go to Poland. I don't understand why this woman would rather be walking with her husband. She is pregnant…she will lose her energy. I felt sad for her!

When I asked her to stay here then, she Says she would rather commit suicide than see any Russian army outside of her house. Later she is insulting me and my friend. They said, 'We will go to Poland. We will rather walk and go there. Hey communist. You'll see our Presidents power!'

Basically, we treat you the way you want people to treat you - with dignity and respect. Because we are humans too. So, we talk with them. We told them it is very dangerous if you're walking because you are pregnant, but this woman is too arrogant. I don't fear Zelensky. I don't fear Putin. I only fear God. Whatever. I hope this woman and her husband survive.

DPR Soldier – Separatist
Donetsk Oblast Frontline
March 21st

My friend was killed. Rest in peace, my friend. Egor Belikov. It's actually sad to see him gone. He shot down one helicopter and a drone. He was wounded so bad, tired and he closed his eyes and he's gone.

I cry knowing he is gone. He did his best. I swear, he really did. I worked side by side with Egor and sometimes we love to bully each other in 2021 for a joke. Now he's left me. His life was terrible. His childhood was terrible. His parents passed away when he was 6. Egor never had siblings.

He didn't run away. He wasn't feeling scared or screaming when a missile hit our convoy. He was only smoking and shouted, 'Nice missile! Oh, Ukrainian helicopter! Long time no see my friend. Did you miss me?' I know him in 2017. It's sad to see him gone. Goodnight, Egor. Sleep well my comrade. Thank you for everything.

Ukrainian Marine
Siege of Mariupol
March 22nd

The Russians can be good fighters, but most of them are cowards and poorly trained and poorly equipped. The way they operate is they attack at first with aviation, artillery, tanks, then only the infantry went as soon as we started to see them off, infantry aviation and tanks began again.

They went in three echelons, first to mobilize against us was the meat, then after them the more prepared ones went, and after the third their specialists came in.

Western Volunteer
March 22nd

I'm new to the front. I've volunteered in Ukraine since day 4 of this war, but this is what I've observed. Ukraine is full, and I mean FULL of lions. This is a whole country of Winston Churchill's. Even the women and children.

The soldiers on the front at the start of this all thought they were going to die. As this was building up, they told me, 'Yes we knew we were probably going to lose, Russia's army is so much bigger.' But they still picked up their weapons and fought anyway…and they're more or less holding. The West thought Kyiv would fall in 3 days. It's been almost a month. It's a whole country of Spartans and it's Thermopylae in reverse now.

The Russian prisoners I've talked to are also surprised. They consider themselves a near peer to the US and they can't quite understand how farmers with tractors and civilians with Molotov cocktails…and the occasional javelin…are stopping them in their tracks.

I've got to hand it to the Russ though. Some of their units are badly depleted and they still keep coming. There are cowards in every army, but there's a lot of brave men on their side. We just have more brave men and women. Haters will say this is propaganda, but they're all at home on the couch. I'm here and I know what I'm seeing.

Andrew Borymsky
Ukrainian Soldier
Kyiv
March 22nd

My name is Andrew Borymsky, and I am a leather armor designer. On February 24th, 2022, my wife and I woke up to the sound of explosions: Kyiv was under missile attack. It took us the entire night and day to set up a bomb shelter in the basement, where my workshop is located. The next day, February 25th, I volunteered to join the territorial defense force of Kyiv, got issued a weapon, and stepped into duty on a defense position.

Weeks flew by, like days. All my energy went into reinforcement of our defense points, and weapons training. Before the war I already underwent a basic military training course and had some experience with firearms. This allowed me to combat stress and act within the safety protocols. I learned a lot during the last month and took the formal pledge to join the Armed Forces of Ukraine.

As all Ukrainians do, I want this war to end as soon as possible. All Russian's must answer for their crimes.

For me, there are no "Good Russian's", and I am openly against blaming only their government. Of course, the Russian government must be judged by an international tribunal, but we must not forget that all Russian's did everything to make this war possible. For this they must answer before Ukrainians and the entire democratic world. For the murdered children, violated women, the bombing of peaceful cities.

Ukraine will win this war. Ukrainians will rebuild everything and return to their normal lives. However, we won't disarm, and won't stop preparing. Because we know that Russian's don't hold on to their word, and some time in future they will surely try another treacherous attack. Ukrainians will always be the protectors of the free Europe. Glory to Ukraine!

Ukrainian Soldier
March 22nd

Many of the prisoners we catch are 18 or 19 and appear to not have a lot of training. Two we had a few weeks ago each had a rifle and two or three reloads. That was all. Not even body armor. Just camouflage uniforms. They said they were in a listening position and ran when we found them so that may tell why they were so lightly armed. One was crying and the other was trying not to cry. These aren't soldiers these are children. Not that I care much. I don't have sympathy anymore.

Art by João "J-Dot" Alves

Ukrainian Firefighter
Kyiv Oblast
March 23rd

Community services continue as long as they can. All day and night we are working going to put out fires started by Russian artillery. This has been exhausting and after long enough you want to collapse! Firefighters never expect to die from artillery but here it's happening regularly. If we do not keep working the fires get worse and worse. We have no choice.

Ukrainian Soldier
Abroad
March 23rd

I am going back home. I am a Ukrainian student abroad and my sister is in Eastern Ukraine. No word from her in two days so I am going back. I won't make it to the city, but I will find a unit to volunteer in. I was in the army for 1 year before I was kicked out. I don't think they will care if I come back now. I don't want to face my sister after we win this war and tell her I was safe at university while she was being shelled. Family is everything.

Russian Soldier
March 23rd

We moved into a small village today. It was on fire, but not from us. Artillery probably got them. No civilians we found, but disturbing things we found in a basement. A woman was beheaded and mutilated. She was violated and then killed. These bastards don't deserve sympathy or mercy. My opinion on this war each day it goes on, goes to hatred for them. But I must remember this is one group, not every Ukrainian. I know these thoughts only go into a journal and won't be thought of very much after this war is over. But if I survive it, I hope the men responsible for this poor woman will be hanged. If not, we kill them in this war.

On other thoughts: morale is very high now, besides this terrible situation with the woman. We have been moving steadily, fast enough that I don't think the maps will be accurate for any amount of time. We've nearly encircled the entire east of Ukraine. It should be done soon, hopefully.

Week Five: March 24 - 30

Ukrainian Civilian
Siege of Mariupol
March 24th

I had to leave my dog behind. We had to evacuate, and the noise scared him away. I searched but couldn't find him. Up to the last possible minute I looked. I lived alone with no family in the country, so my dog was my only family. He's still there in Russian territory somewhere. I worry for him all day and night. I pray to God the Russians or people who stayed behind take care of him.

I understand hate between people, but everyone loves animals. I hope he is fed and has water. When the war is done, I will go right back and look for him. I have seen pictures of Russian soldiers holding dogs, so I hope they treat him well. Or that he has run into the wilderness and is feeding there. I just hope he is okay. I will find him when I go back.

Western Volunteer
March 24th

This message is to all the people who want to volunteer. If you don't have a military/law enforcement background, stay home! This is not an adventure; you're not Rambo coming to save the day and kill a bunch of Russians. Even if you do have a military/law enforcement background think twice about this. I know guys with combat experience from Afghanistan or Iraq who are now back at home. They couldn't take it anymore and I don't blame them for leaving.

To you sitting behind your computer and thinking about volunteering, don't. Stay home, not just for yourself but for the fighting men here as well. You will get yourself or others killed without any experience. You won't get any training because there is no time for it. If you read this while you're on your way to Ukraine. Turn around and go home. ONLY men with combat experience are allowed to fight.

A few days ago we had 4 British replacements, their first day on the front and they got slaughtered. Men breaking down by constant barrages of artillery. I'm lucky to still be alive after a month of heavy fighting day in day out. Leave the fighting to the professionals and find a different way to help.

Ukrainian Special Operations Soldier
March 24th

Our small group when on a Seek and Destroy mission. We got to our starting point and went on foot from there. While we were progressing, we focused on every movement that eye and optics could see.

When we got to our "A" point, we checked all corners and hideouts, but only found looted houses and lots of empty bottles of alcohol. By the looks of it we were certain those belong to Ruskies, they're no different from a pig. We've got into our positions and started observing the location.

After we did that we made a plan and went on a meeting with a SOF group. Group task was – Go through the route that we made, clear the area and get to point "B".

As we progressed pushing Ruskies from trenches (You should have seen them run away) we faced a very drastic picture. Among the dead bodies we found an elderly civilian woman, she was tied to a tree, she died of frostbite. They tied her so that she won't tell anyone their location. (Presumably)

Moving forward, we saw the bags and backpacks filled with stuff they stole from the houses of civilians. More empty bottles. Their positions looked like a pork stall. Our group moved further. When we got to our next point we checked the perimeter and stayed on it. Our group started clearing the buildings. While one group "working" the other holds position and wait for the reinforcements that would hold regained positions. Our mission was accomplished. Bonus findings were:
-   Documents
-   Missile

While we continue to clear the area, we found an elderly civilian couple. 80 years old. The area, "Q" which they lived in was heavily shelled for two weeks. Old man was looking after his wife even though he lost his kidney.

They shared with us their story in what happened during those two weeks. And while they were telling us that, Ruskies started shelling us with mortars, so we gave that elderly couple water and food that we had and moved to our defensive positions.

SOF group commander spent all night looking for ways how to evacuate the couple from "Q" area. He even found their relatives. By the morning we had the plan.

Groups split. One goes, the other covers. All have their sector. Group moves, contact, moves further, contact, cover, point, get in. All around defense. Elderly couple are alive and well. We tell them that we need to move quickly. NOW. The guy says to us, 'I just started cooking potatoes, how can I leave my chickens here? What about the meds?'

All of these issues have quick solutions. They've quickly packed all the stuff they needed. We're requesting Evac vehicle and jump in. Ruskie drones saw us, but it was too late. Our vehicle was faster. We all did a great job and the guys that worked with us on this task – you are the best.

Ukrainian Soldier
Battle of Lukyanoyka
March 24th

Our fight in Lukyanovka. It was a 2-3 assault, we went with our tank, I'm not exaggerating, the enemy had more than 4 tanks and about 5 BMP, our artillery worked well, and we went forward, the Russians fled throwing equipment, the operation was planned perfectly. Their help was coming from other settlements, they were waiting for mines a couple of hours before the road and ambush, they suffered devastating losses, in the first hours we had many wounded but no casualties, we already felt victory, saw Russian abandoned equipment, abandoned positions.

We relaxed a little, as Russian tanks left the landing and broke through the ambush, one knocked down the caterpillar of our tank and killed three people who were next to our tank. The guys were 20 years old; they shot the tank in the forehead with an RPG, but there was a ricochet. The tank duel began.

At that moment, we ran into a strong house to gain a foothold. There were three of us in that house, shots from a tank immediately flew into it, right into the roof, and we were on the floor with a shock wave, just came to our senses, got up and suddenly found ourselves on the floor again with the second shot. We started to run to another house, because we realized that we were noticed, but a shell from a tank flew into that house

165

as well. We only later learned that at that moment, literally where we were standing, three young men were killed because of an enemy tank.

When we approached the main group, the wounded were given first aid, but we consolidated and tried to help our tank, which could not move, but our reinforcements came, they pulled the tank into hiding. The crew of the downed tank moved to the trophy Russian and destroyed two more tanks in the tank duel. It is difficult to calculate how many losses we inflicted on them that day, but it was clearly a success, as half of us fought without such experience.

God was clearly on our side. Our commander was a real warrior, walking in the front row, raising his fighting spirit. It's hard to describe everything, but I'm proud of my commander, I want to go on the attack with him. We dug in Lukyanovka, our help came. The Russians were furious, they started shelling everything that was there, and in the same village I saw hits in the church

Art by João "J-Dot" Alves

Ukrainian Civilian
Kharkov
March 24th

I live not far from the frontline. Not too much time ago I saw frontline troops fighting. Battles are not what I expected them as. Shooting is not always happening. Sometimes it got quiet for a few minutes or hours and then sometimes it was not stopping for what seemed like hours.

I had not even seen Russian soldiers this close to the front until three Russians walked past our street as prisoners. I was expecting younger soldiers, but these ones seemed older. In their 30's or 40's.

I waved to the soldiers walking with the prisoners and they waved back and told me to stay on my street. This is still so strange. 40 days ago I was preparing to go to Western Europe to visit friends. And now I'm watching battles in my neighborhood.

Lieutenant Ken Rhee, ROK Navy
Bravo Team Leader
International Legion
Defense Intelligence of Ukraine (GUR)
Battle of Irpin
March 25th

My 8th op in Ukraine. Its early morning and we meet with a Ukrainian SOF commander at our safe house and get a quick briefing. By briefing, I mean a Ukrainian style briefing. It's basically something like... "We take the MRAP, drive up to the X, get out and kill the Russians".

I'll refer to this Ukrainian SOF commander who is a good friend of mine as Victor to conceal his real name. And just as Victor wanted, I got my multinational special operations team, known as Bravo Team situated and loaded up the MRAP. We leave the Kyiv safe house and do a 20-minute vehicle insertion into the heart of Irpin. On the previous ops, we would dismount the vehicles at least 5 kilometers away from the target and do a long patrol in – but on this particular day we drove up to where the heavy fighting was.

We get off the MRAP and link up with a Ukrainian infantry unit. I order my guys to set up a security perimeter while Victor and I talk to the local forces to gather intelligence on the enemy positions. Fortunately for us, we were given information that there are tank patrols in the area. Our mission was to set up a firing position at specific building and eliminate these tank units.

I asked Victor what the best route to the building was and he said "Just up this main road". No longer a culture shock at this point, I turn to my 2IC and tell him to scout out a route through the neighborhood and to avoid all main roads. Of course, the route would suck as we would have to go through fences and locked gates, but it would be better to do that than to meet a battle tank dead on in the middle of the main road.

We patrol off quietly in a train formation maintaining 360-degree security as we walk in between the houses watching for any signs of Russian activity. I point my weapon at a house where a male and female voices can be heard and had Victor check it out. He starts speaking in Ukrainian and a civilian opens the door. Surprisingly, he was very cooperative and tells us that he knows where a tank is and ends up being our local guide for a part of the infiltration.

As soon as my team arrives at this 6-story building, we conduct CQB to clear it floor by floor. As I creep up to the third floor, I notice a familiar and distinct sound...heavy tracks. I pop back to the second floor and look through a loophole in the wall and see a BMD with its back to me and large letter ''V'' on its tail. I ordered my rocket operators to get ready and run up to the 4th floor where there is a firing position through a big ass hole in the side of the building. Getting eyes on five foot soldiers and 1 BMD, I order my NLAW operator, Matt to fire when ready.

The ambush plan was – NLAW operator fires first and takes out the BMD, then the rest get on line and fire on the foot soldiers. Simple linear ambush. While the NLAW sets up, the rest of the guys take cover on the stairway to avoid the back blast. And we wait for the NLAW to fire...and bang.

Only that it sounded nothing like a rocket. It very much sounded like a sniper round smacking against the concrete wall. Then a lot more rounds fly into the building. I go to check on Matt and then I see him sprinting down the stairway without his rifle or NLAW and a pale face that looks like he just saw a ghost. My secondary rocket operator, Otto takes an RPG and gets ready to fire while I quickly run to a loophole to assess, and the BMD is turning around while foot soldiers are spraying rounds into the building.

I immediately kill two Russian soldiers which was enough to compromise my position and I get my team consolidated on the first floor of the building for exfiltration. The BMD turret hammers the building and I find Otto bleeding out and starting to lose consciousness. Otto was hit by a 5.45mm AK-74 round in the back above his body armor and the bullet lodged into his chest. Alex started administering first aid on him and told me that he needed five minutes.

The concrete building offered limited cover, but the enemy would have us surrounded in minutes which would put us in a very bad spot. I told Alex that we didn't have five minutes and I got the team ready for a hasty exfiltration. Matt was contemplating whether to go back for his CZ Bren and NLAW that he had dropped on the 4th floor when he nearly ate the incoming sniper fire.

I told him to forget about the lost weapons and to take Otto's rifle. Last, I need is for Matt to go back up there and eat a flying grenade. I tell Otto to snap out of it and get up, order my guys to move out, and as soon as we exit the building we get incoming turret fire, mortar fire, and small arms fire. Explosions everywhere. While running in a train formation, we set up dedicated security points to lay down suppressive fire to prevent the foot soldiers from coming after us.

The Russians respond by firing flares above our heads which are followed by consecutive mortar fire. We take a different path than our infiltration which in a way, screwed us as we kept running into dead ends. Any there was no chance to do an about face and go back towards the enemy. So, I order the guys to punch a hole in the dead ends. While we're being rained on by enemy fire, we literally kick down fences, jump walls, trip over obstacles, and then Victor screws up his leg badly on one of the obstacles. Now we have two wounded.

All this running through the neighborhood reminded me of Soap running through the favela in "Call of Duty". This was actually more intense. We finally get to where the MRAP is staged and I have Otto CASEVAC'ed out of the area. The rest of my guys link up with a Ukrainian infantry unit at an abandoned apartment complex. I get my guys reorganized and while talking with the Ukrainian head shed for the next move, I hear my interpreter, Viking tell me...the Russians have us surrounded.

"Tonya Croft"
Ukrainian Civilian
March 25th

Around five in the morning on February 24th, we heard some popping outside the window. My sister and I were just about to go to bed, because at night we worked at computers. It was clear that there were explosions somewhere in the distance. Thus, the war began. Our village is ten kilometers from Hostomel, and we realized that it was airport that was being bombed. A little later, our parents went to neighboring village to buy products. Then there was the possibility. People massively leaving Kyiv, they thought that it would be safer for them in the region... We also think so. But there was not a day when we didn't hear explosions.

Electricity went out on the fourth day of the war, but there was still mobile Internet and we tried to get the news in order to be a little aware. Charged phones through the battery of my father's car. The freezer kept cold for a long time, it saved us a lot. In the first days of March, there were frosts and my mother put the food outside at night so that they would not spoil.

The first time we saw a column of military equipment of the occupant was on February 28, when they stopped on the street near our house. We thought it was our last day, when we heard a knock on our gates. But we were lucky, they went further, because they had a goal - Kyiv.

On March 8th, we lost gas and internet. Since then, we have been cooking in the yard over a campfire. In the morning and evening of every day, we called our friends in Kyiv to get the news. Explosions, rocket whistles, enemy helicopters and fighter jets over the house have become routine for us. And after March 15th, almost every day enemy vehicles drove past our house. We even stopped responding to it.

Everything changed on March 21st at 7 AM. Three or four infantry fighting vehicles, passing by, stopped. As usual, we climbed out the window into the yard and hid with my sister in the guest house. Parents - on the gazebo. Russian soldiers didn't think to leave. They broke the fence of our neighbors (who managed to leave a couple days ago), walked on their territory and went to their garden, began to make trenches.

Parents came to us and mother, with tears in her eyes, said that Russian occupiers allowed us to walk. Then I didn't want to understand that this is reality, it seemed to me that I was dreaming. But we exhaled when the Russian soldier said that they won't kill us. I saw how they were digging trenches; someone went with a mortar closer to the forest...

Our village was occupied. Mom's friend asked Russian soldiers about the opportunity to leave, they allowed. There were not many of us, only three families in three cars. Someone left earlier, the elderly remained - they had nowhere to run...

There was almost no time to get ready - 5 minutes. Mom was crying, all her life she dreamed of a private house (parents bought it only 9 years ago) and now she has to leave it.

We physically couldn't take everything. I took the most valuable - my cat, system unit, laptop and some clothes. But left my heart - all my cosplay, which I did for 17 years, a large collection of Tomb Raider. Sister took her cat too, laptop. Parents - their dog, BUT they left the rest of our cats (there are six of them!), which simply would not fit into our car. We don't know when we can go back there. We don't know if we'll see our house again...

We were helped by kind Ukrainians from other villages in the Kyiv region, who gave us shelter and food for two days! Along the way, we met the Priest, who (with volunteers) eventually helped us get out in a convoy of other refugee cars! We were passing many Russian roadblocks and each time our hearts stopped - they could take away our phones, turn us back or even shoot (such cases have already happened).

On the evening of the 21st we were already in Kyiv. Light, working shops, the Internet - for us it was wildness, because we were in isolation for 26 days! The next day we managed to call our neighbor who stayed in the village. He said that the Russian occupiers had already set up several roadblocks, walked around our houses and marauding our things. I believe that each of them will answer for their crimes, and we will return home to our unbroken house!

Ukrainian Soldier
March 27th

I returned from the front six days before this because I am injured. Not a combat injury. I hurt my leg jumping out of a window. The day before we were shooting tanks in ambushes.

I cannot say where, but I can describe the situation for you. We were on the north side of a road in the trees next to several buildings which we also held. To the east was a small village, the south a field, and to the west was more of the road and a forest on both sides of the road. We were on the edge of this forest waiting.

A row of tanks and trucks came down the road and we waited for the initiation. The rocket shot a tank but had no effect on it. A second and third rocket fired, and the tank stopped. Russian soldiers got out of their vehicles and started running for the ditch in the field to the south. We shot some in the back as they ran. I didn't hit anyone. My job was to load rockets.

We kept firing until we were out of rockets and the position of the enemy became unsteady for them. The rest ran away on foot while the ones in vehicles drove into the ditch to get away. In total we killed 4 vehicles and around 10 soldiers. 2 were wounded and were left behind. They were arrested and sent away.

Ukrainian Civilian
Poland
March 27th

I've had my first bath since early March. My husband and I fled from the Eastern part of the country and just made it to Poland. I'm in a hostel now with him and it took him almost 2 hours to persuade me to have a bath.

It feels so wasteful. All of this water. I type this to you all from my bath now. For so long we saved every cup we could. Now I'm lying in a tub of it and it feels wrong. It feels so wrong to do this while children still go thirsty. Have things like this been ruined forever for me? Have luxury things like enough food, clean water, and electricity been burned away from me? I hope not.

Aiden Aslin, @CossackGundi
Western Volunteer - Ukrainian Marine
Siege of Mariupol
March 27th

Every day feels like it's a repeat of the previous day like in the film Groundhog Day. Now, as Russian forces slowly creep into the city day by day, it's unknown what our future will be.

When the air-strikes and artillery stop echoing and everything goes silent it's almost possible to remember how peaceful it was before here until it gets interrupted by more shelling.

I won't lie, either the silence; as peaceful as it is…also gives me anxiety. At least when there's shooting you know what's going on. When the enemy is silent you don't know what they are planning.

We've lasted roughly for 3 weeks, and a half of that time has been in this encirclement if memory serves correct. While the Ukrainian spirits remain high, I'm unsure what the next day will bring. I can only hope this stupid war ends. Mariupol.

Anastasiia
Ukrainian Civilian
Kyiv Oblast
March 28th

Two groups of soldiers (Russians) passed through my town before I was allowed to leave. We stayed in our house and cooked our food in the yard over a fire. The first group of Russians were respectful of people's property.

They came in tanks and trucks. Many of them. A few tried to enter houses, but they were told to stay out. They just passed through and didn't bother us. They acted like I think soldiers should act. I'm not a soldier. I never have been. But soldiers should act like guests in a town not hurting them.

The next group that came a few days' later in trucks and civilian cars and were not respectful. They were horrible. They entered our homes and took things. They smashed windows and broke things for pleasure. I don't know why they behaved so much worse than the first group. I had friends in Russia before this and none of them ever behaved like this. I will not consider them my friends after this.

Western Volunteer
March 28th

We went to scout positions for a sniper mission, as we moved through Ukrainian trenches looking for spots to get eyes on enemy positions, we heard sporadic shelling around 1km away.

The spots were a bust due to the brush and terrible terrain. As we approached the end of the position, we realize another unit's position is just across a dried-up riverbed. We decide to risk continuing on to see if there was a better position to shoot from.

I started to become a bit nervous as nobody has radios and we could easily be engaged by friendly forces. One of our guys stepped over the berm waving his hands. We were all waiting to be fired in by friendlies. We decided not to push it and headed back to our lines.

On the walk back we thought we heard the engines of BTRs. When we got back to the trenches the spot, we were just at started to come under what seemed to be heavy mortar fire. We think we may have been spotted by a drone or a spotter from the enemy held village. Just another day in Ukraine.

Ukrainian Soldier
Battle of Irpin
March 29th

For me, I still have not shot my gun one time. I haven't even seen any Russians with my own eyes. Not alive ones. I will not lie and say I have been inside battles. I haven't.

We soldiers helped to retake Irpin. We found houses emptied of belongings and trash. Russians had left a mess in houses they stayed in. The people came out to greet us. Many were happy, but quiet. Others were cheering. Mostly old people I saw. People too old to leave and go to Poland or Kyiv. Reminds me of films of World War Two. We walked behind tanks through streets carrying weapons and rockets.

This is not the first time in our past these towns have been rescued from our enemies. I was lucky to be born when I was. I was lucky to be here and proud to defend Ukraine. Ukrainians never give up and say no to die for something good.

The police station here is small and it was used to house Russians. Inside was stuff left behind like stolen chairs, pots, and blankets. They must have left in a hurry before we came. The time to have victory celebrations is not here yet. We still have much to rescue from Russia.

Western Volunteer
Kyiv Oblast
March 29th

Last week I had one of the most peaceful moments of my life in this war. I had woken up for watch; and was standing on the second floor of a building looking out of a window. Chilly night air came through, but everything was silent.

No guns fired. No bombs exploding. No vehicles moving. Just silence. I looked out the window smoking a cigarette. (I know I'm not supposed to smoke at night but fuck you I was exhausted)

I was sitting there just listening. I heard nothing for the first time since I got here. It was a beautiful change from the air raids and gunfire of previous hours. I wondered how many other Ukrainian soldiers and Russian soldiers also on watch in the area were sitting there appreciating this silence. And would we rather not start up all this noise again in the morning. It was such a peaceful moment, and I didn't want it to end. I think I needed the quiet so much that I didn't even wake up the next man for watch. I just stood two posts.

Western Volunteer – International Legion
Kyiv Oblast
March 30th

I will tell a story that I didn't expect to tell. Some Russian soldiers are so poorly trained and equipped they cannot be called soldiers. They carry equipment that our fathers and grandfathers had.

One man we recovered was old enough to be my grandfather. Some say they were volunteers and others tell us they were forced to be soldiers. There are no doubt some very competent, professional, and lethal

176

Russian soldiers in their army fighting here in Ukraine. But where I am, most of what I have seen is the bottom of the barrel.

Russian Soldier
First Chechen War Veteran
March 30th

In 1996 I served in the First Chechen war in the Russian army. Back then, our leaders were imbeciles, our training was poor, and our equipment was not sufficient. Now in 2022, I see the same thing happening to another generation of young Russian men. I live in America now. I have for a long time. The west is 'Oh why don't they just refuse to fight? Why don't they go home?' And 'These Russians are devils and do not deserve life.' But it is not that simple.

First you must understand the hard system of abuse in the Russian army. It is not like in the west. In the army you are beaten for no reason. Sometimes very severely. You are not fed well. They create a culture of obedience through fear of the officers.

The non-commissioned officers and officers are often useless. They take bribes and sell fuel and ammunition for their own pockets. They treat soldiers like cattle. I see these Russian boys on the news and I see men being herded to slaughter; trapped in a cycle of murder that they can't escape from if they asked to.

There are no doubt some very bad men staining the uniform I once wore proudly. But for every one evil man there are 100 scared boys who would rather be home with their brothers and fathers. Too many Ukrainian soldiers, civilians, and Russian soldiers have died for nothing. I see Mariupol and Irpin, and I see Grozny. It's not as simple as saying 'no, I won't.'

I am at a crossroads with myself. I realize that many Russian boys need to pass from this world before this ends. They have to. It's the only way this ends faster. Its systemic fear and self-preservation that keeps this war going on the Russian side, I think. I can't be sure. I haven't been in the army for 20 years.

Week Six: March 31 - April 6

Russian Soldier
Russian Base – Russia
March 31ˢᵗ

We do not want to go. Everyday rumors of us going (to Ukraine) come. I have been in the army for 7 months and I do regret being a soldier. This is something I do not want. I'd like this to be over soon. So soon that this doesn't involve my regiment.

Ivanna
Ukrainian Civilian
March 31st

I am a Ukrainian and a mother. I'm going to share a very unpopular opinion. I fled to the west a few weeks before this began. We have lots of friends west of Ukraine and some in Russia, so I have been living in total safety this entire time and I know that may have skewed my perspective some.

But still, my feelings are my feelings. I see the pictures. I see the videos. I read the firsthand stories of what's happening…and all I can think of is my own children. Had we lived in another country (Russia) these dead boys in the ditches and streets could easily be my own sons…I found myself cheering and calling for the deaths of those Russian boys once.

I feel ashamed now. Somewhere in Russia, 10,000+ mothers are now crying out in anguish and misery. The lives of their boys are gone. Cut short by the whims of a mad man and greedy generals. Their lives had to be cut short, I truly believe that, but I still cannot help but mourn their lives in a small way. I cannot explain why I feel like this. I should hate them. I have every right to. I want them to leave my home very badly.

But I see the pictures and videos of these mangled bodies of 18 and 20 and 22 year olds and I see my own sons. What did they think before the end? Did they wish for their mothers? Wouldn't they rather be home? The pain of this war affects all of us, on both sides.

I stand firmly with Ukraine, but I stand firmly with humanity as a whole as well. This is just a waste. I hope we win. I know we will win. But

I hope this war will be the last large one. I hope this shows the world what a waste this is, and how we can and should be able to speak to each other before we send our children with guns and tanks and planes to massacre each other.

Ukrainian Soldier
April 1st

We are now experts at tank ambushes. Our unit has destroyed over 20 vehicles so far. Armored ones especially. We almost never miss! When you fire the rocket, everything is quiet for a moment. Then our friends with machine guns and other weapons (more rockets) fire as well.

The Russians mostly seem to have no idea we were even in the area. Sometimes it seems as if their guns are not even loaded. It takes a few moments for them to shoot back. Sometimes they don't shoot back at all but not all the time.

The part I do not like is removing the destroyed bodies from burned vehicles. We sometimes destroy entire lines of vehicles and the Russians run away on foot or drive away with what is left and leave everything else behind. Some vehicles are not even destroyed. Not touched. And they leave them for us.

In February 24th and 25th, we did not expect to have a country a week from then. Now I feel like we could march into Moscow and show these guys what real soldiers look like and how we can easily destroy their armored vehicles and soldiers. I expected more from them. The only fear I have is from missiles and they will someday run out of them.

Art by João "J-Dot" Alves

Ukrainian Soldier
April 3rd

It was my and some others responsibility to gather Russian bodies on the road. 9 dead Russians. 1 pile with all their bodies and equipment. It was not what I wanted to do. I did it anyway.

We dragged the bodies from vehicles to the point. Somewhere 300 meters apart. The fat ones I carried on my back. This collection was to have them identified and buried.

Nearby were 3 still alive. Russian prisoners. We all said threats and curses. Today we hear about Bucha and people the murdered there. Children with hands tied. Men with hands tied. Women with hands tied. All shot like the Germans did in the 40's. They called us N**i's and they act like them?

The 3 Russians only live because of the law. If no one was here to report us I would happily sentence them to the same fate. Today we are filled with anger and hatred. I hope this hate never goes away. I hope we use hatred to drive our bodies. Our minds. Our hearts. Our guns. These men are going to regret coming here. Going to regret to be born. This will make things worse for them. I know it. The people know it.

Ukrainian Special Operations Soldier
April 3rd

We had come to a village and started preparing our defense position. Guys started digging trenches, not exactly decent ones but somewhere to hide during the shelling. I don't know how many minutes passed since that but the next scenes got me stunned. The people from the village got to our positions with shovels. Women, men, literally everyone. They asked me, 'Okay where do we need to dig the trenches?' I couldn't say a word, I'm just standing there watching how they detach shovels from their bicycles. I'm saying all good, no need to help but it was too late, and they already started digging along with the guys.

In a few days, we are looking for enemy tanks going our way, I have young guys in my group. They're all shaking in fear shouting, 'Enemy tanks are moving our way, what should we do?' and again, villagers coming our way too, lots of them. They shouted, 'We see Russian tanks moving our way, how can we help?' I'm telling them to get back to your houses immediately, but they're not listening to me. I commanded a couple of guys from the group to push those villagers back.

One of the villagers, a 73-year-old man came to me and said, 'Give me a grenade, I've spent all my life working as a plumber here, I know the infrastructure here well. I'll get closer to them using underground pipes, throw a grenade and get back using the same pipes.' I was lost for words.

The intense battle going the whole day, the enemy artillery shelled the village street, 25 houses on fire, thank God no casualties. We destroy their tanks, vehicles, everything we see. They try to flank us, no luck for them. Guys from our group are no longer newbies, causing heavy casualties to the enemies, so they are retreating. They're asking me to have some rest, I', saying sure, you deserved it. The first thing they went to do – was put out the fires in the village. I'm in tears and joined them right away.

You'll never 'Denazify" the country, where people help prepare defensive positions for the army, an army that after heavy battles help the people save their houses. You'll die here, Russians.

Belarusian Civilian
Mazyr, Belarus
April 3rd

I live and work in Mazyr Belarus. I am not Belarusian but moved here for work and to marry. I work as sanitation in a hospital. I am not allowed to say how many Russians (soldiers) have been here to be helped for their wounds, but it has been many.

Sometimes they come in buses, vans or ambulances. Some that come are out of reach of a doctor's help. Some have not very serious wounds and can walk themselves around. All are addicted to cigarettes. I do not use cigarettes for my health, but many ask me for cigarettes.

I always tell them I do not have any cigarettes. One soldier who has a throat wound survived and was but was not expected to. He asks for a cigarette, and I told him I do not use them. I also told him he won't be smoking in his condition. He told me he hopes the cigarette he finds is the one to keep him here.

I said he should not say these things, but he kept telling me. I do not understand why he would want this to be known. The soldiers do not talk much if they can talk. The ones who can walk just walk outside.

Ukrainian Soldier
April 3rd

I am a tank driver in the Ukrainian army. I am not new to the army. I have been here for 6 years. Many new soldiers come now who were civilians 5 weeks ago. I am the old man here.

I ran the fastest race on earth 2 weeks ago. Part of tank driving is finding cigarettes. It is not an official duty to perform but very necessary for survival and sanity if you understand war. I was walking to the civilians asking if they have cigarettes and Russians started shooting at me with artillery.

I ran like an Olympian back to my tank. I could hear the explosions behind me and I did not want to end up as a tree decoration so I ran. Now it was like an action movie scene like Rambo or something running back. Our Gunner was waving for me to run faster.

I get back inside and he lights a cigarette! I said where did you find this? He said he has had some the whole time. I hit his arm and told him next time he wants cigarettes he can go ask the Russians directly! (I am joking. He is a good man. I did not ask if he had any) That is the story of how I became the fastest man on earth.

Art by João "J-Dot" Alves

Western Volunteer – International Legion
April 4th

Took my flight from the states to Turkey, then to Warsaw Poland. Took a 15-hour bus down by a border town near Lviv. After 3 days of travel and no sleep or food, I came upon a church that took me in and fed me, gave me a bed for the night.

I went about my way not too long after. Amazing people, such kindness is something I've never experienced before. Made contact as instructed by the Ukrainian government and I was off to start my process as a candidate for the UFL (Ukrainian Foreign Legion). It was lengthy and thorough but that's good news, a lot of idiots and fakes that were being processed in that shouldn't be, this is of course in the early days of the legion.

Went to a short "camp" where I would train and meet my future brothers and learn new ways. Took a bit but we built a bond like no other and learned so much from each other. Now we are off on deployment, and we continue to stick to each other like herpes on a whore.

I've fought as a guerilla in Mexico for years to defend my family, but when that was gone, I had nothing to fight for, no reason to stay. I was but a little kid when I learned how to kill, a warrior's culture is how I grew up. Drifted a few years from job to job doing shit I didn't like and things I hated, till Ukraine called. And Ukraine gave me purpose and a calling again.

Here I am. Here we are, fighting for Ukraine. I was placed with a great unit which has a 70% washout rate due to selection and high standard expectations that any professional soldier is expected of them. And I'm proud to be of that.

The violence in Mexico is unmatched in brutality but the mass togetherness of the Ukrainian people is another world in itself. Of course all wars are ugly, and horrible. But this is my personal opinion as I've seen both. I'm proud to be here. I also add that all of my unit members have come here realizing that pay is not going to happen.

Western Volunteer
April 4th

It all started when Russia invaded Ukraine. My best friend went a few days before the invasion started, the 19th of February I believe it was. When videos were circling the internet what the Russians did to the Ukrainian civilians I was devastated, innocent people being killed, mothers and children fleeing the country.

Then the day came that President Zelensky announced the Territorial Defense for volunteers, the Foreign Legion. I immediately felt it was a calling and I went to the Ukrainian embassy to enlist. I bought all the gear/equipment that was required and arranged my departure. I told my friend I was coming to Ukraine to fight; he told me he would help me getting to the destination in Ukraine, what I had to do and what to avoid etc.

I told my family that I was going, and it wasn't a surprise that they were extremely against it, my girlfriend threatened to leave me if I was going. I don't know why but a few days later I called it off, I can't explain the reason for it but I regret calling it off. I felt I let people down like my friend and the Ukrainian people. A few days ago, my friend was killed... I feel guilty now that I didn't go, I feel like I'm a coward if I don't go. How am I going to live with myself if I don't stand for what I believe? I saw the videos and images of what happened in Bucha.

It sparked that flame in me again. I'm doing it, I'm going! I'm going to do this for them and for my friend. I know it will probably be a one-way trip but I have to do this. I accept the possibility of dying and I'm willing to give my life for them. I'm willing to leave everything behind to defend the people of Ukraine, especially all the children. If I can give my life to save a child, so be it. This isn't about being a hero or whatever, for me this is about doing the right thing. That's why I'm going.

Ukrainian Soldier
Eastern Front
April 4th

I am a nurse turned into a combat medic. Before this I also worked in ambulances. I do not carry a weapon beside a pistol. I do not want to hurt anyone. I carry it because they make me carry it.

All types of wounds are wounds I help to heal and save lives. With soldiers the most common wounds are bullet wounds, shrapnel from bombs, and splinters from rocks and trees that become shrapnel from explosions. Working on bullet wounds is much easier than shrapnel.

Bullets in people's bodies do not cause the same damage as a shrapnel can. Bullets fly straight. Shrapnel can come in spinning, sideways, any direction, and shrapnel is always a horrible looking shape. (Jagged, blunt, sharp) These oddly shaped projectiles become more deadly than a finely shaped and straight flying bullet. Shrapnel will tear away an arm or pieces of the body.

Civilian wounds I see are most burns, compression syndrome (being crushed by buildings) and internal damage from missile attacks. (Shockwaves of blasts) If soldiers and civilians are wounded together, soldiers almost always ask for civilians to be helped first. I respect this as the soldier asked to be there to fight and the civilians do not. This is the true soldier attitude.

I try my best to save people but sometimes there are too many wounded people for me to treat alone. Or the wounds are too bad for me to do much. I still help everyone for morale and so I can sleep in the night. Every single day other medics are teaching and helping us newer ones to learn how to help more than we are now. Three weeks ago I had never seen a bullet hole in a body and now I know exactly what to do to help. Advice to new medics is to always try to learn. Always try to help.

John, @R0ogie
Western Volunteer - Ukrainian Marine
Bucha
April 5th

My background is I've been in Ukraine for three years. I served in the Marines with Aiden Aslin and Shaun Pinner. First Battalion, I spent 18 months in the frontline in the trenches on the line the entire time. It's a lot more intense now. A lot more things going on. Air, artillery stuff like that.

They were uncommon things before. As far as Bucha, my story is a rather lucky/unlucky one. About a month before the war started, I went back to UK for vacation for the first time in three years. I got back to Ukraine literally the day before the war started. I landed in Kyiv, and then I went back to my house in Bucha, the home I had lived at the entire time I was in Ukraine with my family.

When the war started, I had seven cats and two dogs. I rescued them from the frontlines in the trenches. The next day I have a train booked to go back to Mariupol to join my unit to be with everyone on the frontline. I went to sleep and then I remember around 6AM I got a phone call from my girlfriend's dad. I looked up at my phone and my girlfriend said to put it down because it's not important. I said, "Its 6AM it's probably pretty important!"

She picked up the phone and I couldn't really hear him, I speak Russian and Ukrainian, but I couldn't hear what he was saying, but I saw my girlfriends face and I knew right away. So, I got a live map and the first thing I saw was the CCTV footage of a Russian tank driving through the border checkpoint in Crimea.

Literally moments later I heard the air attacks. In Bucha there was no air raid sirens, so we didn't have any warning or anything. I went outside, and where I live in Bucha it's not far from Gostomel, so I remember watching Russian helicopters coming in. Russian jets flying over. SU-25's. Ukrainian helicopters. Seeing the missiles coming in. They bombed the airfield and other places.

The first couple of days we spent in the basement. Relatively lucky. We were all jammed in one room in our basement. It was hard to know what was happening in those first few days. We didn't really know what was going on. There wasn't a big military (Ukrainian) presence in Bucha, most of it was concentrated in Irpin on the other side of the river. There wasn't a huge defense in Bucha. The first few days was just spamming refresh on the live map; keeping up to date with information.

Tried to stay in touch with my commander back at the battalion. My last official orders were to stay low, and not to tell the Russians I was in the military. It was obviously impossible for me to get on a train and rejoin my unit, so those were my orders.

I think it was on the third or second day we took our first casualties. The tactic the Russians like to do is fire an inert rocket, a couple of smoke rounds, artillery rounds, whatever, into a civilian area before they come in to occupy it to try to get civilians to leave so they have less collateral damage when they take it. The first casualties were two dead a few injured. I helped to treat them. By the fourth or the fifth day they did a precision airstrike and took out the power, the water, the gas, we had nothing. In total I was trapped in Bucha for the first 14 or 15 days of the war. Then we evacuated on one of the green corridors.

It was just a gradual process of attacking and moving forward for the Russians. It was a very strange atmosphere because some people evacuated in the first couple of days but a lot of us stayed. We formed like a community, and pretty soon everyone was outside of their basements heating food in their yards over fires. It was so cold back then. It was snowing. With no power and heat, you'd see everyone out in front of their basement entrances with stoves or barbeque pits cooking what food we had. I think it was the third day when people started looting the shops, so a sort of volunteer guys with weapons came down to open up the shops to distribute the supplies.

It was the fourth or fifth day, and the worst for me was the nights. This wasn't my first invasion, I was in Syria when the Turks invaded, so I sort of knew the process of it, knew how long things take. I was familiar with airstrikes, artillery, it wasn't anything really new to me. But what was different for me was in all these other warzones I've been to, it was easy to disconnect from it. I was new there, there wasn't anything there that meant something to me and I didn't have a history there.

But after fighting here for years, fighting against the separatists and Russians, then I'm watching Russian dismounted soldiers, Russian tanks, and Russian planes flying over my fucking house where I live. Like a fully modern western city, a place I've lived for years, and the there's Russians everywhere and explosions and airstrikes. It was crazy. Very surreal. Very hard to process.

It was very hard with all our animals. We actually took in another dog. A huge dog, like a bear. It was injured. It had shrapnel injuries in its paw. Its owners had been killed and they fled or left I don't know. I've still got that dog. The dog is in Germany now with my family where they evacuated to.

I started almost like a pharmacy/hospital in my basement. Had a couple of operation rooms. There are photos on my Instagram of that. I went with a few other guys, and we were responsible for about 200-250 people. So, we opened a type of pharmacy. The actual pharmacy, the owners had left, so we had to break into it. We had to steal it but people needed that stuff. We took all the medicine out of there and transferred it all to my basement. That started a clinic and people from all around would come to get help. They'd write lists, and I'd give them medicine from what we had available.

It was a very strange routine. No showering, no washing. Everyone pitched in and helped. It's to be expected that some people didn't do much but cower, you know. But most people helped. They cooked, cleaned etc. It formed into a sort of little community. It was very hard to get information. After the first week we were trapped.

The hardest part was the nights. I'd be fine during the day. I was out doing things, speaking to people, helping, doing something. The night was very difficult. My girlfriend and I would almost sleep on top of each other. We were stuffed in this tiny little basement with seven cats and dogs. Barely any room and it was freezing down there as well. The night was the worst. We locked the basement door to the basement and locked the little storage room with the supplies and where we were sleeping. We were very worried the Russians would come to loot and steal. Anything could happen at night.

At night we would listen to the rockets and artillery. On the fourth or fifth night a Russian jet came and bombed the apartment building 200 meters from our place. Blew open the whole side of it for no reason. It was a complete blackout. There were no soldiers in the area. I didn't see any Ukrainian soldiers the entire time I was trapped in Bucha. Not a single soldier. There were a couple of guys who were partisans, they came to me for medical stuff, but other than that I didn't see any of them. They just bombed the building to bomb it. It blew open all the doors of my basement from the pressure. It destroyed all the windows. The night was horrible. We got relatively lucky. Especially if you've heard about what happened in Bucha, but the Russians never came into our apartment complex until after we had left.

One of the worst moments was when I and a few volunteer guys decided to make a supply run. We were running out of supplies. We needed a chainsaw to cut up wood to make food. I needed animal food. So we were crossing the highway on foot to try to get to this store and we were crossing in two's. About 500 meters down the road there was a Russian BMP guarding the entrances to Bucha and it started firing at people down the road. We got to the gas station on the junction. It had been looted and shot up by the Russians. I went in there and found a few things like packs of coca cola. I sent the other half of the group down the road to the shopping center while we were looking for stuff at the gas station.

The weirdest thing for me was all the roads were covered in tank tracks, and all the concrete was stirred up, that's when it really hit me like, "They're here." It looked like there were so many fucking tracks. An unimaginable amount of Russian vehicles. While we were looting, we heard some gunfire toward the shopping center, so we decided to make our way back down the other side of the road on some low ground, and some of the guys met back up with us. They said the Russians had come to the shopping center and were firing shots to disperse the looters. I say looters, but the majority of the people were there to get stuff that they needed, not to get PlayStations and TV's. So we went back to the community, dished out the supplies and just carried on.

Then the evacuations came up, and about the time the evacuation corridor was open on the bridge, it was half destroyed so people had to walk across sort of one at a time, and I didn't want to take my family that way. We'd have to drive there, leave the car at the bridge, and carry 6 animal boxes and two dogs across. There was lots of shelling down there too so I sort of advised people against it.

Then we started getting information that the Russians weren't allowing men to leave, that they were only allowing women and children, so me and the men started to formulate a plan where we would have to sort of go through the woods around the whole area. So the first day of evacuations a lot of people drove and made it through, they called us and said that the Russians were there at the checkpoints, but they weren't really interested in the civilians, they were more interested in the military stuff, they weren't checking documents, they just let people through. So, with that information we started to get ready to evacuate. On the second day of evacuations, a bunch of people from my community left. About two hours later they came back and said the Russians weren't allowing people to evacuate. They came back and seemed very hopeless.

I had hidden all my military documents and still had a British passport. But I knew that if they stopped me and questioned me, saw my tattoos, they'd figure out I was military. I would just be fucked. I was very anxious about evacuating because I'd have to evacuate THROUGH the Russians. On the third day of evacuations we began the process of leaving.

We left in three vehicles, with some of our neighbors. Covered the cars in white tape. Loaded all the animals into boxes. I was in the middle vehicle with an old couple and some animals. My girlfriend was in another vehicle with some other people. We left Bucha and drove around to another village to avoid the bridge.

We came around and saw a lot of other vehicles, some marked "Children" and they had all been shot up. I can always understand what vehicles has been shot up by Russians because they all had 30mm bullet holes. It was just crazy. Lots of the bodies were still inside of them. We just drove through very slowly and very cautiously. We hit the first Russian block post, and I'll always remember this because it was the first one you come to leaving Bucha, right at the turnoff to Irpin, there was a Russian BMP with about 5 of them sat on it, and more in a pillbox on the other side of the road.

We stopped about 100 meters down the road and they waved us through. They didn't raise their weapons or anything, they just waved us through. We drove straight past them. We drove quite slowly and I remember looking…eye-to-eye with this Russian soldier. He must have been 18 but he looked about 15. He was on the PKM just watching the road…and he looked scared. He looked professional, ready to fight, but he looked scared. Like he didn't have a fucking clue what he was doing here. He was just a kid.

We went on for another kilometer, we got to another intersection with a couple of gas stations, and that's where some more soldiers were with better equipment. Spetsnaz or something. These were professional soldiers. Not like the ones at the first block post. These ones raised their weapons, the commander asked the drivers to get out first. I was in the back seat. The drivers got out. The Russians spoke to them, they just wanted to check the vehicles quickly, and when the commander came to my door, they were checking for weapons. Not checking for documents or anything. Just weapons.

The animals had broken loose. I had dog shit and piss on me. I said in Russian, "I've got animals, please, please close the door." We all had our hands up. The Russian closed the door. They checked the trunks, we were there for about 5 min and they let us through. We passed some more soldiers on the road but they just let us through.

192

It was funny, all the Russians we passed on the road were very well equipped. VDV, fit, professional looking. The first Ukrainian post I got to had a typical sandbag post and it was manned by locals, civilians, with their own weapons. Shotguns, AR-15's. I was like "Fuck, the Russians over there, the Russians are looking good boys." They told me it's okay, they're just manning the road. The actual military is in the woods. We got through there, made it through the evacuation corridor. A lot of the worst destruction of Bucha happened after I left.

Ukrainian Soldier
Bucha
April 5th

I was there in Bucha and saw President Zelensky visit Bucha yesterday. (April 4th) He is someone He has held our military in his hands since this invasion began and my opinion has changed.

He seemed physically sick walking through the streets. He was surrounded by soldiers and cameramen. I didn't hear him speak, I was not close enough to hear. I'm not an important soldier I was just deployed to the area and was near him during his visit.

I saw him walk to different sites where people were murdered. He had the same emotions we all had. We are all upset with what has happened here. His face was one of sadness. I expected a big speech about revenge but there was none.

To me he seemed like a sad man who was disappointed he couldn't save these people so close to his capital. I don't blame him for feeling his guilt; but his leadership helped to keep our military intact during the first days of this "special military operation" by the orcs.

His humanity gives me feelings that not all politicians are so inhuman to recognize human life when it is taken away without a reason. I was not a supporter of this president, but I am now. I know many others with the same thoughts.

These streets are silent. The people are traumatized and have been bullied. We are still finding bodies and graves even today. The Russians say this is false, but I don't think this is false. I couldn't see how this could be false.

"Doc Snickers"
Ukrainian Soldier / Medic
April 5th

How our medic system works: Since we are a volunteer battalion, in essence our medic group and system was built from ground up starting on the 24th of February. Everything we have now has been gotten from volunteers, by ourselves and our money, and a few stolen cars.

Generally, since trained medics are a limited resource, we are a separate unit with our own commander and supplies and report directly to the regimental commanders. We train soldiers in basic TCCC, supply them with IFAKs and prepare ourselves and our evacuation vehicles. From our unit of 30-ish we are divided into3 categories: front line medics (experience with tactical training and capabilities, we have 4-5 guys in this category), EVAC vehicles (on these we have drivers, with paramedics/nurses and a doctor onboard who take care of the wounded) and then staff and logistics personal (which is just as essential).

Generally, front line medics are dealt out according to the need, attached to units who are anticipated to be in the worst of fighting, and they stabilize the wounded and get them into an area where EVAC can get them. Evac also has 2 cars with 4x4 and cross-country capabilities that are operated by two bat shit crazy Valkyries who rip into the battlefield, and we load the wounded onto the vehicles. We have them for two reasons, EVAC vehicles are generally minibuses and such this don't have the ability to go off-road, so these girls are able to take the wounded to the ambulances and thus cut down on time to get the casualty to definitive care (and saves our backs humping them to the closest road).

And secondly, the evacuations with all the equipment and doctors are just to0 valuable to risk them getting to close to fire. The improvised ambulances generally have everything on MARCH algorithm, with advanced airways and drug capabilities. We just got a portable ventilator and semi portable ultrasound thus they will be very important. And they are responsible for advance interventions and stabilization to get the casualty to a hospital.

Obviously, prior to any mission we have to scope out different routes and make connections with different groups in the area as well as, most importantly, have agreements with the best and closest (which is not always the same) definitive care units (field hospitals and, usually, civilian hospitals). Due to general lack of trained medics that are willing to get shot at, we are a scarce commodity and so, we get sent to the line a lot more often than other units.

Week Seven: April 7 - 13

Ukrainian Soldier
Eastern Front
April 7th

Trench warfare is everything we learned in school about it. It is filthy and not fit for human being to live inside. Trenches keep soldiers safe from bullets from rifles and machine guns but do nothing when artillery comes. Even worse when enemies are using drones or missiles now. When you hear something in the air the best you can do is lay down and hope they hit a different group of soldiers than yours.

I served in the army long before this. Since 2014 the first time we were invaded. I have not been in trenches since 2021. I moved to a job that would keep me out of them. I know soldiers are in trenches now. Both ours and theirs. I'm glad I'm not there.

Ukrainian Special Operations Soldier
April 7th

Our group was called up to reinforce the troops fighting in the hardest direction at that point. 1500 Call. 1530 We move out. 0600 the next day, our group is in position. The task is: Two groups move in the set direction to support our troops and kill some more of the enemy that want to take our position. The thing is neither our troops, not the enemies know about us being there.

We have a very tough guide, Mr. "B", a freaked-out guy that can't live without war. Among our and the enemy's positions, our group moved deep. We move during the artillery battle. Whatever you can imagine about the war, we can see it. Trees are falling, explosions are pretty hearable, and debris are everywhere.

We move forward, and finally we are on a territory where only our artillery can shell us (that's what we thought) and this is pretty scary. We are in position. Observing, looking for targets that need to be eliminated. It took us a long time. It was very cold; we've started shaking because of it. We've put our eyes on the enemy recon group, we've sent five guys to eliminate them. That's where the party begins.

We think that we made a mistake during our adventure, so Ruskies sent a helicopter to destroy our positions. The heat was on. We've run so fast but you can't outrun a helicopter. We regroup and change positions. Lots of artillery and a K52 go square by square to kill us. No luck for them. We keep on running and changing positions. Eventually, it worked out. It seems they thought that they killed us. Our position was pretty good for hunting.

Observe. Locate. Shot. Success.

Those beside our prey quickly jump into the trenches. Our mortars were there to help them out. After this, another K52 helicopter came so now it was two helicopter and artillery on us. We moved out, no communication with others until we reach the checkpoint. It was a 10km journey with 40kg of equipment on our back. It was worth it.

Art by João "J-Dot" Alves

Ukrainian Soldier
Sumy Oblast
April 7th

People in the west must understand tanks are still dangerous weapons. Yes, we destroy many of them. But we can only fight them with the right weapons. If we don't have the right weapons there is nothing we can do. They can shoot us all they like and we can do nothing but run or move someplace else.

I have not faced one myself. I have seen destroyed ones, but I know soldiers who have done fighting against them. There are many pictures and videos on telegram and the internet of destroyed Russian tanks, but they are not showing the men who died while destroying them. Tanks still give me great fears.

Western Civilian / Volunteer
Odessa
February 26th – April 8th

"February 26th

I'm a (Foreign) national who's been living in Ukraine with my Ukrainian girlfriend for the past 2 years, were trying to get out but because of general mobilization her father and brother won't be able to leave. Never in my life would I think I'd be trapped in a war. I've never been so scared in my life but your stories from Ukrainian heroes inspire us all here. If anything, I want the world to know how senseless this all is, I know my girlfriend won't leave without me and I don't want to leave what has become my own father and brother behind. The UN has failed us, NATO has failed us, and Europe has failed us. I'll never be a proud (Western Nation) again.

March 6th

Just wanted to update I'm still in (redacted) the ladies in the house have crossed over into Moldova, the men have decided to keep an eye on the house. News here has been mostly word of mouth things seem relatively quiet, we are now armed and waiting. Hopefully I can message you in a few days saying the Russians went home but that's unlikely. I'm starting to accept I'm going to die here.

March 19th

Get my ID checked 50 times a day everyone's wondering what a (foreign national) doing here there's checkpoints everywhere. Can't believe its march 19th already times become weird. Spent the last week helping fill sandbags and prep food stocks for the bomb shelters, everyone here has their eyes on Mariupol what happens there is what's going to determine what happens here everyone seems to think. First chance I get I'm grabbing my brother and father-in-law and heading out.

Other than some airstrikes on military infrastructure the city's still untouched by the war, the beaches have been heavily fortified and there's some rumors about some anti-ship hardware in the city but again I can't really confirm anything information has to be taken with a grain of salt. We're in good spirits, I will say one thing though it's becoming really hard to not hate the Russians after all the suffering they caused here, and I don't think it can ever change.

April 8th

Probably the last update you'll get from me, I'm heading east. These bastards kill women and children without remorse. There's 86 of us from here are heading out we can't sit back anymore it's time we meet these guys head on. Oddly enough I'm no longer afraid. I think I'm already dead, how can they kill what's already dead?

It's pretty crazy just how much foreign fighters have passed through (redacted) to head east. We have fighters from the west, from the Middle East, from the Caucasus. One that I think you'd find interesting is the fact that we have an Afghan with us and an American vet of the Afghan war. Watching them interact is interesting to say the least. The Syrians, who are with us, are easily the most eager to fight, this is repayment for Aleppo. Being one of the few here without combat experience I'm glad I have these warriors with me.

I'm pretty excited to get to the front and prove myself. People will say I'm stupid and this isn't my fight, I should just go home but if every man thought like that who would defend our people

Western Civilian
Abroad
April 12th

Anyone with a ham radio receiver and mic could listen to and even interrupt Russian radio chatter. They were communicating on unencrypted frequencies, and I was part of a group of trolls who would listen in and interrupt transmissions between Russian units. Their frequencies got leaked pretty early into the invasion and you could literally sit and listen to their real time conversations.

We would interrupt them as often as we could. My roommate and I took turns staying up during those first few weeks. We would play music into the microphone, babble incoherently, pretend to be celebrities like George Bush or Sean Connery, and we even started playing audio from movies on a loop. Other groups sat and recorded the chatter. Even managed to record and pass on to open-source intelligence groups some important troop movements.

Aiden Aslin, @CossackGundi
Western Volunteer - Ukrainian Marine
Siege of Mariupol
April 12th

It's been 48 days. We tried our best to defend Mariupol, but we have no choice but to surrender to Russian forces. We have no food and no ammunition. It's been a pleasure, everyone. I hope this war ends soon.

*Taken from Aiden's Instagram account.

Art by João "J-Dot" Alves

Ukrainian Civilian
April 12th

My cousin is one of the soldiers in Mariupol. We spoke several times during the battle, and I could see his mind get sadder and sadder as time went on. In the first week of March, he said they were surrounded. They were going to fight and try to break out but it failed. A few days later he told me they had been hit very hard by Russians and separated from another large group of soldiers. In the last two weeks he told me they had been running out of food and some of them tried to escape wearing civilian clothing.

He said those attempts at freedom didn't work. He said Russian soldiers were taunting them from windows. Then he told me they were eating food made for animals so they wouldn't starve and drinking water from buckets and puddles to stop dehydration. I have not heard from him since our last talk and that was 8 days ago

"David"
Azov Regiment
Siege of Mariupol
April 13th
Documented in July

I want to tell you about my friend, how I met Ahim. He is forever 29 years old. I remember that he woke me up at 3 o'clock in the morning in Mariupol. I slept for two hours that day and was very angry. I ask, "What the hell?" He says, "I was told that you are going to join our group, collect your things."

I set out through the dark in Mariupol to their fighting position. It is so dark we cannot see much. Somewhere an automatic weapon can be heard. Only burning houses light up the path around us.

I was tired and no more sleep and hungry having come to them, Achim showed me where I was to sleep in the new position. I had a mattress on the floor and it seemed so cozy. I took off my gear and said that I would sleep. "If anything happens wake up!"

I overslept until almost eight o'clock in the morning and woke up from noise and loud shots. As I understood, they didn't want to wake me up. The team was very friendly. I felt that these are good people. They put a can of stew and bread next to me when I was sleeping, I realized that I could not eat when my while friends fight, so do I didn't have breakfast.

When I began to look around then I saw that it was a very large, abandoned apartment with five rooms, and most importantly - almost all sectors with clear sectors to fire from. Exactly why he (Achim), as the senior of the group, chose this place. I got up and immediately greeted everyone and saw that an enemy tank and an armored personnel carrier were driving on the street, accompanied by infantry.

I looked out the window and the whole street was burning. Broken cars and broken trees, there was no surviving glass anywhere in any apartment. If someone watched realistic films about the war, then they would seem like a cheap comedy here. I saw all the details of what I could not see at night. A continuous gunfight. High-caliber shots did not even allow us to hear each other sometimes.

I decided not to sit in the building, so I took anti-tank equipment with me and asked them to open the door for me. Achim said he was coming too. You could see in his eyes that he was delighted that I didn't want to just wait until the end of the next day and was eager for a fight...We knew that our allies (another group) were somewhere nearby, and we heard what they were up to on the radio. There are wounded with them, but they will evacuate.

The stretch of road between us was always shot at, sometimes it was dangerous to even put my head out. I felt my heart beat in my chest. I was surrounded by an atmosphere of chaos and war. I decided to quickly run across the area being shot at, took several single-use RPG-22s, and ran back. When the fighting is going on, you don't think about getting hurt.

We began to wait for the tank to come closer to us in order to surprise it as we knew that it sometimes it periodically comes here. An RPG-22 is not an effective weapon against such equipment. I don't know how many times it is necessary to hit in order to do something to harm it, but we had a more interesting anti-tank weapons that could penetrate armor.

We watched from afar the enemy tank and armored personnel carrier shoot residential buildings. They were out of our reach. Peaceful people all hid in the basements, there was no one but us on the street, and somewhere a few birds were screaming, which made the atmosphere even stranger and authentically terrible.

We waited a long time for our enemy, but we decided not to "loom" in the yard and entered the building. Achim and I entered the apartment. I never took the belongings of the former residents, but I was always interested in how they lived. I was permeated by the atmosphere of each room and pictures of the peaceful life of these people. The images played in my head.

I heard some loud noises of equipment, and I was not mistaken, it was a Russian armored personnel carrier. He drove past a broken kindergarten and hid. He appeared so quickly. I thought his task was to cover the operation of the tank. I was in a small kitchen, I opened the RPG-22, and carefully sat down next to the broken window, where the small curtain was barely swaying from the wind.

I heard a hum again. I warned my brothers about this situation that I would be firing. Everything, the iron car is coming back. As I expected, it drove with great speed, and it was noticeable that the driver of the enemy armored personnel carrier was a veteran. I had no more than three seconds. I aimed and hit the rear part of the armor. A big black smoke explosion appeared in that place, but I understood that this weapon is not effective in such a situation and the car drove on as if nothing had happened.

It was already getting dark, but the people fighting around the house were doing their job. At one point, I heard over the radio that somewhere nearby, an enemy group of seven infantry had been spotted entering the entrance of a building. I managed to notice only the last one.

He was carrying something large; it was a machine gun. We decided not to "burn" our position, and to open fire only when the maximum number of this enemy infantry appeared. I sat one of the fighters of my group by the window and asked him to watch. I heard a tank shot and I saw from the fifth floor a burning entrance 50 meters from us. People started jumping out falling on the asphalt.

Night came, the fighting subsided and usually in Mariupol the enemy did not work at night. This was the time when we had the opportunity to send several people for food and ammunition. Achim took two or three people with him and they walked cautiously through the destroyed city. He knew the area well and navigated well. The rest of us stayed to sleep and guard the frontline.

The morning came with the sunrise. For ordinary people the day begins with an alarm clock. For us it's the sounds of enemy equipment, shots, bursts and continuous firing. Tactical noise canceling headphones are a must-have for street fights. Like if you shoot three anti-tank weapons from a building. Forget about your normal hearing for several days.

During continuous battles, you must always wear personal protective equipment (helmet and bulletproof vest), so if you have light plates, you are a lucky person. If you don't take off your bulletproof vest while running and performing combat tasks, the load on your back is very high. Tactical gloves are also a necessary thing, since glass is broken everywhere and we often had to jump out of burning windows, piercing our legs with nails, and no one paid attention to the cuts and pierced legs. It's a, "Child's Prank" compared to the injuries some of our fighters received.

Ukrainian Civilian
April 13th

We are a Ukrainian family living abroad. We have lived abroad for over 20 years now, and my youngest son was 2 years old when we immigrated. He has left home and gone to the front to help our family still living in Ukraine, of which there are many.

He told me, 'Mother, I have to do this.' And off he went. A boy to a man overnight. I begged him not to go, and his father stopped me from stopping him.

Now that he's gone and been at the front for a time, I'm proud of him. I pray for his safety every single day. But he is only doing what I would be doing were I his age and in his position. His father wanted to go with him but I forbid it. Our son has met with his cousins, and they are all together there now, fighting for Ukraine.

I see them all, and I see my grandfather, in his old Soviet Uniform fighting the Germans. He also ran away to join the army to defend our home against invaders. History repeats itself in the strangest of ways and I am very proud of them both. I just hope my son comes back in a better state of mind than my grandfather did. He slowly drank himself to death over 40 years after he came home from Berlin.

Ukrainian Soldier
Border Guard
Siege of Mariupol
April 13th

These buildings will be our graves. Surrender not the choice for us here. Those soldiers hide in tanks. Hide in civilians. We destroy holes in walls to make more confusing defenses. These will be our graves. We will not allow them to torture us for propaganda like a terrorist. If I can send more information I will. We will be dying here. Slava Ukraini.

Maria Petrovna
Ukrainian Civilian
Siege of Mariupol
April 13th

On the 24th of February at 7:30 am I went to the City Park to walk my dog. Unusual was that there was no motion in the city. Usually at this time people drive to work. While walking I met a very old woman. We greeted each other and she told me: 'Did you know that Putin declared war?'
'What war?' I asked.
'Well, war. A full-on war', she said.
I disregarded her statement as one of a confused old woman and went on my way.

After I got back home, I started hearing shots. From automatic weapons and from Grads. My first thought was that once again the industrial complexes of Illich and Azovstal are under fire, since the past 8 years they've been fired upon sporadically.

People in my driveway went out on the street to get a better look. Everybody was in shock. Nobody did expect a full-scale invasion. Then it all started, the daily artillery and mortar fire.

From the 26th on there was no more electricity. Everything got dark. On the 27th there was no more water coming from the tap. On the 29th they cut off the gas. 1st of March they cut communication. It wasn't possible anymore to phone out of the city or receive calls.

After that the horror started. Every day I heard artillery, mortars, machine gun fire and missiles. On the 4th the aerial bombardments started.

They started to destroy the infrastructure of the city. The most terrifying thing was that even the weather was against us. Constant cold and snowfall.

After the gas supply was cut, the men started making fires in the yard so we could boil water and cook food in a cauldron. People started to leave the city on 6th of March. From our apartment complex a few families left, back when it was still rather safe to leave.

On the 10th heavy bombardment started. The heaviest yet. In our houses the windows started to burst and in my apartment beside the windows in my room even the glass on the doors between the rooms broke. That's when I first went to down to a bomb shelter.

The Russians started systematically destroying the city, quarter by quarter. First, they started bombing the Azovstal steel plant, then Illich because they knew that the Army and Azov had taken position there to use the tunnel system beneath the industrial complexes. Then they bombed the 23rd micro district, then the 17th and then the center where I lived.

At first, I refused to leave. I saw pictures of the Ukrainian-Polish border and thought to myself that I'd rather die getting bombed than freeze to death waiting to cross the border. Another thought of mine was that I could defend my home from marauders.

However, on the 23rd of March I decided to leave. The family across from my apartment also wanted to leave. Yet they wanted to take another route as the group I was part of. We tried to convince them to come with us but they didn't listen. That was the last I heard from them. They probably didn't make it, since on the route they took heavy fighting occurred at that time. It was National Guard and the Army trying to defend the people fleeing and keep an open way for Azov.

When we were walking there was fighting all around us. We took the route down the sea and alongside the coast. We also had to walk around mines that had been laid on the streets. I noticed that people that had a trolley with them started to throw of luggage to make them lighter and move faster. While walking down the street I saw a dead woman who was missing a leg. She probably wasn't dead for too long since nobody put a cover over her. Then I saw a young man sitting on a bench.

We wanted to ask him how much longer we had to walk. But when we got closer, I saw the white cloth covering his face. He too was dead. As we continued, I saw about 5 or 6 more dead people. But they have been covered up with blankets and cloths. The most terrifying thing was that nobody was burying them or moving them away. Everybody was too afraid to be out in the open for too long.

My destination was the Morvokzal, since one woman that was with me was able to phone her son and a friend of him would be able to pick us up with a car.

He drove us to Bilosarais'ka Kosa which is a little health resort and went back to get more people out. I haven´t heard from him since. When I went outside on the first night to get some fresh air because I couldn´t sleep the sky was beautiful. Full of bright stars. Yet when I looked to Mariupol, which is only 25km away, I didn´t see anything. For thick black smoke was rising from the city. Although Bilosarajka was already under DNR control, and no fighting occurred there I could still hear the battle noises from Mariupol.

We stayed there for two days and found a driver that took us to Berdyansk and another one that took us to Zaporizhzhia. From there on I got on a bus to western Ukraine, then Krakow, Prague and finally Germany where my daughter is living with her family.

We had to get water at the city park near our apartment complex where I used to walk my dog. It wasn´t without danger because two men from our complex got shot while on a water run. One day I noticed trenches in the park and thought they´re for machine gun positions. Turns out that those trenches where graves since two days later I saw crosses all over the place.

I had food and produce for 2 weeks, mainly grout and flour. Later I boiled broth with chicken carcasses I had bought for my dog.

There was a moment, I don´t remember how far into the siege when a soldiers said he´ll open the doors to a supermarket so people could get food. This saved countless families from starving in my district I´m sure.

Even in a situation like this I didn´t go into the store to get something. I thought I would have enough food and that the army would end the blockade of the city soon. Getting something from the store I felt would be like marauding. In hindsight not getting anything was stupid.

My neighbor Roma, age 34, took about 20 bottles of cognac, some chips and dried sausages from the store. When I asked him why mainly

booze, he said he didn't want to die sober. Also he didn't know how to cook so he just took some things that he can just pop open and eat.
Two to three times a day he went to get water for the people in our driveway and would offer a little bit of said cognac to the men that would go with him.

At first when the aerial bombardment started, we all ran to the bomb shelters. But within a week or so we could distinguish how far away the bombs would land. We started counting the seconds from the release to the impact. 6 seconds it takes a bomb from a SU34 or SU35 to hit the ground. We know it have been SU34/35 since two men in our driveway used to be pilots in the army and they recognized them. They called them "Surik". One of them was tasked chopping wood and he wouldn't even move if he knew the bombs would drop farther away. He just kept chopping wood.

On the 8th of March we all went out to make tea. The men had already made a fire and they were standing in a row and said: "Our dear women, we congratulate you to your day. We're sorry that this year we don't have any flowers for you." And we all sang the anthem together.

Week Eight: April 14 - 20

"Gandalf"
Ukrainian Soldier
Azov Regiment, Intelligence Officer
Siege of Mariupol, Azovstal
April 15th

The situation in Mariupol. First of all, I want to highlight one exact moment. What is happening here, real genocide of Ukrainians. A lot of people asking about the origins of this conflict. Origins of this war. The roots of this war are very deep. Russia, their main goal is to eliminate the Ukrainian nation and all their actions right now, they are showing exactly this.

At least 10,000 people died country-wide in Ukraine right now. Civilian people. At least 20,000 people died here in Mariupol. These numbers are increasing. Russia wants to cover up the results and the evidence of their crimes. This is not just the collateral damage to the warfare, it's not. It's the precisely made operation to kill as much Ukrainians as possible.

They don't bother themselves with a variety of methods. They use everything that they've got. They use airstrikes, they use bombs, and they use freefall bombs for indiscriminate bombings. This is not a precision guided weapon you know. If a one-ton warhead just flies over your head on top of you, it doesn't choose who to kill.

Every day the situation in Mariupol is very dangerous. We constantly can be shot; we constantly can be killed. The civilians are still in danger, despite accusations of the Russian Minister and Russian President that they took control of the city. This statement was made today, but you know, they do not control the whole city. We still control the Azovstal steelworks, and we are still fighting. We destroyed one tank today. Two armored fighting vehicles, and one armored personnel carrier. The numbers of enemy losses are still increasing.

First of all, I want to declare that Ukrainians have already shown their courage to the world. Ukrainians have already shown to the world that we can fight. We can fight against Russia, well-known as the second most powerful military in the world. The most important thing that we want to ask the world is how well will they fight against Russia? Because Russia's appetite will not stop in Ukraine.

Very, very important thing that Russia still helps the numerous thousands of civilians as captured people in Mariupol. They are relocating these people forcefully. They are deporting them to the territory of Russia. At least thousands of people in Ukraine were relocated to the Russian Federation. That is inappropriate. It is unacceptable because people are deported forcefully, not by their own will. Russia's strategy was very blunt and simple.

They are cutting off the supplies of the cities, they are blocking the cities from food supplies, energy supplies, water supplies, and after that people are very easy to manipulate. You just give them a piece of bread and they are going to do anything for you. That is their strategy as an occupant. That is the same strategy they have been using all the time.

I am receiving a lot of questions about the arsenal the Russians are using in Mariupol and other parts of the front. They use a variety of weapons. Starting from the regular small arms like AK rifles, machine guns, up to the tanks, artillery, self-propelled howitzers, rocket artillery, naval artillery here in Mariupol. All kinds of aerial based weapons like free-fall bombs, guided missiles, unguided rockets from the planes.

These weapons are being used constantly. Novelty of the past few days was the use of the strategic bombers here in Mariupol. They use carpet bombings on the city. You know what the problem is with carpet bombings? It is really destructive. It's indiscriminate. You cannot choose where the bomb will fall. Russia still claims that they use precisely guided weapons, but it's not true it's false.

Russia right now is cowardly, hesitating with the final assault on Azovstal steelworks because they know that they will fail. And they WILL fail. You know, if they will have more courage…at least 10% of OUR courage, they would fight with us without all this heavy weaponry. Just with the small-arms, that would be a fair fight; but they're not doing a fair fight. They are showing their cowardly face to the world right now, claiming that Mariupol is taken. Mariupol is not taken.

If someone asks if we need help, yes of course we need help, but we do not need to be rescued. We can rescue others. Thousands of people still, civilian people, hiding in the basements and shelters in the territory of

Azovstal, they escaped from the city to find cover here under the protection of Ukrainian soldiers. They were receiving Russian indiscriminate fire. The most heartbreaking thing in this, is we have limited supplies and we are trying to share everything with civilians, but Russia claims that we use them as a human shield. It's bullshit. It's complete bullshit because you know, a real military doesn't do this, but if you think as Russia, they would do the same. You will think about the civilians as a human shield. They did this in 2008, they already did this in 2014, and they are doing this right now.

My message to the world: Stop Russia. The best thing to do this, is to find your own courage and keep Ukraine safe. How can you do this? Please share your weaponry with us, at least we can fight with these weapons. We need heavy weaponry. We need anti-air systems. We need fighter jets. We need tanks. We need small arms. We need ammunition. We need artillery. With all this arsenal, their imperialistic appetite will be stopped. There will be no more threat to the world, to the free world. There will be no more threat to you, to us. Right now, Ukraine is not just fighting for ourselves, we are fighting for your freedom.

Ukrainian Soldier
Azov Regiment
Siege of Mariupol, Azovstal
April 17th

A story about the Chechens. We were on one side of a wall, the Chechens on the other side. We had no grenades, so we had to do something. My friend had an idea to get them to go away farther from us to give us room to think. He picked up a rock and threw it over the wall at Chechens. We heard them yell and footsteps run away. It gave us time to move from the wall into a building. This was three weeks ago and still makes me laugh in these horrible times.

Western Volunteer
Former Azov Regiment Member
April 19th

I am former Azov. Let me try to explain how it is. Everyone thinks we are Nazis. This is not true. It DOES have origins with neo-Nazi beliefs, but only 10-20% of the men within the unit actually held those beliefs.

You must understand, between 2014 and 2018, one of the only units actively engaged in combat against the separatists in Donbas were Right Sector and Azov. Azov was a unit that took volunteers. If you wanted to fight, Azov was the unit to be in.

I'd say the vast majority of Azov soldiers in Mariupol now are not subscribers to the belief that Russia and her bots claim. Most of them are just normal men who wanted to defend Ukraine and Azov was the fastest and best way to do that. The internet shills will claim otherwise, but they formed an opinion based off of Russian state media and read one article on the internet and took it as fact.

I'll stand by my next statement: Azov is full of good men. Good, well-rounded men who just want to defend Ukraine. People can have whatever opinions they want. But I served in the unit for a while and I only ever came across two or three guys who subscribed to the Neo-Nazi beliefs.

Even if they were Neo-Nazis. It's still better than being a Russian soldier or a supporter of Putin. Pick your poison.

Russian Soldier
Siege of Mariupol
April 20th

I arrived in Mariupol on the 6th of April, we were here to assist a motor infantry unit to push harder as they were stale from the fighting. All I immediately see is the dead meat (bodies). It's in the air, it seems because of the big amounts of corpses, then when you get try to get used to it you see more dead and dogs eating them.

This place is destroyed by the constant bombing. It's so heavy I feel my bones rattle.

I have shot men (his enemies) in the first week of the fighting and almost got hit myself, a guy on the second day in my unit got killed by a sniper and then another wounded. We tried to rush the position with an infantry team. The house was booby-trapped, and two men got exploded by what I think was a homemade bomb stuck to a door.

I want to say the Ukrainians have made a good fighting army; better than we expected. Every day the Azov and the Marine Ukrainians have picked the infantry off with snipers and lots of small arms fire. Whoever is left of the Azovs; I'm sorry to say will be mutilated by the Chechens. They aren't not in good spirits anymore.

We eventually left Mariupol with on 18th to go to the new offensive with one killed in action and one wounded. I hope I can never return to that place not even in my mind.

Art by João "J-Dot" Alves

Week Nine: April 21 - 27

Ukrainian Soldier
April 22nd

I haven't written (to Battles and Beers) because I had nothing to say. Now I have something. Ukraine is stronger now than in February. I see it every day. In February, I thought we would not hold a week. The crossing over the border came fast and strong in so many places.

I admit. I was a defeatist. I did not have the attitude we would win. I was ready to run. Now after fighting and seeing our army and what it can do, I believe we will win. We have had rest. Yes, some battles are very tough. Irpin was a difficult area, but we can rest. I have had many days of rest since 24 Feb.

I have had new training. New arms. New uniform. New everything. And experience and rest. Russian soldiers do not have this. More and more we are seeing them tired and hungry. We are seeing them exhausted with blackened eyes. We can rest in our country. They cannot.

They have 2 months of battles some of them. How does it feel to see their comrades shot from the sky? Lay unburied in the fields? Their big victory is only Mariupol. Outnumbering the defense 10 to 1 and they still cannot 'clean' the steelworks. 20,000 dead on their side and what have they done?

It is a matter of time and will for who will win. We have both. They do not have either. The conscript army cannot occupy a country who will die defying them.

Ukrainian Soldier
April 23rd

I feel nothing when we see bodies of Russian soldiers. Weeks ago, when this started, it made me vomit to see them. Even new dead bodies just liquidated. Now, after Bucha, Mariupol, Irpin and so many others, nothing. Now I drag them from where they die to a pile. I feel nothing. To me it's like dragging sacks. The only sickness I feel is that they are tough (stiff from rigor mortis) when they should be soft like when they are alive.

It only makes me sick because of the rotting meat now. Not because they are humans and especially not because they are Russian. I have not seen battle up close. Just the time afterwards when the frontline soldiers fight. I have moved too many bodies of Ukrainians and Russians to feel sick anymore. Sometimes we find them after days. They bloat and bubble in strange parts of the bodies. A neck will bubble to the size of a head. Like a man swallowed another head before death. Or a stomach that has become so large it almost tears a shirt.

Ukrainian Civilian
April 23rd

On 24.02.2022 I woke up at 4:30 in the morning when my mother and brother came to my room. *The first explosion.* A little panic gripped my mind. It was impossible to believe what was happening, my brother Mykola 22 years old, said not to turn on the lights and pack my things he handed me a flashlight and walk away. *The first explosion.* Still not realizing what the hell was going on; I took a backpack with carefully folded notebooks for school and laid them out on the table.

I only packed my computer, tablet, and chargers into this backpack. I went to my mother's room, she was sorting the documents and at the same time calling my sister Varvara, 18 years old (She was with my grandmother at Obolon, on February 24 she had lectures at the medical university). My mother told me a list of what I should take with me, and I took the suitcase from the closet and went to gather.

We live in Vasylkiv in a small village near Kyiv, we have our own house, and a military airfield is a kilometer away from us. Unfortunately, it all started from Vasilkov.

After a while, my mother went to pick up my sister and grandmother from the underground. And my brother and I continued to gather. There was a third explosion. My heart fluttered. Tears well up in his eyes. My brother said to print out a map of the road we will take. The plan was to get to Vinnytsia, where my uncle has a house.

After some time, my aunt Anastasia came to our house, with her sons, Leo 17 years old and Jacob 13. My mother has not returned yet, it was already 10:00. We were waiting for my aunt's husband, who is a soldier and my mum. When they arrived, we continued to gather and load things into two cars. My family at the time had three dogs, Troy (Shepherd) and Holdie (Malinois) and one puppy. They had to be left at home; we left them a lot of water and food.

We left the house at 13:30, only nine people and my aunt's dog. The road is terrible everywhere were pits and it was almost impossible to go. We almost got to Vinnytsia, and everything went wrong, I did not understand why, but our route has changed; now we are going to Lviv. It was a difficult 16 hours and 48 minutes.

We came to the registration center in Lviv, we were registered and sent to a school where there was a humanitarian center. (This is the first time I am in Lviv) We were greeted as a family. They gave out blankets, pillows, huge packages with the necessary products, personal hygiene products and a lot of food. We slept on sports mats, on the floor, but in the warmth and for a while we felt safe, until the first air alarm at 2:00 am. My heart skipped a beat, and we went down to the bunker. We were there for a long two hours.

They cooked us food three times a day and if we did not take in count the air alarms everything was fine. The next day my brother and my aunt's husband went back to Kyiv for territorial defense, my mother was their driver and she had to return. She was gone for 2 days, not going to lie I cried. The fear that something could happen when my mother did not pick up the phone bound me and hit me hard. Every day we went to humanitarian centers and offered our help.

So, a week passed, and we found an apartment and moved there. The company where my brother works paid a whole week's rent, but after the first night there, my grandmother got a call by her graduated student who lives in Poland and volunteers. She said she found people who can give us rooms in their house. And two days later we packed up and left for Poland.

When I was told about leaving Ukraine, I cried for a long time, I am leaving here my house, friends, pats, my whole life. And now I am leaving to another country without knowing when I could return. Panic and fear were all I felt at the time.

We made a terrible mistake going to the main border; we stood in line for one day and one night, in the terrible coldness, but advanced only a kilometer. One day me, my sister and cousins gone for a walk we decided to go to the border and see what the situation was there. It was very bad, we were gone for one and a half hour, and our car didn't even move. We told adults to go to another border some kilometers away from this one, but this time prepare: buy food and water...

At that time, my mother was driving for 32 hours without normal rest. We arrived at a restaurant, ate, charged phones, and drove on. We were also on this border for 1 day, but this time when I woke up, I could already see the border gate. After finishing the registration, we drove to Poland. We drove for another 8 hours to the city of Mikhailov, where elderly couple Mrs. Lila and her husband Mr. Zbyszek met us. They took us to a room, and we were finally able to relax on the beds under the duvets. Finally rest, safety and peace.

We were on the road for 72 hours

A week passed, my cousins and I went to school. And in our house in Ukraine, we settled my mother's friend, with her family. By that time, my dog Holdie had run away (We still don't know where she is) I hope someone took her home. Troy stayed protecting my house from robbers, and my mother's friend looked after him. Everything was fine despite missing home, brother, and friends. A month has passed, my sister is nineteen.

April 12th:
My sister and I are watching a series, after an episode she went to the kitchen and left the door open, so I heard her talking to mum.
"He was shot, Elijah found him in the field..." (Elijah is my sister's boyfriend).
When she came back, I asked who she was talking about...
My dog is dead. He was shot by my neighbor. The next second my hands are shaking, tears appear in my eyes, I can't breathe, panic attack. This day I lost part of my world, it's broken now, and it won't heal. I went to school the next day, acting "normally," how hard could it be?
Well, you see my dog was the world for me, I loved him more than my life, and now, now I don't have him near myself. It's exhausting thinking about it.

Ukrainian Soldier
Eastern Front
April 24th

We are always digging. If we stop for one day we dig. If we stop for several days we dig. Most often we dig in defenses ordered by officers to defend parts of villages, roads or other important areas.

I have dug more holes and moved more earth in 50 days than I have in 26 years being alive. Soon, you become experts at digging trenches. They are not outdated ideas. Trenches can save you.

More than one-time trenches have saved us from drones or artillery. Good concealment is also recommended. We once dug a trench right through a destroyed home and used it as part of an observation post. In that part of the trench, we placed chairs from the home, and a kettle and pot. We could heat food because of the half standing walls that concealed smoke. We make do however we are able. Maybe after the war I will work for the government to dig trenches for pipes or irrigation. I am a professional earth mover now. Beware Russians! I will bury you!

Ukrainian Civilian
April 25th

I was born in Donbas. In 2014, people drugged by Russian propaganda believed that they could "secede" like Crimea. Although Crimea was in fact occupied by us. But whereas Crimea had a pro-Russian government, not everyone in Donbass wanted to capitulate.

So, FSB officers (for example Girkin) started to kill the local government. Our government declared the killers separatists and launched an anti-terrorist operation. Russia at the same time started bringing heavy equipment to Donbass and arming the separatists. They were also coordinated by FSB officers.

After a bloody two years, the shelling subsided. Since 2016, the "militias" have had this tactic: they bring in artillery to residential areas, fire from there at Ukrainian positions and leave very quickly, watching the return fire come into a residential area. Blaming Ukraine for the shelling of civilians in the process. Later, when Ukraine stopped responding in this way, they started shelling their own cities, blaming Ukraine.

This sounds absurd, and I would not have believed it myself if I had not witnessed it (there was shooting from my yard).

I personally witnessed all these events and saw the Russians pin Ukrainian flags on their tanks and shoot at houses. This was done to sow hatred against Ukrainians among the inhabitants of Donbass. When they came to the Kyiv region, they did exactly the same thing. My friends from Kherson tell me that they do this. Their tactics do not change.

They used people as human shields, and even a couple of years ago, when I went home to Donbas, a Russian military officer poked me and my mother with a machine gun.

After the full-scale war, I helped the residents of Bucha who managed to escape. It was horrible, hundreds of young girls were afraid of their own shadow because of the violence they had to endure from the Russian troops. They have been out of Kyiv for almost a month now. However, we continue to find traces of their atrocities to this day.

DPR Soldier / Separatist
Siege of Mariupol
April 25th

Today "Azovstal Inmates" fidgeted with their asses. Again, we entered into negotiations, from 1500 hours, we stopped shelling, and it became quiet. We began to discuss the terms of capitulation and the place. At first, the Nazis did not like the place - the central entrance, they wanted another one, then the time - they offered to move it to tomorrow or even to Wednesday.

It became clear that they were trying to deceive us. But we are not fools, therefore, during the negotiations, they controlled Azovstal; from drones we saw a strange fuss near one workshop - the Nazis tried to tow the tank in order to drag it from workshop to workshop. Since our command received a picture from the factory in real time, Tu strategic bombers immediately joined the negotiations.

Art by João "J-Dot" Alves

Ukrainian Soldier / Medic
Siege of Mariupol, Azovstal
April 26th

We are in a critical situation. Under constant shelling and bombing. Guys are starving and many injured. Doctors operate day and night in premises where it is impossible to even live normally, let alone perform surgery. Infusion solutions are almost out of stock. The material for bandages and headbands is washed sheets.

The wounds are starting to *rot*. There is no time and therefore our hope is only on guaranteed green corridors and departure to a third-party country. We ask the President to address the world leaders with a statement, and the leaders to guarantee the safe exit of military and civilians from the city!

Ukrainian Soldier / Medic
Siege of Mariupol, Azovstal
April 26th

The hospital is surrounded. Among the doctors and nurses who are here are the wounded. Even with injuries, they help day and night. There is absolutely no septic tank. Wounds rot. The evacuation of the wounded is under constant fire.

Ukrainian Soldier
Azov Regiment
Siege of Mariupol, Azovstal
April 26th

Death and war is not black and white. It is not like you think of it in your head, being a world covered in clouds and dark skies. It's much worse than that.

You die in sunlight. In bright skies and sunshine. You can be driving or sitting, completely minding your own self and die from a rocket, a bullet, or artillery. There is no music to accompany your coming doom. No warnings.

Urgent tasks remain unfinished. You just stop being. You die and become meat. Everything about you is gone. You are no longer yourself, you become meat rotten in the sun. It can happen anytime. No experience, weapons, or friends can save you sometimes. If you are going to die you are going to die.

No, it is not like cinema or books. The plot does not revolve around who you are. You just die like a letter on a page being turned and there is nothing you can do about it. But what we (the living) can do is remember. We can build monuments to these people who give their lives so hideously.

We can say we will remember the sunny days those men died. To so many of us a sunny day with birds in the sky will never be as it was before. It will never be peaceful again because we know death creeps in the shadows of the trees and in the ditches and in buildings.

All we can do for the guys who died so ugly in the sun is be cautious of the shadows and remember they did not pass and rot for no reason. Even dead dogs will feed the grass. No, these men did not die for no reason. Our children will remember that, I'm sure.

DPR Soldier / Separatist
Izyum Front
April 26th

I do not know that in other sectors of the front, but in the Izyum-Slavyansk direction, there is a systematic destruction of the personnel of the Armed Forces of Ukraine. Losses are at least 1 to 7, and sooner or later this will have a very significant impact on the morale of the Armed Forces of Ukraine.

There is one problem that needs to be solved and that problem is enemy artillery. For 75 years we have not fought under conditions where the enemy has the restraint to inflict serious rocket and artillery strikes both on the positions of our troops and on attacking battle formations.

Counter-battery combat, the destruction of enemy guns and artillery crews, is a priority task for the RF Armed Forces. After its solution, the Armed Forces of Ukraine will become an order of magnitude more difficult, and no ATGMs will be able to contain or even seriously slow down the advance of our troops.

On the other hand, right now we are getting a unique combat experience. None of the developed powers since the Vietnam War has attacked in the face of active enemy artillery opposition.

Speaking about the losses that the Armed Forces of Ukraine are ready to suffer without signing surrender, it is necessary to take into account the fact that Kyiv is not completely independent in making decisions.

Kyiv supplies meat for the war, no other functions are assigned to it. Therefore, the Armed Forces of Ukraine may well lose from three hundred to five hundred thousand people, subject to total mobilization. Scary numbers, but it's a fact.

Already now, among the dead and captured, the bulk are mobilized middle-aged men. Frightened, dirty, hungry, with a doomed look. And in fact, those who were captured pulled out their lucky ticket.

A typical example from a conversation with such a lucky man: "Our unit was thrown into the forest belt, the defense sector was indicated, after which the officers left. For three days we lay under fire, we lost half of our personnel. Then they saw Russian tanks and surrendered."

The only way out of this situation (the way out for the Ukrainian soldiers) will be mass disobedience and banal desertion. In this case, we will save the shells, and the soldiers of the Armed Forces of Ukraine, their own lives.

Ukrainian Soldier
Azov Regiment
Siege of Mariupol, Azovstal
April 27th

I think I might die here. The Russia said they will not storm Azovstal steelwork but now they are 20 meters away at places. I don't want to die or be wounded. Our room of wounded smells like rotten meat. Other soldiers said Russian soldiers yell to us from buildings that we must be hungry, and we have lots to eat inside. (Bodies) I can't believe this has happened. We must be rescued soon, or we all will die here. Please God.

Ukrainian Soldier
Azov Regiment
Siege of Mariupol
April 27th

The best way to work on the enemy (attack) is when they cross roads in the open. Most roads here are wide and taken more than 20-30 long steps to cross, and they will cross all together in one group.

My group learned quickly to use these opportunities when we were defending an area. We allowed them to cross halfway across the road before we fired. This way, the entire unit would be in the open at once. If you work on them too early, the others won't run into the road. If you work on them too late, you will not have as many enemies to work on.

The best is when the first man is halfway across. You can work on them with the AK-74 or machine gun and get at least one every single time. It is much harder to work on enemies inside of buildings. It's easier when they try to cross into new areas. They can be brave, but they are not very smart.

For us, one man leans around a wall and works on an area with his weapon. While he does this, the others cross behind him to move safely. If we start getting shot at, the man leaning at the starting point can cover us as we advance or retreat. I never saw the enemies do this and it seemed like such a simple and obvious thing to do.

Art by João "J-Dot" Alves

Major Bohdan Krotevich
Chief Of Staff, Azov Regiment
Siege of Mariupol, Azovstal
April 27th

I am a serviceman who went from a soldier, an infantry platoon commander to a regimental staff officer. All these 8 years, I and my unit are constantly in the combat zone. We have witnessed and participated in all the fighting in the southern direction of the environmental protection zone (Azov region). Currently, my unit is the Azov Regiment, for the third month it has been defending Mariupol completely surrounded by the enemy.

I saw and talked to the Russian prisoners. It can be called an easy interrogation. In fact, to get information from a Russian soldier or officer, it is enough to capture him and feed him. Then he tells all the names, radio calls, cities of concentration and all other information that interests us. For a Russian soldier, his personal life is more important than the so-called "special operation" of his country's leaders. They understand that they (Russians) are occupiers. However, everyone is crying that they knew nothing (referring to conscripts) and sent them to study. I documented all the interrogations; I will definitely post them online when Mariupol is unblocked.

If you take my personal experience for 8 years - I have repeatedly been in battle as an infantryman, during the Shirokin offensive and defense operation.

If we talk about the situation of the last two months. The battle in the city is a continuous battle of artillery, enemy aircraft, as well as storming positions. Artillery has been working on all positions for more than two months, and aviation - can this be called a battle when the command post is continuously hit by artillery?

When there is an opportunity and the good judgment of the commander, I try to visit the positions, although I am a staff officer - it is extremely important to see everything with your own eyes. I was repeatedly shelled at the positions, but I will say that the command post is fired at more often and with heavier artillery. As far as I can remember, one day the Chief of Intelligence and the Battalion Intelligence

Commander and I advanced into the position of the enemy surrounded by our forces.

We had a prisoner who had to pass the radio station to the enemy so that we could offer them to surrender. It was at this time that two enemy armored vehicles broke through from the encirclement in the direction of the enemy forces.

The only thing I regretted was leaving my RPG-26 with the driver. However, at first glance it seemed to me that the personnel on the armor was alive, so I worked on them with the Ak-74. It later emerged that the enemy had tied up its dead to armor and was trying to take some of the living inside of the vehicles.

In any case, one of the armored vehicles was destroyed by an officer of the operational department of our headquarters, the second vehicle left the encirclement. After that, according to the standard operating procedure, the enemy aircraft worked fired all over the area, but that is already a common thing for us.

Then we sent the prisoner, he handed over the walkie-talkie, the enemy refused to surrender, so the next day our artillery and reconnaissance groups with infantry completely destroyed all his personnel. By the way, it was one of the units of the GRU (Russian Special Forces). They have courage, but not enough intelligence. I am the chief of staff of the regiment, so every fighter of the Azov regiment is my brother. Some fighters have already received 5 wounds, recovered and continued the fight. Our contusion is not considered an injury at all.

Speaking for me personally - my best friend, the head of the operational department died covering the group during the storming of the building against the SOBR unit of the Russian Federation. The assault was repulsed by the defended position, but he died as a true warrior along with his comrades defending his native land. Since the Azov Regiment is based on the principles of brotherhood and personal example, most of the officers of the regiment's headquarters are directly in position and fight side by side with infantry soldiers. Unfortunately, the losses among the staff were also not small. This is not the first time my friends have died, but I am calm about death.

During the entire defense of Mariupol, our fighters confirmed destroyed 1,150 and wounded 517 enemy manpower, as well as destroyed 49 tanks, 23 armored personnel carriers, 36 armored infantry fighting vehicles, 5 infantry fighting vehicles, 3 tigers, 17 units of trucks, 3 typhoons, 6 armored vehicles, 2 lynx, 1 battleship, 3 UAVs, 2 MTBL; damaged-1 SU 25, 29 tanks, 24 BMP, 12 APC, 3 tigers, 8 trucks, 2 typhoons, 2 tigers, 2 lynx, also captured trophy 2 tanks, 1 BMP.

In general, during this period, many fighters of various positions, whether artillerymen, infantry, staff officers - proved themselves as gods of war. I think everyone will tell me better than me about the meeting with enemy tanks.

The main thing is not to make our lives more important than the security and protection of our country and to be proud that we have the opportunity to defend our homeland. Chechen leaders are the current army, but some Chechens fought directly on the front lines and were killed by our guys.

Russian Special Forces are brave but stupid. Regular troops are not brave at all, and they are very stupid, they are thrown in like cannon fodder. Azov - the gods of war without exaggeration. Destroy four tanks a day - actually documenting this on video recording. Our fighters are doing more than you can imagine.

I personally support the idea of cold hatred against the Russians. There is no point in explaining our position to a mad dog - it is better to shoot him without notations and explanations.

Ukrainian Marine
Siege of Mariupol, Azovstal
April 27th

We are surrounded, but we are not broken. They cannot break our spirit. They will disappear in the ruins after death. And we will live forever.

Week Ten: April 28 - May 4

Diana Piskovesk
Ukrainian Civilian
Wife to Azovstal Soldier
April 28th

My husband and I communicate very little. Because they have a weak connection. He emphasizes that the situation in Mariupol is very critical. Urgent evacuation of military and civilians is needed.

I was in Mariupol during the first month of a full-scale invasion. Now I am in another city already. In fact, I don't have a special story. Because our stories are quite similar for civilians who were able to get out of Mariupol in time.

I am lucky and I am alive. But I am waiting for our military to be able to get out of Mariupol alive. And I'm waiting for them not to be betrayed.

I am proud of my husband. He is courageous. And with dignity bears the brunt of the war in a completely surrounded city. But I'm afraid for him. Like everyone who is waiting for their loved ones from Mariupol.

Anastasia
Ukrainian Civilian
Wife of Azovstal Soldier
April 28th

My name is Anastasia. I am the wife of a military soldier who is now in hell itself, in the besieged Mariupol.

My husband Artyom is now in the Azovstal factory together with his brethren. There was no information from him for almost a month, on the 7th of April, he wrote to me...He told me that he is alive, healthy and that everything is fine with him. On April 9th I was informed by his command that he was wounded. Although we have just talked, he did not say a word about the injury. The injury is severe. It is a shrapnel wound that has been treated and sewn up, but the fragment remained inside.

Without an X-ray, it is impossible to perform an operation, as well as to find out whether the pelvic bone is intact. The nerve has been broken and because of it he does not feel his legs anymore. He did not complain even once.

But my husband did not believe that he would see me or our son again. He even wrote a farewell letter to him. I forced him to rewrite it, to write about his hopes and faith in our future. About where we are going to travel, and about plans for the upcoming years. For two days I did my best to return his faith and hope for salvation…After this he wrote told me that he wants us to adopt a child who lost his parents in this terrible war.

Now he is dreaming about how caring and loving parents we are going to be to the baby...He dreams of hugging his son and me…He dreams of syrniki (cheese pancakes) He writes that he dreams about food. And that he really wants me to cook him lots of syrniki when he will return.

He also told me that there are a lot of abandoned stray dogs where they are, and that he and his friends feed them. They give them what they can. These abandoned animals come to them in the hope that they will give them some food, and they give them the last.

After being injured, my husband could not go to the toilet. I was very worried that the intestines would not be affected, but the doctor said that this is normal, since there is not much in his intestines. After 8 days without laxatives, he finally went to the toiled and luckily there was no blood which means that the intestines are not damaged.

We had a beautiful city, Mariupol...A city where we lived a happy life, where our cozy home was! This was the city where my soul remains…and my heart. Was...lived….it is all in the past tense now. But I have hopes for the future, I hope that our relatives will return! Our house in Mariupol no longer exists, like most of the houses of the city's residents…we only have memories of our happy life now. Personally, for me, life without my husband is meaningless.

I will not and I do not want to live without my loved one! And in order to restore my husband's faith in life, I wrote to him that he must survive, because without him, I will kill myself. He must come back alive.

Olya
Ukrainian Civilian
Future wife of Azovstal Soldier
April 28th

My name is Olya, I am the future wife of one of the soldiers of the Azov Regiment, who is now in Mariupol city, in Azovstal.

It's so heartbreaking for me to see and hear how he has changed and suffered…When I last spoke to him, he told me, 'Damn, I really would like to drink some clean water now, even half a glass.'

Their values now do not coincide with the values of modern life in 2022 and it is terrible... But despite these changes in values, his main value has remained to fight for his family, his country and Europe. Even drinking dirty water and chewing hard bread gives him new strength and motivation to fight for all of us!

Olena
Ukrainian Civilian
Girlfriend of an Azovstal Soldier
April 28th

My name is Olena. I'm the girlfriend of one of the defenders, who is in Azovstal now. It is very painful to understand that I'm in a safe place, but he is in that hell, in Mariupol...A week ago when he texted me in the middle of the night with the words:

'We've been attacked by phosphorus bombs yesterday and tonight we're gonna have a hard fight, sorry babe, I don't know what's gonna happen next, so I want to tell you that I love you so much.

Please, don't think I'm just talking, I had big plans for us, I bought a ring for you 3 months ago and I wanted to put it on your finger when I'm back home on vacation, it's in my pocket now, here, in Azovstal. Kissing you...'

We have been together for almost 4 years, I hope he will come back alive and do what he wanted to do.

Ulyana
Ukrainian Civilian
Girlfriend of an Azovstal Soldier
April 28th

My name is Ulyana. I'm 20 years old. My boyfriend is a defender of Mariupol. We have been together for 8 years. We don't have children yet, but we want to. We had a lot of plans for this spring, but the war started, Russia came to our house.

One day my boyfriend told me about how his regiment brother died right before his eyes. At first, his regiment brother was wounded in the head. The doctors, with their stock of medicines, did not know what to do, how to treat him so that he would not suffer.

He was put into a medically induced coma, then some help came from Dnieper to transport the wounded, but it was not possible to transport him, as Russia dropped an air bomb on a car where were a driver and a couple of wounded were, and they all burned alive.

Zoriana
Ukrainian Civilian
Wife of an Azovstal Soldier
April 29th

My name is Zoriana and my loved one is now in the Azovstal factory, defending Mariupol. We met on the shores of the Azov Sea, and now he is still there, but he is not hugging me, but does everything to stop the ruthless enemy. I love listening to him telling stories, but I understand that these are stories from a brutal war. He told me about how his regiment brothers were wounded, about how he saved civilians...They help civilians, feed abandoned dogs and live with faith and hope for salvation and peace.

Now his dreams do not coincide with those that once were. He dreams of sleeping, eating fresh and hot food, playing board games again and watching his favorite TV shows. He also wants to hug his mother.
If I could, I would give him all of my strength, because now he is starting to lose it. It hurts when he writes to me "I'm going crazy", it hurts when he writes "I looked death in the eye today". I have tears in my eyes when I see a small "+" in response to my question about him, which means so much.

He is a man of high values, but the price is just too high.

He protects his family, stands for his country, Ukraine. He hasn't been in touch with me for two weeks now and I don't know what happened to him. I reassure myself with the hope that he is still alive and will return to me. I want him back; I'm waiting for him.

Leaflet Dropped on Ukrainian Soldiers in Mariupol
April 29th

"Ukrainian soldiers and officers:

Kiev lied to you and left you to die in Mariupol. Group 'East' and the reserves of VSU (Ukrainian Armed Forces) are destroyed. THERE WON'T BE REINFORCEMENTS/HELP. You are completely surrounded. If you continue to resist you are bound for death. Over 450 Ukrainian service members dropped their weapons and surrendered in Mariupol. They are alive. Your only chance to survive is to put down your weapons. Follow the instructions on the other side.

Instruction:

1. Remove magazine from your weapon.

2. Hang your weapon on your left shoulder with the barrel pointed downwards.

3. Raise your hands above your head with a white cloth.

4. Slowly approach the positions of our troops and follow their commands. Service members of the armed forces of the RF and DNR know of these conditions."

Art by Mike Liu

Ukrainian Soldier
Eastern Front
May 2nd

I have been a soldier for 8 years. In these years I've seen every kind of enemy except for the Chechens. There are different kinds.

The conscript. They are trained like shit. Not good or motivated soldiers. They have no night vision, and we capture them armed with two or three reloads. Their medical bags are always very simple. They will run.

The professional soldier. These are VDV, or Special Forces. Sometimes they have night vision. Sometimes they have telescopic sights on rifles. It's mixed between their competence and bravery. Most are brave. They are thrown into battles like the conscripts and machine gunned the same as the first group. Only at night do they have advantage in training. And only with night vision. Most of us do not have it, and when they do, we are at the disadvantage.

The separatists. These are different. They are equipped often like conscripts but perform better than VDV and some special forces. They are experienced. They are the men I have fought for 8 years in sniper battles and artillery duels. They lived in trenches and are not shy from violence.

The Chechens. I have not seen them for myself or even been near them. I have been told they are too busy taking pictures for their friends and shooting whole reloads at empty windows to actually be part of the war. Their reputation here has declined to nothing.

Ukrainian Soldier
Azov Regiment
Siege of Mariupol, Azovstal
May 2nd

I wish I could talk to Russian soldiers. Yes, our enemy. I wish I could say the only thing they are doing right is becoming a song on a Sabaton album.

I want to speak to them. Truly I do. I want to ask them how they can do this. We live in the modern world together. We are not our grandfathers, yet they seem so willing to die like our grandfathers. You will perish here, Russian soldier. You will never see your home again and your children will be raised by other men.

Your children will ask, where is father? And mother will say, in a field in Ukraine being fertilizer for the famine they caused in the 30's. (Holodomor)

Yulia
Ukrainian Civilian
Wife of an Azovstal Soldier
May 2nd

I worry about my husband but in fact my fear for his life and thoughts that I'll never seen him again are accompanied by my honor and love. I married my husband Arseniy for his bravery, loyalty to his country, also for his willingness to protect the weak, and to protect Ukrainian values and freedom. Therefore, it is such an ambivalent feeling. On the one hand it's a very big fear to lose him as the closest person, on the other hand it's an honor that he is there (Mariupol), and I think that's the way it should be.

Arseniy also thinks that he is in his place, he doesn't regret a minute. He is fighting in the east from the very beginning of the war, from 2014. He had graduated from university and went straight to war. Of course, it was hard for him, he was tired, he was wounded, and he went through a lot and is still going through even more right now. But he finds the strength to fight on, he doesn't lose hope, he doesn't lose strength and general willingness to fight on. So, I really hope that all his hopes are not in vain, and I will see him again.

I contacted my husband today in the afternoon, he said that right after evacuation of civilians, the Russians began dropping heavy bombs on Azovstal'. They began firing artillery from ships and from the Mariupol area itself. They came in tanks and very heavy shelling began. Some people died, some people wounded, casualties from civilians and military. The horror that took place before the evacuation with renewed power, continued. That is what he told me.

My husband continues to be proud of his service, he doesn't regret that he went to war. But he went to war because of his views, because of the importance of protecting his values, Ukrainian values and freedom, independence and human dignity. He believes in it; he believes that every man with weapon in hand must defend these things, otherwise we are slaves, and this is what Russia wants to do with us. We are all proud of him, my relatives and his are too. We are all happy that he is the man that defends us all.

My husband contacts me from time to time and I always tell him how I love him. I am trying to be brave like him and I always tell him that I am waiting for him at home. I want to have a family and kids with him, I want us to win this war and I am glad that he is involved in it. That is what we discussed together.

I want to tell the World that there is Genocide in Mariupol. Russians had killed more than 20'000 civilians. There are still a lot of people in Mariupol and Azovstal' and Russians have been shelling them with all types of ammo from the air, sea, and ground. Also, they dropped multivolume (cluster) bombs. There are around 700 wounded in Azovstal' with amputations, gangrenes, they are just rotting alive and die every day, because there is no help.

A lot of soldiers and civilians were killed, and their bodies are still rotting in Azovstal', because Russians do not allow them to be taken out and burry them properly. Those people are trapped in there (Azovstal'), they need to be evacuated. We need to save not only civilians but soldiers too, because they are people too, they have lives.

In addition, I would like to tell that Azov Regiment, where my husband serves is not neo-Nazis group. It is official state unit of the Ukrainian Army, which is completely subordinate to the General Staff. The myth that Azov is neo-Nazis is Russian's propaganda, which is trying to tarnish the reputation of Azov, because they are one of the most capable and trained in Ukraine and Russia hates it. Azov is a regiment in which different nationalities serve, such as Jewish, Greeks, Azerbaijanis, Armenians, Crimean Tatars, and Georgians.

It is an international regiment, and many organizations donate money to it. One of the biggest donations came from LGBTQ organization. Everyone is supporting Azov here, because we know that they are not Nazis, they protect us it is part of Ukrainian Army. The only Nazis we have in Mariupol now are Russians. Russians are acting like Nazis, they kill, rape, and rob.

Alice
Ukrainian Civilian
Wife of an Azovstal Soldier
May 2nd

My name is Alice, I am 24 years old. I come from the city of Bakhmut, Donetsk region. The word war, I learned back in 2014, but then our city was not affected. In May 2020, I moved to the city of Mariupol, to my then boyfriend. My husband is currently at the Azovstal plant and defends the city of Mariupol. We have a 10-month-old son, Timothy.

We lived a happy life until February 24th. On this day at 6 o'clock in the morning my sister called me and said that the war had begun, she lives in Kharkov. And I was alone in Mariupol, because my husband was on duty in another city.

In order not to be left alone, I went to my friend, whose husband serves with mine.

When the heavy shelling of the city began, the eastern region was the first to suffer, but we lived far from it. Around the end of February, we started spending the night in the corridor, because it was scary to be near the windows. On March 2nd, the light and water were completely gone, but we had supplies, so it was normal. Since we lived on the 5th floor, we sometimes went down to the neighbors on the lower floors. About the number of March 4-5, we woke up in the morning from a loud sound, looking out the window - saw that the shell flew across the road from our house to the private sector.

The decision is to go to a safer place, thank God that my friend can drive, and she had a car. I, my son, friend Tamara, her daughter Sasha, two dogs and a cat, took with them a minimum of things that were prepared in advance and went to the shelter of the store ATB.

We spent two weeks there. Without light, water, heating. At the beginning, when there was still gas, the guys went to cook in neighboring houses, and when they turned it off, they cooked on the grill. Fortunately, we had enough food, drinking water was a small supply. But they also collected rainwater, technical water and melted snow.

Once a day or two, if we were very lucky, we managed to heat the water, then we could drink tea or make porridge for the child. Once a day we tried to cook soup, first of all we fed the children, sometimes we

241

managed to cook something else. I was lucky that my son was breastfeeding, his food was always with me, and I also had a supply of diapers.

We slept on a wooden pallet on which we spread several blankets. Some slept on small benches. Morally it was very difficult, in the dark, without the opportunity to wash the child, normally wash your hands, we lived like moles, already learning to walk without a lantern, to the touch. There were enough children in our temporary home, about 6-8 years old, the youngest was my son.

During our stay there, we began to feel like one big family, all united and helping each other. We also had several cauldrons and dogs, they also lived together. Several times my husband managed to come to our shelter for 5 minutes, he brought some food and diapers. We exchanged notes with him, in which we shared our experiences. There was no connection in the city then.

Early in the morning of March 10, we all woke up to a very loud roar and a deafening roar, as it turned out later, it was a plane that dropped a bomb on a cafe near our shelter. My husband came the same day, this picture is in front of my eyes every time. I come out of the basement door, I see flying window frames, nets, burned cars, a broken road, and he runs to meet me, in military uniform, with two packs of diapers, and a bag…in the bag were two batteries, thanks to which there was light.

This was the last time I saw my husband…in the following days air strikes were repeated more and more often, after which the door to our basement jammed the lock, and then almost took off the hinges.

At such moments I thought that our life would never be the same again, it was very scary to live in ignorance, not to know if your family and friends are alive, if you will ever see the sunlight again, if you can enjoy a peaceful life again…A few days later, the Russian army entered the city, and their tank stopped near our shelter. The shelling of the city still continued, it was loud every minute, we have already learned to distinguish between different types of weapons.

There were days when it was impossible to go outside for a second, such days were especially hard, without boiling water, sunlight and normal food. One day we went on a small outing, wanted to visit their homes and pick up some things. It was sad to come to the house where my family lived happily, the house where our child grew up, our memories, everything has a special value, not material, but emotional. After all, a separate story was connected with each of them.

It's sad when your child had everything, and at one point it was all taken away. When we walked home around the city, it was very scary. The shelling did not stop, and the city was no more. I walked and could not believe that it was all reality, not a nightmare. Corpses lay on the roadsides, houses burned, burnt down, people cooking in heaps near the entrance by the fire, trees, pillars all lying on the ground. The house of a friend, from whom we hid at the very beginning of the war, lost one entrance. I could not believe that the city that grew, prospered rapidly, at one point turned into a complete ruin.

Since the city was under a complete information blockade, according to rumors, conversations of different people, we learned that they bombed the third maternity hospital, a drama theater where a huge number of civilians were hiding. Percentage of phone charge managed to catch the connection! I called my family and found out that my sister and her husband had already gone to Mariupol, but they were not allowed to go. From various sources, we learned that people leave in an organized column, it was decided to also try to leave. My sister and I agreed to meet in Melekino.

Tamara's car was not badly damaged compared to the others. The rear window flew out and shattered the side window, covering it all with film, we stuffed the car like sardines in a jar. Me, Tamara, Timofey (my son), Sasha (daughter of a friend) and another married couple with a son. Golden-Belgian Shepherd dog, cat and two other small dogs.

It was scary, the roar was still going on. As we drove around the city, the picture was even more horrible, the children were blindfolded so they wouldn't see it all. Some houses were burned to the ground, corpses were everywhere, on roads, curbs, huge holes, funnels, potholes on the asphalt.

We left the city about 4 o'clock, there was a huge column of cars. In order not to waste very little gasoline, they pushed the car, where it was difficult to start, and where it was easier - pushed. That day we drove to Melekino and stayed overnight there, sleeping fully clothed even in hats, as there was also no heating, the lights were turned off sometimes.

The next day my sister and her husband came, and we went to Berdyansk, at each block of the post thorough inspections, men were forced to undress to their underpants in order to identify tattoos or a trace of a machine gun. Examined phones, messengers, calls, messages, gallery, if you found any photos taken in the city -at the best they could ask to remove or confiscate the phone, and at worst. That's why I have not saved a single photo, with our two weeks of life.

By the way, from Berdyansk to Zaporozhye we got 11 hours, as well as a convoy of cars and buses. But we are lucky, we are alive! Next to me was a reliable friend Tamara, my mother now calls her "fearless Amazon."

My husband got in touch on March 22, called, heard his voice in his throat rolled a lump, all 7 minutes of our conversation, I just did what I sobbed. At that time, he was already at the factory, they were already surrounded, in a ring. Problems with food and water already then began.

The next time he got in touch was in early April, then there was no telephone communication at all, he wrote in messengers. He does not tell any special stories, no details of their whereabouts either. Every time he writes that he loves us very much, misses us, wants to live a peaceful life again, and that he wants to eat an ordinary sandwich.

Quite sad in those moments when he asks what they say about them? Are they going to save them? And I do not know what to say in such moments...They really believe, hope and wait that they have not been forgotten, they have not been abandoned, and they will definitely be helped!

Being in such inhuman conditions for three months, he always thinks first of us, worries that everything was with us, that I did not worry about him, which is why he always writes that he is fine, although we all know as it really is. They eat once a day, sometimes it is adjika and cabbage borsch, potato soup with sardines cooked in a bucket on a burner from a bottle and antiseptic, dog food, cakes of missing sour cream and flour, and technical water, at best.

I ask, I beg, I pray the whole world! Help save our defenders, heroes and courageous warriors who have taken the brunt of themselves, who have stood for our country for so long! They all want to live! They want to see and hug their relatives and friends again!
Give my baby back to Dad!

Tamara Parakhenko
Ukrainian Civilian
Wife of an Azovstal Soldier
May 3rd

When the war started, on February 24, my husband was a civilian. In December last year, his contract service ended. We have been together for 11 years; we have a daughter. She is 7. We just bought an apartment, which we collected for a very long time and began to make repairs.

At the time of the Russian invasion, my husband could not go to war. He could take us out of Mariupol on the first day. Could not appear in his military unit. But he decided that he could not sit idly by while his former colleagues defend our country. He said: "and who, if not me, will defend?" Then he gathered his things, and I went to take him to the military unit.

The first time was a connection with him. We could call each other; we could write messages. We knew each other was doing relatively well. But for security reasons, he did not reveal his location. From February 27, they began to arrive from heavier weapons. And more severe destruction of schools and houses began. And every time I was afraid that he would not get in touch, but everything was fine.

On March 3rd, the house opposite caught fire. A projectile hit him. And you know, the worst thing at that time was that there were no fire trucks. No one else extinguished buildings. They just burned out. Nobody could help.

Since I stayed in the apartment with my daughter, with my wife and the eight-month-old child of my husband's colleague, I realized that it was already dangerous to stay in the apartment at that moment and I needed to look for another shelter. We quickly packed our things and first decided to drive away from the house where the execution was taking place.

My friend worked as a deputy store manager. And she had a basement in the store. So, I decided that I need to take the children there. And she took it. When we arrived at the basement, there was still room for us. I left the children and returned to the house for blankets, pillows and necessary food. On the way to the basement, we came under fire. A shell exploded right behind our car.

245

Unfortunately, since the second of March we have had no electricity. Phones hung up. I could no longer contact my husband. So that he knew where to look for us, I wrote our location on the door of the apartment with red lipstick.

And just as he did not know where to look for us, so I did not know how he was and where to look for him. Unfortunately, since the third of March, our information vacuum has begun.

Already in the basement, we were able to contact through third parties and tell our husbands where we are. So, they know where to look for us. On the sixth of March, I went to the apartment for food. But my area was shelled so hard that I didn't get into the apartment. I went back to the basement with nothing.

On the way back, I saw how the car braked sharply, and my husband got out of it in all his equipment. With weapons, but body armor and a helmet. I was so happy that I ran to meet him. I hugged him and cried. Then he said that everything will be fine. That soon help will come and they will cope. Now I know that help did not come to them, but at that moment I hoped for the best.

He walked me to the basement and that was the last time I hugged and kissed him. He promised that he would come to me as soon as possible. He is a romantic, so he gave me letters written at a time when we had no connection with him.

Living in the basement, we hope that everything will end soon. That everything will be fine and we can return to the apartment. Our basement was without windows, and there was no light. And we lived in complete darkness, when you don't understand whether it's night or day. We had small flashlights, we cooked with them, moved along the corridor and went to the toilet.

I have an old car. Old Opel Omega 1992. It worked very badly. And at that moment I hoped that when everything was over, I would be able to return home even on foot. I decided to remove the battery from the car...And remove the fog light from the car. Connect it directly to the battery. And then in the kitchen in the basement we got light. It was a good time.

On March 8th, a colleague of Pasha (my husband) arrived and gave our daughter a gift from Pasha - pencils and gave me letters. He said Pasha was fine. What is food, water and cigarettes? What they are doing. Hold on and wait for help, and when help comes, they will quickly expel all Russians from our cities, and everything will be fine. He asked what we needed, and I asked him for a battery, because my car was already discharged and didn't light well, and we have nowhere to charge without light. I also sent letters to my husband.

On March 10th, we woke up early from a very strong explosion. We vomited the doors in the basement, the whole basement was cowardly, and everyone was very scared. It was an air bomb that landed in a cafe near us. The cafe began to burn, there was a strong wind and because of this, a high-rise building next to the cafe caught fire. Our store was right behind the high-rise building. We have prepared all the necessary things in case our shop from above catches fire.

We understood that we would have to leave the basement under the shots, because we would simply suffocate with smoke if the store started to burn. On this day, we did not prepare food. We just sat and waited. Listened. On this day, Alice's husband arrived, brought us a battery, brought sweets, letters from my husband. Told them they were fine. They are waiting for help...And he left. No one else came to visit us.

And our life began when we wake up in the morning, cook food on the fire under shelling, feed the children, somehow, we do something all day and wait for the evening to say that another day is over. We wake up from the sounds of shots, then we wait for our husbands to arrive, at least one of our colleagues. We are preparing to eat...And sometimes they shot so hard from planes, artillery and tanks that we didn't go out and cook, because it was scary.

It seems that on March 15th our territory was seized, and Russian tanks and Russian cars began to drive around us. We were told that they go from apartment to apartment and do sweeps. In their language, "they are looking for nationalists and fascists," what they do next with them is not known to us. Alice and I were very afraid for our men. Because we didn't know anything about them. We didn't know if they were alive, where they were...We no longer had contact with them. And we were afraid not to see them again.

On March 16th, there was heavy shooting around our store, we did not leave the basement for the whole day. I understood more and more that I need to leave the city and take the children to a safe place. We didn't know where to go. And they didn't know how to do it. We had no gas for the car and my battery was already completely dead.

I had claws for lighting a car at home. And I decided to try to go pick them up. The road to my house was hard. I saw a bunch of burnt houses, electric poles were broken. Shot cars were abandoned. But the worst thing is that I saw a bunch of corpses...These people will never return home to their families. No one knows where they lie...It was terrible.

Approaching my house, I saw that an air bomb had also flown into my house. I took everything I needed for the car and returned home. After everything I saw, I realized that even if my car did not start, I would leave the city on foot. Even if it's difficult.

There was no contact with her husband. And I did not know how to tell him that I would leave or leave. On March 18th, we lit my car and started the car from the pusher and left. I drove on the last gas that was in the car. There wasn't much of it. At the exit from the city there was a large queue of people wishing to leave. We stood in line for 5 hours. To save fuel, we pushed the car. And then they left.

Even when we were at home with my husband, we agreed that he should save himself, and I should save our daughter.

We were safe on March 21st. We got to Zaporozhye. Then, for the first time, my daughter and I slept warmly, with light. We washed for the first time since the beginning of the war. For the first time we slept not to the sounds of the plane. Life in Mariupol taught us not to be afraid of hail or artillery.... We were afraid only of planes.

As soon as I was able to charge the phone, I wrote to my husband in a telegram. But he was not online.
And he answered. I cried. He was alive! Everything is fine with him. Then I learned that he was in Azovstal. There are many of them. They are relatively safe. But they are constantly fired upon.

He periodically gets in touch every two or three days. He writes messages and then gives someone a phone and they send. I also write him messages during the day, and then they all come and go when connected to the internet. But there were cases when he was not online for 8 days. And I'm afraid.

When messages come from him, I cry. In one message, he wrote that I should buy a gift from our daughter, pack it in a parcel, and say that it was sent to her by Dad.

He and I are veterinarians by education. I work in my specialty, but he doesn't. But at this difficult time, he is treating people. He makes drips, sews wounds, and treats wounds. Saves lives as he can. He's always busy, so he doesn't get in touch. I haven't heard his voice in a long time. When he is not in touch, I write to all acquaintances and strangers who appear online, from whom I can find information about Pasha.

To date, he has not been online since April 21, because more and more people are injured. He is very tired of taking care of them. But he tries to write to me through his colleagues that he is all right. But they are very bad there! They run out of food, water. They smoke tea there...

We are trying to shout about Mariupol. We are trying to draw attention to the military in Azovstal. We don't want our heroes left there to die. Everyone says that they are the strongest and bravest. But we do not want to be the widows of heroes! We want to live with our loved ones. I want him to hug his daughter. That he hugged me.

This war took away everything material from us. Now I have an old car, which breaks down forever, but which saved my daughter's life and took away 2 more families with children. And a package with things. But I do not want this war to take away the person dearest to me. I am almost 30 years old; I spent a third of my life with Pasha. I don't want to lose him. I don't want him thrown there. Everyone is proud of them, but no one wants to save them...I don't want to!

Pasha Paralhenko
Ukrainian Soldier
Letter to his daughter – Husband of Tamara Paralhenko
Siege of Mariupol, Azovstal

"Hi daughter. I love you and miss you very much. How are you? Very nice drawings, thank you. I'll put them in my bulletproof vest for good luck. You are brave. Are you teasing your mom?
I love you"

*Pasha, Husband to Tamara Paralhneko. Letter written on March 8th. Documented May 3rd

Victoria
Ukrainian Civilian
Fiancé of an Azovstal Soldier
May 4th

My name is Victoria, I am the future bride of a soldier of the Azov Regiment. His journey towards the Azov regiment began in 2014, when, as a young man, he realized that it takes a lot of courage to protect us all.

Now I myself want to protect him. Every day he tells me how much he wants to eat some bread. He says that when he will return home, he wants to start baking homemade bread. Every time we get in touch, he writes, "I have been very lucky again today." And I try to persuade him that it is all thanks to me, a white witch who guards him in battle. He protects all Ukrainians, and I have to protect him.

Week Eleven: May 5 - 11

Ukrainian Civilian
Wife of an Azovstal Soldier
May 5th

I am the wife of a warrior who has been courageously defending Mariupol together with his comrades for two months now.

We started living together only half a year ago. And got married just two months before the war. Our dreams are about a big cozy house in the mountains, and about children.

All the time we spent together… The hugs, touches, kisses. Everything so warm, so dear, and you think that you want to be this happy all your life. Naively believing that there will always be peace and calm blue skies. Every evening you wait for him from work, and then run around the apartment following him everywhere.

Snuggle up to him like a kitten and after a bath, run into his warm arms, and ask him to comb your hair. Hear the phrase "I will be the best father to our daughter." Feel how he hugs me and puts a blanket on me, kisses me while I am asleep. Feel his steel protection and know that I will follow my husband anywhere. My heart is with him.

My husband is my home. And now I feel homeless, helpless. I want to give up everything to bring him back to me alive. He is going through hell. He went to serve in the Azov Regiment consciously, knowing their values and ideas. Knowing that he wants to protect his country and his people. He wants to know that our children will have a peaceful and carefree future.

His life is at risk every second, like the lives of everyone who is with him. My husband sees death every day, sees torn, rotten bodies, and sees the most terrible things on this planet. He sees how people die without water, without food. How they suffer from pain and how they can't sleep. Courageously holding on, he feels wild injustice, injustice towards all of the deaths, the deaths of his close comrades, the deaths of civilians, the destroyed cities and houses.

I'm there with him now, though not physically. We are each other's support. For me, there is no greater faith in this world than my faith in my beloved husband.

251

We have great confidence and desire to pass this test for the right to live until the end. A happy end. Until our victory. Together.

It's hard, it's insanely hard there. And even I will never understand what is going on there. Not a single living soul, except for those who are in Azovstal understand it. I ask and want one single thing, to help them get out of there, help them stay alive. To give everyone who does not see the sky above their heads the opportunity to breathe freely and be safe.

In the meantime, I will only really live when my husband gets back, now I definitely just exist.

Major Bohdan Krotevich
Chief of Staff, Azov Regiment
Siege of Mariupol, Azovstal
May 5th

Situation at 16:45, 5.5.2022. Enemy has broken through. Heavy fighting is ongoing. Enemy has taken parts of the factory. They are using human meat/wave tactics. The fighting has not stopped. On the territory of the factory remain women, children, and heavily wounded.

Art by João "J-Dot" Alves

Natali
Ukrainian Civilian
Wife of an Azovstal Soldier
May 5th

I lived in Mariupol for 3 years. On February 23, my husband and child sent me to my hometown of Kharkiv to visit my mother. We didn't even know then that the war would start. On the morning of February 24, around half past four in the morning, we woke up to the explosions. At first, I didn't even understand what it was. When we saw that all the people who were already going to work at that time were scared, we realized that the war had started.

I called my husband who was in Mariupol at the time, said that we were being bombed, he was very scared for me and the child, told me to take the baby and hide somewhere. We lived in the basement for about two weeks. But then, at their own peril and risk, they decided to leave the city, because it was no longer possible to live in the basement under fire and air raids with a small child. Because the child was afraid to come out of the basement at least on the stairs! A military man and he certainly could not leave the city! We left Kharkiv for a more carefree city, but we are staying in Ukraine and waiting for our dad!

It hurts a lot when you don't know if he will return home alive! They have no connection and can't communicate! He has repeatedly told us that he is alive, but this is very rare. They ask for help but no one helps them. Our father is a hero, we don't need any benefits to come home alive! We are very much looking forward to his home! We love him very much!

Ukrainian Soldier / Medic
Azov Regiment
Siege of Mariupol, Azovstal
Appeal to Turkish Government
May 5th

Dear Recep Erdogan.

I don't remember what the day of war today is. Some people are dying of starving, dehydration or traumas. Wounded soldiers are dying because we can't cure them, because of insufficient medicine. We stay in conditions which are incompatible with the word "life". We don't have time no more. I don't know if there is tomorrow.

I am a Crimean Tatar; I am a Muslim. I have a medical education and now I'm helping the people in Azovstal. I had never seen death before this war. I have been working as an Ambulance doctor and I always did my best to save people's life. And now it is so heartbreaking for me to see how people are dying one after another here, because we don't have enough medicine, because of rotting alive…in 2022.

We suffer of air, ground and sea attacks every minute. I'm begging you to do the procedure for taking everyone out of here, including the military. Do an extraction. Stop this horror, please.

Only 263km away from you there are innocent people who are defending their country, men, women and children. We didn't want this; we didn't attack anyone. Turkey has been always getting on with Ukraine, we are close friends who support each other. We don't know who appeal to…So I appeal to you for help. I believe that Allah will repay it to all of those who help us now.

Former Russian Soldier
United States
May 6th

I'm a Russian immigrant living in the United States. Proud American citizen. (Believe it or not, there's a lot of us) I was conscripted into the Russian army in 1995. I'm not here to offer any political or strategic opinions, but only to talk about the trauma I know all the soldiers are going to have to deal with in the coming years. I know because I am a survivor of Grozny.

In Grozny, I saw nothing but criminal acts on both sides. More than once I saw captured Chechens shot against a wall or in the street. More than once, captured soldiers, my friends, were butchered like hogs within earshot of us. In war, you are both the murderer and the victim, sometimes. I know these soldiers are going to have nightmares. I know that some won't be able to please their wives because of impotence. I couldn't for a long time. They will never hold their children the same way again because they will have seen children blown to pieces.

They will never walk the streets again without at least a small thought in their head a rifle is pointed at them from a window. They will never be able to be fully truthful about what they saw and what they did. Out of shame, anger or guilt. No war story you ever hear is the complete truth.

I and other Chechen war veterans will attest to this. I know men on both sides of this war are just thinking one thing. 'I'd rather be home.' Because war is not like the movies we see here in America. You don't die with glorious music playing and in slow motion. You may get your jaw shot off and scream for hours until you bleed out. You may get crushed by a tank or burn to death trapped in a house. Worst of all, you may fight among your own homes and families like these Ukrainians.

Those kids in Mariupol. In that factory. If they make it out of that building, they have my prayers. They will not be the same coming out as they were coming in.

War will turn all of these boys into shadows of men who have blood on their hands. I feel so sorry that another generation of people will be traumatized. Traumatized because the fires of government grew too big and burned everyone it could.

Ukrainian Soldier
Azov Regiment
Siege of Mariupol, Azovstal
May 7th

If we all die or get captured, I have this to say. We are proud of our soldiers. We are proud to defend Mariupol and I do not wish I didn't come here.

To Ukrainian soldiers in other parts of the country: Avenge your brothers. Destroy every invader you find. Force a generation of Russian children to grow up without their fathers. Glory to Ukraine.

Major Serhiy Volyna
Commanding Officer of 36th Separate Marine Brigade
Siege of Mariupol, Azovstal
May 7th

Just my thoughts: How do I feel? I feel like I'm in some hellish reality show where we military people are fighting for our lives, taking every chance to rescue ourselves and the whole world is just watching! Such scenarios are used in movies and TV series. The only difference is that it's not a movie, and we are not fictional characters! This is the real life!

Pain, suffering, hunger, torment, tears, fear, death - all real! What surprises me? Cynicism!!! There are no limits to human cynicism! There are generally accepted rules, they are the same for everyone, certified by a bunch of laws, signatures and stamps, but they don't apply here! Then what are they needed for? What am I hoping for? Amazing!

That the higher forces (in the broad sense of the word), will find a solution to our rescue! And this hellish reality show will end… Higher forces, we are waiting for the results of your actions…Time is running out, and time is our lives! MARINES - ALWAYS FAITHFUL! GLORY TO Ukraine!

P.S. White flags, for the evacuation of civilians, are used for the fourth time, during each evacuation of people. The price of the latest civilian evacuation is three killed and six wounded military. Mariupol garrison did everything possible to rescue civilians. We ask everyone to do their best to evacuate the military.

Sandra Krotevich
Sister of Major Bohdan Krotevich
Siege of Mariupol, Azovstal
May 8th

My brother is now in Mariupol in Azovstal, and he has been there from the very beginning of the war. He was also there before the war. I am mentally with him every day and around the clock, I can't tune in to a normal life or work knowing that he and his regiment brothers are under constant air bombs and shelling for over 70 days now without any the basic human living conditions.

He doesn't feel well there. He is human and the lack of sleep, food, water, medicines affects his health. He does not complain, because he has always been strong and has never shown any weakness in his words or actions. But I see how strength leaves him, how hunger affects energy loss, how the lack of normal nutrition affects his health.

I write to him every day and I am so happy when he answers me. Between my message and his answer, 12-36 hours can pass, and all this waiting time I cannot eat, sleep, work, live, but when he answers, my heart falls like a stone. We all understand that this is a thin thread and at any moment it can break. He is in constant danger.

There are lots of things he told me about... That civilians that are there with them live in inhumane conditions, that they share their food with their, water and medicines. That small children, newborns do not receive proper care, because of the lack of opportunity to provide it there. That they have a lot of wounded, who, from the first days of the war could not be evacuated, and in the conditions in which they are, they cannot be cured. Many have to be amputated in order to somehow extend their life. Many people need major surgeries. Therefore, pain is their constant state.

He told me that they successfully carried out military operations and helped the 36th brigade to leave the encirclement and join them, same with the police and border guards and the rest of the military, who did not surrender to the enemy and continued to fight for Ukraine.

I am worried about the inability of the whole world to influence this situation. We all live in the 21st century, the age of technology and opportunities. You all see how they stand strong, the whole world admires them, their courage and heroism.

So why do you have to become dead for the world to stop simply expressing sympathy, rather than to start helping and finding a way even if it is unprecedented, but a way to save such heroes now, and then admire the living legends, not the dead.

I know that it is possible if the world really wants it. With these words we turn to the world, this is what worries us all, wives, children, mothers and the entire Ukrainian people. Do not give them hero medals posthumously, they defended the right to be alive for over 70 days now, they became legends and everyone, all Ukrainians, want them to live.

My brother was forced to become a military man. In 2014, the Russians occupied our home in Crimea, and now they have come again to occupy the whole of Ukraine. They simply took away his whole future. After the academy, he was going to become a civilian sailor, he studied to be a skipper, but life changed his plans - the war came. He had to take up arms and put on combat boots at the age of 20 and all 9 years (from 2014 to today) live in constant tension and learn to protect himself and other people.

He is proud to be in the Azov Regiment, the most powerful unit in the world. And he is happy that this is a monolith of friendship, understanding and professionalism. The Azov Regiment is capable of performing the most difficult tasks, which in fact today they are demonstrating to the whole world. With a complete blockade that lasts more than 70 days now, they still manage to demoralize the enemy.

The enemy is afraid of them which is evidenced by the stories of local residents and radio intercepts. There are also lots of horror stories about Azov, which the enemy himself comes up with. Azov continues to destroy the enemy daily in the occupied city and does not allow them to feel safe the whole time.

The world has united. The world got to know Ukraine and the Ukrainians. The world must find a way to make the aggressor comply with the rules of this world. There are not so many warriors like the Azov Regiment man out there in the world. This is the gene pool of the world, outside of the nations, creeds and skin color. Their principles are based on morality, the principles of a world, civilized society and the military code. That is why the world must find a way to get them out. The titan warriors of Azov stood up for all of the people they could save. The world must show them that this was not in vain, not only in words, but also in actions.

We believe that goodness and wisdom will win, we feel the support of everyone who helps us and feels our pain as their own. We hope that faith in goodness will win. We believe that we are not alone and all of you will find a way to help us in deblocking Mariupol and rescuing our courageous men from the Azov Regiment and other units.

Dima
Ukrainian Soldier
Azov Regiment
Siege of Mariupol
May 8th

I had the desire to join the army since my childhood, when to the choice of which unit to go to, I chose the Azov Regiment because I liked their approach when it came to warfare.

The first few days I spent adapting. We came to the unit with a friend whom I met in Kyiv, and they almost immediately began to prepare us for the basic course of combat training, which had to be passed by the recruits to get a chevron (badge used in military to indicate rank or length of service) of the Azov regiment and the uniform.

In all matters the commanders helped us as well as our roommates with whom we immediately found common ground. So, it was relatively easy. For our training, the commanders assigned to us specialists in various weapons, who gave us literature to read and study and conducted practical classes. First, we needed to know by heart how the regular weapons (ZU 23 2, PKT and AKS 74 U) need to be disassembled and assembled, and then there were trips to the firing field.

Everything was easy for me thanks to the people who taught us and my desire to learn. Then there was the basic course of combat training where we engaged in physical training and studied tactics, topography, tactical medicine, the regulations of the Armed Forces, and had shooting lessons.

We lived on the polygon in a strict regime, so the very period of the course was the most difficult experience for us as we thought at the time.

On February 24th, we were at our base and all day we were transporting weapons, our belongings, ammunition, etc. to Azovstal. In fact, we did not really believe in a full-scale offensive and thought that everything would be limited to Donetsk and Luhansk regions. So, when in the morning, my friends started calling me telling me that there were bombings in Zhytomyr, Kyiv, and other cities I was a little shocked and at the same time I at once felt hatred towards Russia.

All of our guys were motivated and ready to meet the Russian troops. Although it is difficult to call them real soldiers because they do not follow any of the rules of war by killing civilians and prisoners, destroying entire cities. When I was in the Mariupol hospital, where in addition to the military were treated many civilians, including children, the enemy's aircraft dropped bombs on us and there were dozens of such cases in Mariupol alone.

I was lucky to take part in battles in the suburbs of Mariupol. At that moment I personally had no thoughts except from the fact that I saw the enemy and I had a goal to destroy him. Roughly speaking, at that time we were very successful.

I saw Russians alive during the fighting and I managed to look the prisoners in the eye. I felt only negative emotions then because I saw what they were doing to our people, villages and cities, but it did not escalate into violence because I understood that this person surrendered and even if there are many lies about it out there, but all of our prisoners were treated well.

I was frightened by the scale of the destruction, the crippled and dead children and the elderly. After seeing this, I began to hate this war even more as well as those who brought it to our country. Those with whom I served were ordinary guys. Everyone had their own personality, had their own interests and views on life, but we were all united by the desire to be professionals and defend our country.

Most of us had girlfriends, wives and children. We all made plans for our future life. I was close with some of the guys, we went to the gym together, went on vacations, and helped each other. The war really revealed our true selves, and I was pleasantly surprised by how each of us showed himself.

I gained more life experience from this war. Most of the problems that exist in peaceful life turned out to be trifle. The war taught me to value the people close to me, fight to the end and to always present a bold front. There were wounded and killed. Pain and the desire for revenge are the only things I can say about that.

I would like to convey my best wishes to the military, I wish for them to return alive and victorious. To the civilians, I would like to remind that our country is at war and that they need to understand that our army needs a strong rearward.

To those Russians who have the ability to think, I would advise to try and understand that the enemy is not Ukraine and NATO, but those who are in power in their own country. And for those who believe that Ukrainians are not a nation and Lenin invented Ukraine, I will just remind you of one well-known motto "the will of Ukraine or death."

I am worried for all the guys who are at the front, and especially for those who are now in Azovstal and show us an example of heroism and steadfastness.

When I got wounded, I was angry with myself because I will no longer be able to help our guys anymore as I understood that the injury was severe. I don't remember very well what happened, but I remember that something from a drone was dropped on us. We were evacuated from Mariupol by the helicopter.

Western Civilian
May 9th

I am a psychologist who specializes in trauma experienced by soldiers/veterans. What these soldiers are experiencing in Azovstal is unprecedented in modern times. They are sitting in a hole in the ground, constantly under attack, slowly starving to death and watching their wounded comrades literally rot in the damp and dark.

You can see the change on their faces. The sunken eyes. Curled lips. Men resigned to slowly starve, rot, and die. An indicator to me of their hopelessness is many pictures we see are of untrimmed beards and uncombed hair. Part of this is due to the combat environment, but also a 'What's the point?' attitude I'm sensing is growing.

If these men survive, they will not be the same men who went into that bunker. They will need decades of mental health counseling, and I fear that the number of survivors may slowly dwindle in the years to come…We must all remind ourselves, yes, they may be heroes of Ukraine. They may be surviving against all the odds stacked against them. They may have iron wills, but they are just men.

This will affect them in ways modern mental health specialists will have no experience dealing with. They may lose their minds. After this is over, we must convince them to come back. Not all the scars they will carry can be seen.

Ukrainian Soldier
Azov Regiment
Siege of Mariupol, Azovstal
May 10th

The whole civilized world must see the conditions in which the wounded, crippled defenders of Mariupol are and act! In complete unsanitary conditions, with open wounds bandaged with non-sterile remnants of bandages, without the necessary medication and even food. We call on the UN and the Red Cross to show their humanity and reaffirm the basic principles on which you were created by rescuing wounded people who are no longer combatants.

The servicemen you see in the photo and hundreds more at the Azovstal plant defended Ukraine and the entire civilized world with serious injuries at the cost of their own health. Are Ukraine and the world community now unable to protect and take care of them?

We demand the immediate evacuation of wounded servicemen to Ukrainian-controlled territories, where they will be assisted and provided with proper care.

Ukrainian Civilian
Evacuated from Mariupol
May 10th

Mariupol is my home. I studied abroad for the last two years, but it is home. My brother and cousin are soldiers there. I have not heard from them in a while. My boyfriend is there also, and I worry for them all. My home is destroyed. The city I grew up in is destroyed. Everything I had known and loved in that city is destroyed and the boys I love, their fates are not known. I made love with my boyfriend on the beach there last year. Now I see it is in ruins. My old school is gone. My mother's house is gone.

My friends and almost everyone I knew there is gone. Our whole lives are destroyed, and I am 22 years old and now my city and childhood are gone forever because it fell too close to a border on a map with greedy neighbors.

Ukrainian Soldier
Lysychansk
May 10th

I am UA military engineering + EOD officer. I have served one turn in Donbas prior to the recent invasion. Recently, I have accomplished a mission which made huge impact on Russian losses and completely screwed up their plans to encircle Lysychansk. Initially, there was intelligence from frontline units that there are Russians on the other side of the river, and they gather various vehicles. So, my commander asked on 6th May me as one of the best military engineers to do engineering reconnaissance on Siverskyi Donets River.

Together with recon units for backup, I went to explore the area of Hryhorivka and Bilohorivka on 7th May. Frontline units in Bilohorivka reported multiple RU vehicles gathering on the other side of the river. I explored the area and suggested a location where Russians might attempt to mount a pontoon bridge to get to the other side. And, used rangefinders to figure out river is 80m wide, thus Russians would need 8 parts (10m each) of the bridge connected to get to the other side.

With that flow of the river, I knew they would need motorized boats to arrange such a bridge, and it would take them at least two hours of work. Took me a day to check everything. And I had to do it on 8th of May as well. So, reported this information I had to my commanders. Also, I told the unit who observed that part of the river that they need to be on the lookout for sound of motorboats.

Visibility was shit in the area because Russians put fields & forests on fire and were throwing a lot of smoke grenades. On top of that, it was foggy. They had to hear the sound. And they did on May 8th early morning. Right at the place I said. I was there to check it as well - and I have seen with my drone as Russians do the pontoon bridge. Reported immediately to commanders.

Looking back, I think my recon and hints to the river unit made the biggest impact. I outplayed RU mil engineers. Russians attempted to place a bridge RIGHT in the place where I guessed.

River unit didn't see RU units but was able to hear motorboats and report it immediately. Artillery was ready. We have been able to confirm Russians mounted 7 parts of the bridge out of 8. Russians have even succeeded to move some troops and vehicles over the river. Combat started.

In about 20 minutes after recon unit confirmed Russian bridge being mounted, HEAVY ARTILLERY engaged against Russian forces, and then aviation chipped in as well. I was still in the area, and I have never seen / heard such heavy combat in my life.

After one day of combat, 9th May morning the bridge was down. Some Russian forces (~30-50 vehicles + infantry) were stuck on Ukrainian side of the river with no way back. They tried to run away using broken bridge. Then they tried to arrange a new bridge.

Then, Aviation started heavy bombing of the area and it destroyed all the remains of Russians there, and other bridge they tried to make. Rumors say it's about 1500 RU dead. Their strategic objective was to cross the river and then encircle Lysychansk. They miserably failed. 10th May pontoon bridge was completely down. That's about time when you started to get all the pictures from the area.

I was on the ground, doing the work there, alongside with other Ukrainian heroes. I did my part and it had significant impact. Proud to serve Ukraine!

Ukrainian Soldier
Kharkiv
May 11th

We were in trenches on a small hill near Kharkiv not long ago. Not a big hill, just a rise above and trees behind. We had no place to piss and shit in the trench, so we went in the trees behind. Someone said we should shit in the trench in cups, but no one wanted to smell that and what if they spilled? So, the trees are where we went. 'Mykola' went into the trees to shit. He was gone about 5 minutes and we heard artillery shoot in front of us. This was not strange because we had not been hit in days, but we always heard artillery fired. Now we heard the artillery coming at us and we all yelled to Mykola to hurry the fuck up.

It (artillery shells) starts hitting in front of us and Mykola is still not returned yet. For 15 minutes it hits, and Mykola is gone. When it is done, he comes back with no pants on. We ask where he was. He told us he ran further away from the trench. His pants on his ankles so he left them behind. He comes back after to find his pants and artillery had moved them into a tree!

So now Mykola sits with no pants. We found him something to wear and now when he goes to take another shit, we tell him to bring another pair of pants. He said next time he will shit in the trench.

Western Volunteer
Kyiv Oblast
May 11th

I've met a lot of amazing people along this journey. Our first day when we arrived in Kyiv, on April 8th we were immediately under our first air raid warning as soon as we arrived at the compound we would be staying at. This is when the reality of the situation for the people of Ukraine really set in. I knew that this was a common occurrence but didn't expect them to be as common as they were.

We all went downstairs and settled into a WW2 bomb shelter that was in the bottom of our building. One thing that amazed me about it all wasn't that we were down in this shelter but the fact that later that day we had went to a local tactical store and another siren rang out and the Ukrainian civilians were still casually going about their days like nothing was happening.

This is the heartbreaking reality of living under Russian aggression. A couple days went by, and we found ourselves on a train towards Kyiv to link up with our contacts and a group we would be working with. We got settled into a building in Kyiv and got linked up with a Ukrainian contact who was having Ukrainian territorial defense members brought to us for training in Close Quarter Battles, Combat Life Saver, and small unit tactics.

This should be known that these Ukrainians were civilians just weeks prior and had little to no medical or military training. A couple guys had already been to combat and shared their stories from the front. EVAC for guys even with amputations takes days and by then the limb is surely lost or worse. A lot of the tourniquets these guys receive from whatever sources they may be are complete junk and break as soon as you tighten them. They are designed to look like the C-A-T tourniquet which works well but these aren't even effective.

It's a shame that companies are taking advantage of this war and sending out supplies that don't meet the standards. We were able to supply a good bit of these guys with US IFAKs and proper tourniquets, supplies, etc. to assist them on the front in which they will inevitably go. I have so much more to tell but don't want to overwhelm you with all of it all at once.

They shared with us videos of the conditions on the front lines and shared with us pictures and videos from the front. We managed to get new groups of guys to train daily. In just a few days with each group we had them performing CLS, the entire process, and proper CQB / MOUT procedures like they were pretty well-trained rifle squads. Another heartbreaking thing is a lot of these guys don't have proper SAPI plates, nor helmets to protect them from shrapnel and the caliber of rounds they would be facing. We are working to source these items, so they have a better chance when they go to combat.

We met other commanders of different units who need their guys trained desperately and are extremely grateful for western volunteers who are coming to assist and advise with these types of classes and courses. The will and determination of the Ukrainians is unlike anything I've ever seen. They are so motivated and determined to win the war. They don't say if they win they say "When We Win."

And I find that to be a beautiful thing. They would share pictures of their families and we sat and shared life stories and experiences and bonded over their local foods and drinks. I had no personal connection with Ukraine when I arrived, but now I can say I will gladly train, and fight for Ukraine and their people and their fight for freedom and peace from the Russian aggressors.

As controversial as this will be and I know everyone has mixed feelings about it, but this is EVERYONE's war and everyone who is able needs to support Ukraine in some shape or fashion. Charities, volunteering, humanitarian aid, and yes even fighting. In my own opinion we are seeing the beginning of something that won't stop with Ukraine and it needs to be stopped before it's too late. What you see from the media and on the news doesn't even scratch the surface of how terrible this really is and it's the most heartbreaking situation I've ever been involved with in my entire life.

Week Twelve: May 12-18

Anton Kryl
Ukrainian Soldier
Azov Regiment
Siege of Mariupol, Azovstal
May 12-14th

I am 22 years old. At the age of 19, I already took part in the deployment with Azov to the front line.

But this situation is very unpredictable for my experience. Before this, I had not seen an enemy tank so close, I had not heard the voice of enemy infantry so close. I had not helped my friend in a critical situation. Here everything is a first for me.

It's very scary not to convey the feeling when a tank fired at me. As over time, literally a change of position and you change roles with him, and for the first time you shoot at him, the adrenaline is running high. When you see the Russian infantry running, just running at you without a bulletproof vest, a machine gun somewhere in front shooting at you, it takes a second to think about what to do in such a situation. You do not know what to expect.

It was very important who I was with at such moments, with whom I shared a sip of water, a piece of biscuit. When I was confident in my friends, I could do anything.

And most of all you dream if something happens to help him, to do everything possible and impossible to help. When you see only pain every day, ordinary people and you can't help them, it's sad. I was overwhelmed with anger and hatred for the enemy for everything he had done in my city.

You experience these emotions only for the first two weeks, when you do not understand who your opponent is, where he is, and how he acts.

The first time I saw a tank it was 400 meters away. We were in a high-rise building then, kept the defense, the first feeling is of course fear and thoughts where it can be safe. At this time, he (the tank) started shooting at our house from the 9th floor to the first. It shot at random so there was a chance to 'dodge'.

It's a pity that the tank was cowardly, he worked quickly and left. There was no opportunity to attack it. After the tanks' work, the infantry always ran away, and we coped well with it.

The enemy has always had one tactic, the first tank destroys everything in front of it, shoots anywhere, in these moments you can try to destroy it, which is what we worked on. Sometimes one shot is enough to catch fire, it's a very good feeling when you're a tiny person who destroyed such a huge vehicle. Unfortunately, we "Azov" did not have enough people to close and defend positions, in such cases, border guards, Marines and so on were sent to us.

Some lacked the strength, courage, and desire to even just watch the enemy, it was very difficult to work with them. It is good that there were not many of them.

We were in a house one time (already a completely different position), here they also have a tactics, and the enemy changed into civilian clothing and quietly explored the environment around the battle.

The closest I ever got to enemy infantry. Here they also have a tactic, they changed into civilian clothing. They decided to occupy our house very quickly, the house was on two floors, and we had an advantage. They decided to get closer, and we opened fire on them, the screams began.

'What are you doing?'

'Come out, give up!'

We just kept quiet and waited for them to come closer. After a very short time, I decided to look out our windows from the second floor, saw two "people" there, and opened fire. Because they also noticed me, they hid in a shelter, behind a small barn, a fight broke out. I decide with my friend to knock them out with grenades.

They were forced to flee from our actions, but they did not manage to escape far because we were ready for their maneuver and met them. We successfully repulsed their attack that day.

Later we inspected them, they were completely without bulletproof vests. On one's head was a World War II helmet, two magazines for a machine gun, and the machine gun itself is a brand-new AK-74. How can such a fighter be released into battle? He was clearly inexperienced and went to the slaughter.

Another time in battle, we were then at the "school". (Position name) According to the morning "tradition", a tank came at 7-8 in the morning and tried to knock us out, as this was not the first day, we were ready for this position.

Imagine a school territory with the letter "n", respectively front, left flank, right flank, from the right flank a tank drove up straight on the road almost at the stop to the school 70 - 110 meters, I looked into the collapse of the wall and was very surprised that the tank stood alone without infantry support.

We quickly decided that we needed to work on it, I took a new "matador" RGW 90 toy, shot him under the tower, to my surprise, he calmly left, but we were still glad that he would not come to us today. As it turned out, we were mistaken, he decided to shoot at us from the front of the school, because of the trees about 200 meters, the second floor of the school was almost completely collapsed, we waited and decided to fire on it three times. We chose a position, got ready, shot, all three didn't hit.

We had to retreat very quickly to the first floor, ran to the stairs down, a tank shot behind us, and a shell broke through two walls and exploded behind us. Everything is in smoke. We shout to each other to understand whether everyone is alive and safe, after a while, the dust settled. One of my friends had fragments in his legs, but he was alive. I was luckier just a shell shock, the one who was closest to the epicenter of the explosion from the wave his helmet just flew away and the fragments covered the back of his head.

That day was one of the most terrible. We understand that we need to provide assistance to the wounded, but in such a situation we are powerless. At this time the infantry assault is still beginning, and the issue of evacuation of our wounded comrade fades into the background.

I wanted to throw a weapon in the first minutes when you see this, then the acceptance of this comes, and incredible anger towards the enemy.

There was only one moment in our thoughts when we moved from the right bank of the city to the Azovstal factory across the river in rescue boats. It was our last chance to escape across the river to the stronghold setup in the factory. A lot of people moved for quite a long time. The last group remained, at that time the enemy raised his drones and naturally noticed the groups and started shooting. I think they shot all they have. Artillery, rocket launchers, mortars…the group on the other side of the river came under direct blows were very seriously wounded.

They asked for help to evacuate for a long time, it was very painful to listen to this on the radio and not understand how to help them under such dense shelling. Only a moment of silence, I immediately ran to the shore and our commander was there. He was supposed to meet the last ones to cross, and they came under fire.

I said that they need help urgently and asked who could sail in a boat for the guys. Most refused, I understand that there was a very strong shelling, and no more boats were to be risked, but the commander looked at me and said, "Swim."

I could not refuse, it was decided to swim together, and we took everything off ourselves and went to the opposite shore. As soon as we took the wounded and loaded them into boats on the other side, the second wave of shelling immediately begins. I don't know how lucky we were that we crossed back in a boat under heavy enemy fire, this is some kind of miracle. The commander immediately took a group of people and led them under fire to the factory, to help.

Miraculously, then almost the whole group got saved. I don't know what would have happened if the commander hadn't told us to swim together under fire for the wounded. There would have been no one to help and they all would have died on the shore. You probably think, "He is the commander, he shouldn't do this. Risk his life like that." But that day there was such a dense shelling that only a few would decide on such actions, risk themselves for the sake of others. I hope you could imagine that day and how it happened.

The hospital in Azovstal is an ordinary bunker, everything is dirty, there is no place to lie down, the wounded lie on the floor, there are no medicines. It is very difficult to provide assistance, enemy aircraft are always working.

We are forced to go to the top in order to hold positions and watch the enemy 24/7, to this all you need to get food under the rubble and water.

The mood of the guys is normal, stable, no one is going to give up, and everyone is ready to fight, to protect their wounded at the plant, themselves and their brothers.

The days pass the same way, in the hope that you will not die from another air strike, if you go out into the street, you always need to run. Snipers are working, and an enemy drone. There is low chance of survival here. When there was fear and I was with my friends, there was no feeling that I was afraid of it very much.

The only moment I felt true fear was in frontline positions, I heard on the radio that my brother, Bogdan Tsimbal, was wounded, and they couldn't do anything at that time. I became very scared. It scared me so much to think that I might lose him, I've never been so scared.

Fortunately, everything is fine with him, he is already safe. He was evacuated by helicopter. I don't know how he survived that day; I don't know how I would have fought further that day if everything had happened differently.

Here, in short, we are always relying on each other. We are in history, and we have done everything possible and impossible. After we are pulled out of here, I will immediately marry my girlfriend, everything will be Ukraine!

*This last interview was conducted on May 13th. Anton was killed in action on May 14th, 2022. Rest in Peace, my friend.

Art by João "J-Dot" Alves

"Iniquity"
Ukrainian Soldier
Azov Regiment
Siege of Mariupol, Azovstal
May 14th

Anton and two close friends of mine were attacked by a combat drone. Anton died on the spot. Another friend of mine was killed during the evacuation because of serious injuries. We took the third soldier to the evacuation point and now medical specialists are trying to save his life. This is a huge loss for me personally and for the entire regiment. They are like brothers to me and now they are dead. He was one of the best fighters who supported the defense of Mariupol from the first day.

Bogdan Tsimbal
Brother of Anton Kryl
Azov Regiment
Siege of Mariupol
May 14th

My brother was a guy from Mariupol who was not afraid and went to defend his country at the age of 18. He was not afraid of anyone! He was an ordinary guy from the city who was supposed to live and build a great country, he dreamed of marrying his girlfriend whom he loved very much. He loved his four-legged friend Odin (Pitbull).

He was very worried about me; he and I were always together. We fought together in Mariupol. We could never be apart for a long time. I love, respect and miss him very much!

In the war, he was a great warrior, burned and destroyed a lot of equipment and eliminated a lot of the enemy in the video where Ukrainian soldiers counterattack from the parking lot, he throws grenades at the invaders.

He died as a hero; he will be remembered. And most importantly, he never bragged. Our opponent will die as an occupier. Let's take revenge! From my experience in the war, it is very difficult not to lose human qualities. But my brother and how he lived and died deserves to be known like everyone else.

Ukrainian Surgeon
Kyiv Oblast
May 14th

Working as a trauma surgeon in civilian life meant lots of car crashes, accidents and injuries like that. Now I work on battlefield wounds, and these are worse than anything I had seen before.

Gunshot wounds are relatively easy to treat depending on where they are shot. I hear stories of medics on the front line having to choose who to carry out and be evacuated, and who will not survive. I can't verify this. Only stories. Hopefully not true.

Traumatic brain injuries from explosions have become more and more common as Russia steps up their use of conventional artillery on the front in the east. We get more and more patients with shrapnel wounds and internal bleeding than we did before.

Most of the soldiers I treat here are fighting in the northeast part of Ukraine. I am very proud of the staff that works with me. My subordinates do a good job of working many hours, and they never complain. I complain the most out of all of them, and I only work during surgery.

We only have one rule and that is to never be visibly upset in front of the soldiers who are wounded. They have done the hard work of fighting face to face with the enemy. We have the gruesome, but safe job of fixing them as much as we can.

My father-in-law was a surgeon during the last war, (WW2) in the battle of Sevastopol, and I often think of decisions he had to make in situations similar to mine. I have lived a long life in medicine, and to see so many of these young lives cut short hurts my heart.

We do the best we can. Always. We always do the best we can. Our patients deserve our best. A lot of medical equipment we have has come from our neighbors and friends to the west. We are eternally grateful.

Ukrainian Civilian
May 14th

My brother is on the front. He contacts me as often as he can, but he has been silent for 6 days. He is not a volunteer soldier. He is a professional one. In the Ukrainian army since 2019. He told me that one day all men in the country would need to defend Ukraine, and he wanted to be trained before that day came.

He was 19 then. He is 22 years old now and has been in combat a few times since Russia invaded. We had a method of communication set up. 'Alive. Working' meant he is in combat area and cannot speak but is okay. He sent me this message every day or every other day.

He told me Russian artillery is the worst. (Worst to endure) Russian infantry is scary but only within shouting distance. He said the closer the two armies become the worse the fighting gets. Everyone prefers to keep the enemy as far from them as possible. He told me several times he has been in such a close distance they have thrown grenades and insults at each other.

I am proud of my brother. He was not a brave child growing up. Deep water scared him. Heights scared him. Even the dark scared him. So, I respect that he has courage now to do the things many others are afraid to do. He says that everyone is scared and it's not courage that keeps them fighting. It's necessity.

He has told me that courage plays a small role in fighting. You move positions because you have to, or you will die. You fight because you have to, or you will die. You load ammunition because you have to. You dig trenches because you have to. My brother has changed a lot. I really respect him. I am confident he will survive this war and come home to tell us all his stories.

My brother is a Ukrainian soldier, and I am proud of him. To me he is Ukraine, and I will always praise him.

Ukrainian Soldier
Azov Regiment
Siege of Mariupol, Azovstal
May 16th

We have survived everything so far. We are all prepared to follow any order. After this is over, if I am dead, I am dead. I can't make plans. I won't know the difference. If I am alive, I will marry my girlfriend and get a dog. I don't look into tomorrow because it has not happened and may not happen for me. I think about today and what I can do. We all must. It's an easier way to live. Especially here.

Ukrainian Soldier
Azov Regiment
Siege of Mariupol, Azovstal
May 16th

My best friend died in rubble by a bomb. We crossed a street on the final retreat to the factory (Azovstal) and I ran across first and he ran second. A bomb hit near the ground and killed him instantly.
I couldn't go back and help him because there was not much left of him to help. I couldn't bring anything with either because we had to leave the area immediately.

I will die or be a prisoner soon. I would prefer to have died with him. We joined the military together. We trained together and went to school. We would have had fate make it, so we died together too, but that's not how it ended up working. If we survive captivity or are rescued, I will find the spot where he died and make sure to build something on the spot to remember him.

Yuri
Ukrainian Marine
Siege of Mariupol
Former Prisoner of War
May 16th

At the time of the outbreak of the war, we were already there on the front line of defense, we called this rotation. They began to actively fire on us from artillery a week before the start of the war.

On February 24, everything was as usual, but at 4:30 in the morning the enemy began an offensive along the entire front line, they opened fire on us from hailstones, mortars, self-propelled artillery installations, that's how we started the first day of the war.

Since we were in an open field from the shelter, we had only trenches and poorly protected dugouts, which the enemy destroyed during the day, thus preparing the bridgehead for the advance of enemy infantry and tanks.

Thus, repulsing the infantry attacks, we held out until 16:00, at about that time, an order was received to retreat to more advantageous positions in order to regroup and take up defense, since our positions were destroyed by the enemy at that time, everything was just on fire.

We began to collect the remaining surveillance equipment ammunition, communications equipment and weapons and leave the firing zone, while destroying all secret documentation.

The retreat was organized without panic, everyone knew what to do, while the enemy tried to the last to prevent us from doing this, constantly fired at us from artillery, but we went out and that day in my unit, after all, everyone was alive and not one wounded.

Our task was to get out of the enemy shelling to a safe zone where our armored vehicles were waiting for us for evacuation. When we got out, we boarded our armored vehicles and drove out under fire. After that, a command was received to gain a foothold in the area of \u200b\u200bthe settlement of Pavlopol, only on the other side of the Kalchik river, the bridge and the pontoon crossing were already mined and they were waiting for us to pass, after which everything was blown up in order to prevent the enemy from crossing the river.

There we took up defensive positions, choosing more advantageous positions and dug in, while observing the enemy and transmitting information to the top leadership, while detaining the enemy in this settlement for another 4 days in the flesh until February 28th and it was only one company without tanks and heavy weapons against superior enemy forces with tanks, aircraft and artillery, then some units still called us a legendary company, since they found out that we still held out in an open field for 4 days.

So, on February 28, at 4 AM, a command was received to leave these positions and we began to move towards Mariupol on our BTR-80s. Arriving in Mariupol, we occupied the northern part of the Ilyich plant, where we held the defense in the flesh until the breakthrough on April 12th.

In Mariupol itself, it was very tough. If I may say so, we did not think that the enemy would destroy the civilian population. It was the most difficult and morally very pressing when you see the innocent children of old women killed, but at the same time we only became angrier.

Our morale was at its best, we only dreamed that the enemy would attack us on an equal footing, but they simply bombed us with aircraft, artillery and missiles. Every day we had more and more wounded and killed, since there was no way to evacuate the dead, we buried them right there at the plant, and the wounded were treated and saved with what we had. Our doctors did everything to save the lives of the soldiers. But we believed to the last and waited for help to come, and therefore we fought to the last.

Some soldiers, after three wounds, again took up arms and joined the ranks, because they could not do otherwise until there was someone to fight, we lived. Then problems with food began, some drank water once a day, but we kept at the same time morale was high, we supported each other, motivated each other.

The worst things started for us at the beginning of April when the ammunition started to run out. According to intelligence data at that time, the ratio was 1:17, the enemy then withdrew his remnants from the rest of Ukraine and threw everything at us. I can't even describe to you how many of them there were, we saw them, we saw where they were shooting from, but we couldn't do anything about it since we had light weapons against the infantry.

The assaults were constant, they climbed, we killed them with great pleasure, but then they drove the infantry like Baranov tanks, and it was endless, while everything was under constant fire from aviation and artillery. At night, they did not storm our positions; leaving us for aviation and artillery, but every day with sunrise, attempts began again to storm our positions, which we successfully repulsed with minimal losses for us.

Since we didn't have any food or ammunition, the command decided to prepare for a breakthrough and the last battle, we all understood that not everyone would survive, but no one wanted to give up just like that, so everyone was set up for combat on their last journey.

April 11 at 3 AM, we had to break through, but as soon as our equipment began to move, we were covered by aircraft and artillery. While we lost the remaining ammunition that remained for the breakthrough. That night we had a lot of dead and wounded, most of all we lost people on that night.

The commanders decided to return to their original positions, and we just held out on April 12, I don't even know how the most powerful attack was then and we didn't have anything to achieve, I don't even understand how we managed to survive.

On the same day in the evening, it was decided to go out on foot, on the remaining equipment, it was a very small percentage of what would work out, but no one wanted to give up, and we all began to break out in small groups. My group of 10 people started moving at 23.00, we understood that there was little chance, but at least we would die in battle or return home.

Since the Russian army was poor and not all units had thermal imagers, we relied on this, since we had them, so we went out at night on the first night we passed 3 posts and the enemy ambushed right under their noses, the distance was 50-70 meters, they didn't see us.

On the first night, we managed to walk 15 kilometers and reach the river as planned. At dawn, we landed and lay down to rest, while we took turns observing the area. At 9.00 in the morning, we heard a military truck coming our way, we took up firing positions and we were getting ready to go into battle, he approached us, 30 people unloaded from him, we thought that we were noticed.

They lined up and began to shoot through the landing with small arms and an under-barrel grenade launcher, but since we were lying under their noses in the bushes, everything flew over us and it turns out they didn't know that we were there. It lasted 30 minutes, then the shooting stopped. They again got on the truck and left.

After that, we nervously smoked and began to wait for darkness to continue moving. Morning with dawn we hid and rested, and the day was calm. Somewhere at 16:00 a group of 20 Russians passed by us; we missed them because they did not notice us. After waiting for darkness, we again continued to move towards the Zaporozhye region. We had to go 180 kilometers to our troops.

At that moment, the enemy was already hunting for us, but we did not know this yet, everything was calm. We replenished water supplies near the river and moved further along the route. The terrain was very bad, there were many open areas and roads where we could be seen. We tried to pass these areas very quickly, and in one of these areas a well-prepared enemy ambushed us.

It was the Russian Special Forces that just started shooting us in an open field, not long ago there was no chance to prepare for the battle all lasted about 7 minutes. Five of my guys died and 5 were wounded.

I was the most seriously wounded, I got hit the groin, my strength began to leave very quickly. The enemy continued to shoot at us and tried to finish off the fighter who was lying next to me. I was able to give him a command so that he would shout that we were surrendering. I wanted to somehow save the lives of my people.

After that, they said not to move, and they would come over to us. After that I felt my strength leaving me and I was dying mentally. I said goodbye to everyone and began to fall asleep. But why did I wake up every time and realized that I had to fight to stay alive, I again gave the command to the fighter to ask to help us.

I remember then I still gathered strength and put a tourniquet on my leg. Then they approached, since I was seriously wounded, they stood for a long time before me, they debated to finish me off or not, but they decided not to finish me off. They bandaged my wounds, and my fighters carried me for two and a half kilometers, while also being wounded, but no one left anyone. That's how me and my people were captured.

After I got to their hospital, they took 2 bullets out of me, the rest went straight through. On the same day after the operation, their services came to interrogate me. Since I was still under anesthesia, the interrogator was bad with me, after which they hit me several times and left.

This was the only time when they interrogated me, but their military personnel constantly tried to destroy them morally, they also came in with a knife to cut off their ears to scare, it all brought them pleasure, so I stayed in captivity until April 27.

On April 27, at nine in the evening, they came to me again to interrogate and asked my military unit. After that they took a picture of my position and rank and then left. Then a security guard came in and said that they would shoot me tonight and I began to mentally set myself up for it.

We traveled from Donetsk to Russia for 6 hours and they brought me to Taganrog to a military airfield. Then from there by plane to Crimea, and from Crimea by truck to Zaporozhye region, and only there I was told that there would be an exchange.

We were exchanged on some destroyed bridge, so as if my legs were shot through, I had to be carried on a stretcher and there it was necessary to lift me to a certain height over rubble on the road, but the guys didn't have the strength. I asked them to put me on the asphalt there I began to crawl this section to my guys (Ukrainian) then they put me on a stretcher again, and so I was returned. On the 29th I was brought to Kyiv to a military hospital here and I am still there.

Art by João "J-Dot" Alves

Ukrainian Soldier
Azov Regiment
Siege of Mariupol, Azovstal
May 16th

We have performed combat tasks for Ukraine, at the cost of the lives of young men and women, for the benefit of the cities that now live in silence and with whole houses. I hope all defenders of Mariupol will soon see their relatives and loved ones. We have done a lot for Ukraine. Ukraine, do the same for us.

Major Bohdan Krotevich
Azov Regiment, Chief of Staff
Siege of Mariupol, Azovstal
May 17th

I forgot that I need to explain everything to the world like to a child. Stop feeling pity on us, stop whining, especially for the soldiers. You do us no favors. The military men are not kittens, they are military elites of Ukraine, the guarantee of Ukrainian future and children. I hope the centuries of wars will help us understand it. Women, please raise your kids with love to Ukraine first and foremost, and not to yourself. The main thing is not to "come back alive". The main this is to not surrender.

*Posted on Major Krotevich's personal Instagram, and then sent to Battles and Beers for documentation.

Western Volunteer
Donbas Frontline
May 18th

You know… since I've been here, I've met many 'super soldiers' claiming they have done so much for Ukraine. Claiming operations, claim to save children…the list goes on. But they have not done such things at all.

I am a combat volunteer based in Donbas, but on my Instagram, you will not see my face. You will not know my name. I believe our face and name does not matter. I simply let people know I'm a British volunteer and THATS IT.

Unless I fall for Ukraine my identity will remain anonymous because unlike many volunteers I see online I'm not here for fame and followers. I've took no donations from nobody, I'm in Donbas broke as fuck with no way home and no way to even buy a chocolate bar, but I see guys living in hotels from donations. It knocks me sick.

Why are you here? Are you here to help the people or is it all a publicity stunt? I came to Ukraine a few days after the 2022 invasion began and at first it seemed every volunteer was true to their word, now it seems we got guys flooding in looking to find their fame out of the people's misery.

Fedir
Ukrainian Soldier
Doctor of Sciences - Frontline
May 18th

I am a professor of Uzhhorod National University, Doctor of Sciences. I've been teaching at the University for 27 years. On the 24th of February I was greatly shocked by what had happened, got to my work and gave three lectures to students and afterwards I got together with my friends and we went to join the Ukrainian Military Forces.

In an hour after going through necessary procedures we appeared in the military base. On that day which is captured on the viral picture I was giving a lecture on tourism ology to my students. I had three lessons after night patrolling without proper sleeping. I taught classes over zoom on my computer while in a position in a trench.

*This story is in reference to the viral photo of Fedir sitting against the parapet of a trench while teaching a zoom class at the front.

Ukrainian Firefighter
May 18th

How do I say this to people? We are so tired, sometimes it would feel nice to lay down and not wake up. Russia has bombed more residential neighborhoods and the fires get out of control. We cannot control them sometimes. We just save the people we can and let it (buildings) burn.

Dogs jump from windows on fire. Cats as well. People too. It is the hardest part. Seeing living things suffer as they do because of the behavior of our enemies. We are not complaining about our work. We are just very tired. Fighting fires is different in peace. The fires are not so often started on purpose. They are accidents. We cannot be angry with fires for starting by themselves.

This is different. These fires are made on purpose and that makes it harder to do this. (Emotionally) Because there is anger involved. Someone started these fires to hurt people. Someone stated these fires to damage our infrastructure and way of life. It makes me angry.

Sometimes people help us on their own. They carry away civilians or tell us where people may be who are trapped. There won't be a drop of water in this country left to fight fires if this goes on for much longer. We could drain the Pacific Ocean and still be fighting fires.

But I am proud, yes. I am not a soldier. I am not brave enough to fight tanks or bullets, or even other men. I have not been a fighter before in my life. I am proud to help my country and save as much of it as I can. When this war started, I was going to be a man who designs websites. Now I am a fireman, and this job does well for me.

Week Thirteen: May 19- 25

Andriy
Ukrainian Soldier
Azov Regiment
Siege of Mariupol
Evacuated due to wounds
May 20th

We have been in combat readiness since the 20th of February, we were ready to meet the enemy. It all started with the meeting of the enemy at checkpoints at the entrance to Mariupol. So, without meeting the enemy, we took up positions in front of Mariupol and consolidated them.

I realized that I had made many mistakes that could have cost me my life. This was my first combat experience, but such a plan. We learned to fight in the city almost on the go. The main mistake that I had was to move anywhere and anywhere without fellows. You always need someone around, even if you go nearby.

The day I was shot in the head, all I remember is that a bullet hit me in the head from a window. The pain was not as strong as I thought. I fell and everything was like in slow motion, there was the same squeak as in the movies in my head, realizing that this may be the end. It was hard to breathe, I won't pass it on, but it's really hard...

My brothers heard me fall, dragged me away and began to examine me for medical help, but the wound was in the head and all they could do was help me get to the evacuation site. Strangely enough I took off my helmet and was still able to go down from the 7th floor...my head was very foggy, I'm grateful to the guys that they pulled me out.

Art by João "J-Dot" Alves

Ilya
Ukrainian Civilian
Mariupol
May 22nd

The first time the war came to my house, I was 13 years old, it was 2014. I lived in a small town near Donetsk, and alas, my city came under occupation. I left from there in 2016 to my father in Mariupol (He is also a migrant, but already from the city of Donetsk). My father is a musician, he used to work in a police band, but since 2019 he moved to a military band, because they pay more there.

I myself am a journalism student, I'm a big fan of the NBA, but now that's not the point. So, February 24, 2 hours before the announcement war, my father was urgently called at work, I didn't pay much attention to it, because it was the 3rd time in a week. But unfortunately, this was the last time I saw him at the moment.

I managed to leave Mariupol around March 16th. It was horror. From the end of February there was no heating, from March 1st there was no electricity, internet, water and gas. We cooked outside, under fire. When we left our house, the city looked like an apocalypse, because all the shops were robbed, no one did anything about it. I left the city on foot; I was able to leave on a ride.

The last time I personally spoke with my father was on February 28, all the following times - in the SMS version through his commander. In peacetime, his main task is music, but they constantly had military exercises, so they can be called full-fledged soldiers. All this time I was worried about him, but most of all I was afraid for Azov.

Words cannot convey what guys from Azov are heroes, but more on that another time. They surrendered on May 17, then I learned that he was slightly wounded in the leg. Now they are waiting for the exchange, I hope they are in normal conditions.

Week Fourteen: May 26 – June 1

Ukrainian Soldier
Battle of Lyman
May 26th

We were ambushed by a BTR hidden in a street. It fired its gun, and it tore my assistant's leg off from above the knee. We fired back with a rocket and tried to get him (the wounded soldier) off from the street and into cover.

We carried him by his arms around the corner but could not retrieve his leg. The next hour we were trying to get him to safety. He became tired and closed his eyes and was unconscious. Our ambulance came and picked him up. It was an ambulance team made of western soldiers.

They got him into the ambulance and drove away with him. He is alive still and recovering. He has asked to rejoin us when he heals. I told him on the messenger that he was crazy and should retire but he said he will come back to find his leg. We joked about his leg and how it is still out fighting Russians all by itself. Soldier humor is what keeps soldiers sane.

Art by João "J-Dot" Alves

"Krusader"
Western Volunteer
May 28th

93 days and still counting. The enemy proves brutal and relentless but the spirit of the Ukrainians are strong and unwavering. Since the very beginning of this war, I've witnessed firsthand all the stages that have come to pass. Starting with Russia's failed blitzkrieg operation and disastrous attempt to capture Kiev onto the Russian advancement in the south being pushed back from Mykoliav into Herson.

It certainly seems that this war hasn't gone anywhere according to plan for the Kremlin. Nowadays our time is spent ducking and dodging drones. Our villages are bombed continuously by heavy artillery and air strikes.
You must adapt quickly to this new type of warfare, or you will meet a certain grave.

The more damage we do to the Russians the better. The only way to keep these Russians from swallowing the entire country and killing tens of thousands of more people is by giving them the fight of their life. At the end of the day, the Russians fear us and are scared of death. The Ukrainians don't fear the Russians and are ready to die for their country.

Connor
Western Volunteer
June 1st

I got out of the US army shortly after Putin escalated the war in Ukraine and decided to go over there and help with humanitarian aid. I'm not an expert on Ukraine, nor do I have any awe inspiring or sobering combat stories, but I hope to add some perspective on the effect that this war and the preceding revolution has had on Ukrainian society as a whole.

I had previously spent time in Ukraine as a missionary, so I knew the culture fairly well and had a few contacts over there. I also speak Russian and a little Ukrainian. So, I packed a suitcase full of food, and got on a flight to Poland where I met up with one of my old missionary friends, who was doing supply runs into the country from the Netherlands. While I was there, I helped organize and deliver food and supplies for internally displaced refugees in and around the city of Vinnitsa. I also spoke at a local church.

During my previous trip to Ukraine in 2016, they were still recovering from their revolution two years prior. They were in the middle of reforming their government. I personally witnessed the establishment of their newly reformed National Police Service, after the old corrupt police force was disbanded.

When I arrived in Ukraine this past May, much had changed in ways I didn't expect. Some of the infrastructure was noticeably more modern than before. Over the past eight years Ukrainians have been taking measures to weed out corruption and improve the economy, and results were beginning to show. The highways were noticeably smoother. Another noticeable difference was the booming patriotism; Ukrainians were already patriotic, but now everywhere you look, you'll see billboards, murals, and other artwork featuring prayers for the nation, images honoring the courage of their military servicemen and first responders, celebrating their Cossack heritage, or quoting the phrase "Russian warship, go fuck yourself". The patriotic war song "Chervona Kalina" could be heard in every corner of the city. They also took down most, if not all of the Soviet monuments and statues.

As for my experience with the war itself, I was far removed from any fighting or bombing. The situation in Vinnitsa, where I stayed, was surreal. Apart from the occasional military checkpoints and air raid sirens that no one reacted to, life went on almost as normal. It was easy to forget that three away Kyiv was still being peppered with missile strikes. The only other noticeable war related oddity in Vinnitsa was the overcrowding due to the refugees.

Conflict and tragedy has a way of uniting and bringing out the best and worst in people like nothing else can. Ukrainians were united in the overthrowing of their dictator Yanukovich, and it seems to me they're united now more than ever before. As awful as this war is, I believe Ukraine will be a better nation for having endured it. As someone who has prayed and rooted for Ukraine since the start of their revolution in 2013, I'm encouraged by the progress they've made as a nation; and even though it's not my country, I'm proud to be even remotely associated with it.

Week Fifteen: June 2 - 8

Ukrainian Soldier
June 3rd

Seeing someone get shot is strange. War in many ways is like driving. You've seen the product of a car crash but almost never see it happen. For me it was the same with casualties. I had seen men wounded afterwards but never seen them become wounded.

A man I didn't know was working on enemies from a window in our building. A table was pushed up to the wall and his gun was laying on it while he worked.

He fell backwards and rolled on the ground grabbing at his shirt. I didn't know what had happened to him. The other soldiers who were new as well also were confused. We had not been in battle before. A Sergeant ran up to him and dragged him into the hallway and began to instruct us on what to do to help.

After the situation he spoke to us about what to do in the future. He was angry with us for not helping but told us he understood we were new and like children in this situation. We had no experience to deal with this. What was strange in my mind was the soldier was fine one minute. And the next minute there was a small hole in his arm and chest threatening to kill him. It is hard to understand how situations change so suddenly.

Anton
Swedish Volunteer
June 5th

I'm a 21-year-old male from Sweden. Previous experience in emergency medical care and former safety guard at oil refineries. Motivation to go to Ukraine: To help the affected people and hopefully help Ukraine regain independence.

In late April of 2022 I decided to go to Ukraine after getting a position in an armed ambulance unit based in Dnipro. I entered through Poland and went to Lviv. Of course, I was afraid and worried but while meeting all the refugees from the most affected regions I got the motivation to push through the fear. From Lviv I went to Kyiv. I remember seeing all the horrors of war on the way, mine fields, burnt out tanks and thousands of bullet holes. I've never experienced anything close to this and I'm sad that this was the reality of the people here. At my arrival to Kyiv, I was met by a fellow Swedish volunteer that helped me get connections within Ukraine and it was really nice to meet another swede because it had been a lonely journey.

I was informed that the Dnipro ambulance project was delayed, this wasn't a surprise and I presume it had something to do with the missile strike at the train station a couple days earlier. My Swedish friend offered me a position as a medical instructor for Ukrainian volunteers. I gladly accepted this responsibility as it could lead to saving lives at the front. I won't however take any credit for this as I personally think the other instructors did the most important bits and I want to thank them for their service.

At the camp we met with volunteer instructors from all over the western world and they were great men. I remember the Ukrainian volunteers being very enthusiastic in learning everything we thought them and all of them showed what a great people they were. All Ukrainians we met were very thankful and helped with anything they could, like driving us and giving food to us even though we probably had more than them. I felt great after meeting everyone at the base, and I couldn't be more convinced that we were doing the right thing.

My view was however challenged after meeting a few other international volunteers while on a visit to their camp. They clearly didn't care about helping Ukraine, they were just here to kill and thrive in combat. They had arrogance I've never seen before and were the opposite of everyone else I've met here. Smoking and watching pro war propaganda they sat and eagerly waiting for the front. I felt my character being challenged and I questioned if I was just a coward who feared true warriors or if they were just a bunch of lost souls. I guess they are doing the right thing at least? Heroes or demons? I'll leave you to decide what they are.

My time in Ukraine was cut short by my bank account hitting Zero and I had to go home. All the expenses including my gear had cost about 3,000 dollars and no sign of getting any from my group. I gained and lost a lot from my service.

Ukrainian Soldier
June 5th

Artillery is Heaven falling to earth and hoping you live through it. When the enemy works on your positions with weapons like this all you can do is get as small as you can in a trench, in a hole, or other cover. There is nothing you can do but take it. You cannot run away in most cases. You have to lie down and take the explosions and pray. The destruction is worse with trees and buildings.

Trees become shrapnel splinters that rip holes in you. Buildings become grenades with their bricks flying. The man who invented artillery is in hell I am sure of it.

It is frustrating. The enemy can sit long distances away and work on your positions while smoking cigarettes or having snacks, while we on the receiving end are trying to stay alive and whole.

Courage cracks under these bombardments. It feels like God is sending these weapons against you. Bullets are personal. They are aimed at you by another human. Artillery seems like something from another world. It is very hard to stay brave.

Ukrainian Soldier
June 5th

Drones have changed the way working on positions is done. I spoke of artillery and how it is terrifying. That is true. Drones are worse sometimes because you will hear nothing. You will see nothing. And then your position is exploding.

We are fortunate to be on equal strengths with drones with the Russians. Many civilian drones are converted for military use and drop bombs on the enemy. They are useful because there is no noise or warning.

Artillery is fired, the enemy can hear it. Drones can fly right above them and drop a bomb and they don't know until it explodes. This tactic works for the Russians too. Drones are just as scary as artillery, but probably more deadly because almost every bomb is a hit.

You just don't know when a man is looking at you through a camera. That is the scary part. My brother is in a unit where 6 men were killed in a trench because of a drone. They were lying down sleeping and they never woke up or knew what happened.

It is exhausting. All of your senses are always working. Listening for artillery. Listening for bullets being fired. Listening for drone noises. Looking for enemy soldiers. Looking for drones in the sky. The frontline is where the work is done, and it makes you very tired.

Art by João "J-Dot" Alves

Western Volunteer

June 7th

The funniest thing I ever heard was from an American. We were in trenches during the daytime. Nothing was going on, really. Sporadic artillery. Some gunfire in the distance. It was pretty chill where we were as far as wars go.

Anyway, so it's almost our second full day in the area, and a few of these former US military guys are chatting with another American down the trench. Then I hear this crystal-clear SpongeBob impression scream within hearing distance of the Russians:

'Gary! You are going to finish your dessert, and you are gonna like it!'

Week Sixteen: June 9 - 15

Ukrainian Soldier
June 9th

I'm eighteen-years-old and I signed up to fight because I'm from the occupied territories. My parents are still in the occupied areas. So, I'm fighting to get back to them and also free them. I have been fighting for a month and already.

At first, I was hiding down in the subway system which was the bomb shelter. I then went and signed up and after being trained they sent me directly to the front. Out of all the other soldiers around me, I am the youngest one. They look at me equally and as their comrade.

There aren't any moments that I regret coming out here. Before I was out of occupied territories, I had to help load up all the dead bodies. So, I have already seen enough. Nothing scares me, nothing bothers me, and nothing concerns me. I'm here to fight.

Ukrainian Soldier
Battle of Severodonetsk
June 10th

I have been a soldier since 2017. I am experienced in war before February and because of this I lead a machine gun team. We were on the frontline in Severodonetsk. My machine guns work well together.

Not the whole army works like this. Many units still do not use machine guns like western countries do in terms of working on the enemy in the advance. I was trained by American Marines how to use machine guns and PICMDEEP. (Employment principals)

We were advancing near Ivonin Park to work on the objective. The area was a Russian stronghold with many buildings. I placed my machine guns right of a storage building to use the angle of the road to our advantage. Two machine guns.

We had sight for 900+m. We stayed as others went NNE along the road on the right side of the road. Halfway down our sight we saw 10-12 Russian soldiers moving in a line toward us down the road coming toward us. They must not have known we were waiting in front of them. We fired before the others in front could. My machine guns killed half of all enemies in seconds.

My experience set up the situation to be success. But my soldiers using their mind and discipline are what saved lives on our side. I am proud to be their leader. Another machine gun on machine gun battle happened and I will tell of that as well.

We were forced away from that area by armored vehicles and infantry. Many of them almost immediately after our machine guns killed that group. We had no choice but to run backward to the trees.

We had moved back to positions we had earlier that day. On our way a Russian machine gun killed two infantry. We had no cover until the trees, so we all had to keep running. It was a bad moment for us. Many wounded and injured.

Our machine guns saved us from being worked on at close range. I placed one team behind a long, and another team in the hole. I ran from team to team to direct their shooting and to act as a target to give our machine guns time to find theirs back in the city. It worked. Soon most of our soldiers were back at the defenses and returned the feeling. (Returned fire) My machine guns worked in talking pairs until their (the Russian MG) stopped and was dead or retreating.

It was not a good day, but our machine guns did their jobs, and many more Ukrainian soldiers would be dead if our teams were not disciplined with firing and choosing targets. All of my guys and me lived through that day.

Western Volunteer
Battle of Severodonetsk
June 10th

We are outnumbered as fuck here in Severodonetsk. We were told the Russians pulled troops from Kherson and Kharkiv and other areas to get the city. It's like the battle here is swinging back and forth if that makes sense. From my experience here this place is by far the most intense. They want the city bad.

They don't care how many people they lose they want it no matter what. I can say now that I'm here in the Donbas area now I understand why they call it the meat grinder. When I was in Mykoliav I was in the second line on the front, every so often we would get artillery rounds, but it was rare, they didn't start hitting Mykoliav hard until after I left and the Russians began their new offensive.

But comparing Mykoliav to the Donbas area is a whole another level. When we do our CASEVACS (casualty evacuation) normally we drive a few blocks away from the fight, and normally they have our wounded waiting for us to do a quick grab and go.

But the artillery is what is really scary, because you can hear them going everywhere but again you don't know where they are going to land plus you have to watch out for drones, it's hard to tell if it's ours or not which is also scary as fuck.

But again about Severodonetsk this is my first actual urban combat experience, this is a whole another level, words cannot even describe how intense the battle actually is, one minute we have the upper hand and in a split second we are falling back because we are getting overwhelmed. It's scary the second we jump off the trucks, but then your adrenaline kicks into overdrive, helping you focus while the artillery and gunfire are going coming from everywhere.

When we go for wounded we don't know what to expect, and also at times we have to go look for them as well if it safe enough, but most of the time it isn't since the Russians are pushing hard.

I'm actually more scared of a BTR than a tank. So, with the tanks they are normally alone but a BTR is never really alone they got guys either in them or around them but never alone. It's hard for a tank at times to move around on the streets to swing that cannon around but the BTR has no difficulty swinging it and aiming it at you. We normally run when we see a BTR. Fuck that, hell no.

Ukrainian Soldier
Battle of Severodonetsk
June 11th

I am not a trained sniper or spotter. I am a soldier with good aim who was assigned with another good soldier to work as snipers. We have no official training in the job but are good at it from watching soldiers who are trained.

I returned from Severodonetsk after fighting there to rest. We (his partner) work on the enemy as a sniper team, always in communication with another team of real snipers. It is a good job. Our jobs are not to just work on enemy positions, but mostly to watch and report what we see. During our battle we only eliminated one enemy. It happened such as this. Our spot was inside of a three-story building. We watched a street ahead of our own soldiers behind us and below us.

Ahead we saw a head around the corner looking at us. It went away, and then came back. We looked through the magnified optic and saw he was speaking into a radio. His head was still looking down the street toward us when my partner shot him.

He fell down right away, and it was a success. Then he must have been rescued because he was dragged back around the corner. It was not eventful or worth speaking about but that is what happened. Other teams have more success than us. We learn from them everything they can teach. We are still new to this job.

Ten soldiers and our sniper team (sniper and spotter) moved down from the third floor and tried to cross the street to the rest of the unit. Crossing streets is very dangerous in the daytime. You are seen by human eyes and drones. When we leave buildings the first man looks outside down the street both ways, then at the sky for drones. Left, Right, Up. Then he runs. The others follow seconds later. First man runs. 1…2…3… second man runs. 1…2…3…just like that. Not always, because we can't let them learn our ways so we always changing how we cross. That's why I can say and share this.

This time a BTR from so far down the street we could not see started shooting. The man in front of me had his backpack completely shot off his back. It scared me because I thought it was his body (torso), but he kept running.

He didn't even see it was gone because of the adrenaline and how scary the moment was. When we were into safety we began to laugh together. We all made it. The only casualty was the backpack with our night vision inside of it.

Whenever we cross, we check to make sure our equipment is okay. As a sniper my most useful tool is my magnified scope. I was taught to make sure it is still tight and not loose. If it is loose, I cannot do my job. The commander said he was taught 'Weapon, Gear, Body' from foreign soldiers. This is now a skill we also practice.

"Viking"
Georgian Volunteer – International Legion
Battle of Severodonetsk
June 12th

I hate air force even more now. Fuckers bomb us relentlessly. There's a single Russian tank in the city that's been giving us trouble for a few days now.

Unlike what we've seen so far, this tank crew is solid. I mean they know what they're doing. Always changing position, shooting from cover where it's impossible to hit them back. They killed some of ours and I helped drag their bodies out...They're literally ripping holes in our defense, and we can't seem to catch them.

Can't help but respect this tank crew. First time I have met a worthy adversary in this war. All the more reason why I am so eager to blow them up.

It's weird. We've reached a point where we have mutual respect. But this tank crew is driving me nuts. Can't use NLAW, too much metal in the way. Too many buildings for Javelin. Gotta go old school. But I'll have to ambush it. And they make it impossible. They are a fucking great tank crew. Pity it's on enemy side.

Art by João "J-Dot" Alves

Ukrainian Soldier
Kyiv Oblast
June 12th

I notify families of their dead family member. I am one of the people responsible for talking to families when their family member dies in the military. I would like to be at the front. I would like to do anything than this.

I tell a mother her son is dead. I tell a father his son is dead. I tell a wife her husband is dead. It is the worst job in this war.

The families do not believe me sometimes. They tell me it is a mistake, or I am lying. They say this through tears, and I am not joking. I am not good at this job. Their faces make me wish I was the dead one instead of their family. I request a new job often because I cannot be the messenger of news like this anymore.

Ukrainian Soldier
Battle of Severodonetsk
June 13th

We watched Mariupol on the news. Now Severodonetsk has become the same battle in many ways. I will say the truth and not lie. It's very hard and I am scared.

We have many casualties and the Russians. The frontline is always moving forward or backward. Some days you will be in a building, and another day the building is the home to Russian soldiers.

Ukrainian Soldier
Battle of Severodonetsk
June 14th

Behind us is the river. I can look behind me and see it. In front of us less than 300m away are the Russians. The fighting is getting worse and desperate from both sides. I do not think we will be trapped here, but there is no place for us to go but forward.

I think maybe we will be trapped. But that means forward is where we must go. It is strange to feel. It is clear in my mind that we must keep fighting no matter what. We must not back into the river but go forward.

The mood is still good here. I am glad to fight for Ukraine. My brother's wife's family is in front of us, behind the Russians. I want to reach through them and say hello to them. (His brother's wife's family) So, we must go forward.

People fear another Mariupol for us. But we must not think of such things. We still have strength and desire to fight! Just as the Azovstal defenders did until the very end.

"Mickey Mouse"
Western Volunteer
Battle of Severodonetsk
June 15th

There are corpses out here two or three weeks old. The lines are so fluid in some parts that the killed are just left there, seen by the enemies when the take the position, and then seen by their friends once more when the position is taken back.

On the eastern side of the battlefield is a tree line. I'm not familiar with the area and haven't even seen a map so I don't know how far the city extends. But where we were, there were trees.

We got orders to dig around that area and right next to the spot I chose, I could smell it. It was a fucking body. It was nighttime, and I couldn't see it well, but I figured it didn't matter anyway so I kept digging.

As the sun came up, I saw it was two bodies next to me. Black from rot and the stench got worse as the day got warmer. The lips were so shriveled that you could see their teeth. Animals and insects had been at them, and it was honestly just horrendous to see what happens to a body when it decomposes.

It was two Russians like 5 feet from each other. I couldn't stand just looking at them, so I moved them both into my hole and filled it in. I spent the rest of the day in a friend's hole. When he asked why I hadn't dug my own one I told him the situation and he didn't object to my being there. All I can think and say is this. When I was in Afghanistan, I remember parts of it being really shitty. I remember sometimes tears welled in my eyes and I wanted to go home. This is ten times worse than that.

Art by João "J-Dot" Alves

"JJ"
Western Volunteer
Battle of Severodonetsk
June 15th

Its feeling like my days is numbered and I'd like to say some things. About me. Former military. Afghanistan veteran. Combat experienced. Three days ago, I was in a trench line listening to artillery. I got to thinking about the perspective of the enemy. Just a few hundred yards away are the Russians. Living through the same bullshit I am.

They've killed my friends. I've killed their friends. People say things about the leaders of these warring governments. Good things. Bad things. It's all politics. There's no politics out here. The grunt in the dirt has no say on what's going on. I'm here because I disagree with what their leader wants to do.

They are here because their leader told them to be. Both of us would rather be home, but we aren't. We are here eating piles of bullets and missiles because of some guys in suits. When I got here, I hated the Russians. They did some really vile things. But people don't quite understand soldiers. All of us would rather be at home with our families. And I just sort of had that realization today.

I've seen dead bodies before. Dead Taliban. Dead Afghan civilians. But that culture was so far removed and different from ours I couldn't really identify with it. I saw some dead Russians lined up by the road and I was shocked. I thought, 'These guys could be me.'

It's weird, man. I aim at them through my optics in modern military equipment, uniforms, and I see myself. Does that make sense? I guess what I'm trying to say is I don't harbor any hatred anymore. Just pity. Pity for them and for us. The sooner this is over the better.

I'm not making excuses or minimizing the crimes that have been committed. I'm just saying that I personally hold no hatred for them. I know I don't have as big of a stake in this fight as Ukrainians (except for my life) I'll keep fighting them as savagely as I can, but I don't hate them.

Week Seventeen: June 16 - 22

Ukrainian Soldier
June 16th

I understand what war is and what fear is. But raising voice for the right cause is something that any human should do. Endless calls to the President's, military and other hot lines gave nothing. So, I'm writing this text.

In April 2022 my unit assembled for training and further military service. People were settled in the trenches. Newcomers were digging those trenches and fortified them with materials that they bought themselves or which were brought by volunteers. Everyone was happy to do anything they could while waiting for the training.
The training never happened.

Most didn't get a chance to make even 30 training shots. We had 3 days training in combat engineering. Anti-tank and machine gun fighting - even less. When we asked about how we should fight without knowledge, the officers told us: 'Guys, you'll get it with time, no one will send you to the front anyways.'

Same time I've seen how officers were writing into journals hundreds of training hours that never existed. This miserable approach of USSR years surprised me, but my thought was: this is Army! We probably will have more training. I was wrong. We were recommended to watch YouTube videos and learn from there.

After a month *of such training,* we were sent to the south region. Our battalion is getting into the real fight under the heavy shelling. One soldier got blown up because he didn't know that cluster grenades can't be touched.

When majority of men began to say that they don't know what to do and have no weapons - the threats of courts and jail were commanders' answer. The reality of this threats made its work.

My objections that people are being sent to the certain death like Zhukov's army, I was named a coward and told that I'm bringing down fighting spirit. One of the commanders of the battalion threatened my life. I was told that my new assignment will be with him, and I will be left somewhere in the field. To protest I wrote a report for transfer on the basis of my total disagreement with the officers and that I am a father of four.

Ukrainian Medic
Battle of Severodonetsk
June 16th

Moving wounded who are not able to walk is extremely difficult at the front. We have donated stretchers from hospitals and foreign countries and that makes it easier. But this is still not an easy thing to do.

In the city, if a man has been shot and cannot walk or his leg is broken, we have to carry him behind the frontline. The difficult part is doing this safely and having the evacuation team finding us.

The area is rubble and destroyed buildings. Moving through this safely and not being seen by drones or Russian snipers just makes it more difficult. Sometimes evacuation is impossible, and the casualty has to wait hours before we can move him. Some don't make it.

These are the hardest moments. He is asking for help, but you have to keep telling him it is not safe to move, or we make more casualties. Some wounded understand this, but others are too full of pain to have reason and begin screaming to move him to a hospital.

It is very hard on your mind during these moments because you want to help him because he is your fellow soldier, but at the moment it is impossible.

We do get most to safety. We move the wounded to a point safe for the evacuation team and give him to them. Sometimes they even come to us. Driving right up to the position and getting him quickly. Helicopter evacuation is impossible in most of the city. Our helicopter is our legs.

Art by João "J-Dot" Alves

Western Volunteer
Battle of Severodonetsk
June 17th

I'm part of a group of volunteers fighting in Ukraine around Severodonetsk. Former US Military. Seen and been in some pretty decent combat before but not like this, man. Not even close.

The Taliban were very amateurish in firefights and their IDF, if any, wasn't very accurate. Don't get me wrong, the fights there were tough but nothing like facing a uniformed military.

There are jets and drones here bombing us constantly. Tanks, BTR's, BMP's, everything you can think of, they've brought it here. I've gotta say though, as scary as this shit is, it's kind of fun. Just getting handed rockets and as much ammo as you can carry and just basically being told to hunt Russians beyond our position.

We go out, do our jobs, and come back. The thing that pisses me off the most is the Russian aircraft. They're constantly flying around and bombing shit. But my favorite thing to do is shoot rockets at enemy vehicles. In a way I kind of feel like the GWOT roles are reversed.

Here I get to be the guy sneaking around bushes and tree lines taking pot shots at troops and tanks. And here they get all the cool vehicles, air cover and IDF. In a weird way it's given me a new sense of respect for our old enemies. It took some serious balls to face us in a firefight and they did it with less than what I have now.

Kind of wish we had a battalion of them here with us. Wouldn't that be a sight? Honestly if some just magically showed up, I don't think I'd be that upset.

Ukrainian Soldier
Battle of Severodonetsk
June 17th

My brother was killed at the Donetsk airport in 2014. It is different for me and for most Ukrainians. I hate them. I have been a soldier since 2019 as soon as I could be a soldier. I have fought in the east for years. I am older now than my brother was when he died. I live every day for my brother. Western soldiers from USA and UK and more cannot understand how we feel because they do not live here. I am glad they are here. Thank

313

you. But the feelings of the soldier on Instagram today do not represent me.

We want the occupier out. To do this we have to hate them. We cannot say please leave because they will not. So, we move them out by working them with guns, bombs, tanks, and our blood. I will die like my brother if I have to. I would be proud for that.

The Russians and their friends took my brother. But they also gave me more brothers because of their invasion ambitions. I will call them brothers until I die. The soldiers I fight with are my brothers. They are the best and only brothers I have. They fight on and so will I.

I do not wish destruction on all Russia. I just wish they will leave and never return. Western world needs to understand how we feel. This is not a fight from former brother but mortal enemies now. Fire and water. Two cannot live here at once. Only one and everything will be Ukraine.

"Viking"
Georgian Volunteer – Ukrainian Foreign Legion
Battle of Severodonetsk
June 17th

I think that's the only thing that really affects me mentally. I dragged out 3 Ukrainian SOF casualties. Blood all over me. Young men. No emotions, no feelings. Seeing abandoned animals just fucks with me man. Or a cat dead on the street caught in a shelling. They don't close their eyes when they die. Their mouths are open. Looking in petrified shock. It's absolutely heartbreaking man.

I don't understand how people can leave them behind. I have 3 cats. I'd rather stay to look after them than leave them in such a situation. And cats are pretty independent. They don't really need us. But a dog? Fully dependent on your care. Last safe house we lived in came with 2 cats and a German shepherd. One of the cats was really old. Didn't have any teeth left. I had to make soups for him.

The dog was so stressed. I mean constant artillery. And their hearing is so much more sensitive than ours. Plus, we understand what's going on and they don't. He would turn in circles and bark at the air. Poor thing.

This GSD was letting us feed him but wouldn't let us touch him. He actually bit one of our guys who tried to pet him. He was so angry he went for his sidearm. I don't think I've ever snapped onto target that fast in combat man. I was really gonna shoot his ass if he shot the dog. I have absolutely no tolerance for animal cruelty.

Western Volunteer
Battle of Severodonetsk
June 17th

I will describe a feeling strange to people. It's not 'Fun', but it is, if that makes sense. Surviving something you shouldn't have survived.
I was running across a street and literally almost ran right into a stream of bullets hitting a wall in front of me. I basically baseball slid on the ground to stop myself. I got back up and ran back to the building I came from.

As soon as I cleared the door more bullets came right in after me. As soon as I was done shitting myself and wishing that Russian soldiers received poorer marksmanship training, I couldn't stop laughing.

It was the weirdest thing. I had almost died twice within 10 seconds and my first reaction was to laugh. Everyone around me was laughing too. Man, I felt so pumped up. Like pumped up and stupid enough to run back out there and try that run again.

Adrenaline is a hell of a drug and thank God we decided not to run back out that door or else the dude with an MG trained on the door would surely have cut me in half like a piece of toilet paper. Don't believe the propaganda. They can shoot. And shoot well.

After the adrenaline wore off, the exhaustion hit me and so did the reality of what happened 30 minutes before. I had almost died twice. I was very lucky, and it reminded me to take better care of myself and observe my surroundings more before moving out of cover. Not everyone gets the chance to get a lesson like that and live to learn from it.

Scott A. Laurent
Photographer
Northeastern Front
June 18th

We're in a damp little cellar, chatting about all and everything. The radio sporadically spits some things in Ukrainian, but this time all become quiet and pause and listen. In one voice they utter a 'blyaaat!' and stand up as one. One of them just tells me, 'Two wounded' as we put our helmets and go up and out.

Some long minutes later, under the cherry trees and the sounds of whistling mortar rounds, a beat-up, spray-painted van comes in drifting. The guys open the rear doors, and I can hear a kind of long, low groan, half pain half fear. A soldier comes down, walking, bent forward. His neck and face is a mess of bandages and blood. He holds his fucked-up forearm, dangling, numb from the tourniquets and the wounds.

They unload another soldier lying on his side on a stretcher, he's nearly half naked, huge wound on his lower back, a piece of metal poking out of one of them. He doesn't move, doesn't make any sound and at that point I guess he's either dead or unconscious.

A frontline medic stumbles out of the van, walks aimlessly. His pale grey eyes are empty, cold sweat all over his face. He is full of dust and shit. He limps toward me, and I notice his leg is soaked in blood. 'You alright?' I ask him, pointing at his leg. His eyes locks into mine. 'It is not my blood.' He's completely shellshocked. Another one dropped his AK and is emptying a bottle of water over his head.

Meanwhile our team is taking care of the wounded, calmly, professionally, they assess the wounds, cut off the clothes, change the bandages.

I shoot slowly, try to make myself as small as possible. Also, I try to stay sensitive and only take useful and respectful pictures. I don't want to stick my camera in the face of someone whose life, at that very moment, is taking the most painful, frightening turn. I go around the soldier on the stretcher, so I can see his face.

He looks pretty young yet hardened. Dirt all over his mouth and nose. His eyes open, looking in the distance. No expression, no pain, nothing. He breathes slowly. I wonder what is going on in his mind.

They put the soldiers in the second ambulance to drive them to the hospital in town. The first one is lying on the spare wheel and a blanket. I can see a dozen tiny bleeding holes on his back. The two blasted medics and the last wounded are shoved inside too. The slam the doors shut. As they go, the driver tells us to go back in the cellar before the Russians shell us too.

Ukrainian Soldier
Battle of Severodonetsk
June 18th

The occupants have many different weapons they use against us. Worst is the artillery. Hundreds of explosions make the land look like the moon, and one shell can kill 20 men if they are not covered. The impact is impossible to predict. I will say I am scared of this.

Machine guns are used in big numbers. Most Russians don't use them properly and because of this they are mostly dangerous if you are in the open. The same for rifles. After 300m rifles need to be used by professionals to be very dangerous.

Snipers. Some of them have thermal scopes. We have lost men on patrols and in the trenches at night because they are locking discipline and stood too long or were just unlucky. I have not seen a badly trained sniper yet.

Aircraft can be worse than artillery because you can see the jet coming for you. I cannot find words to explain what this is like to see. You can just imagine.

Drones are used in numbers too. We try hard to conceal positions from the sky with whatever we can. Blankets. Wood. Metal.

Last is tanks. Fighting a tank for me is scary and also an adrenaline injection. To be so small and destroy something so big makes you feel accomplishment and pride. What we need is more weapons and more training. Too many soldiers do not have the training they need to survive.

317

Western Volunteer
Battle of Severodonetsk
June 19th

We were on a clearance of 8 buildings (a block) in the city of Severodonetsk with a platoon minus. We cleared 5 of 8 buildings ourselves and with our drone saw 10 enemy walking into one of the last two, which we supposed was a Russian OP beforehand.

Once we had cleared 5 of the 8, we heard them and had noticed a generator, food and water, and a vehicle with an emblem of a known Chechen group. We estimated 20 or so enemy so we planned to hit them.

After opening their front door with a few rockets and heavy fire into doors and windows, my team and I cleared out building 6 of 8 next door so our two buildings faced their two across the street (about 20 meters away). As we cleared to the roof, we started exchanging fire with both buildings more-so the one directly across from us.

After attempting to head back down the stairs, we received very accurate sniper fire (we think, or just a really good fuckin shot) into the window in the video. We exchanged more and more fire. Backing up a bit exchanging fire on the roof myself and a mate of mine are pretty sure we got two in the top floor windows but neither of us could confirm our kills. While on the stairs we lost communication with friends and were stuck.

Still exchanging fire, we lost one of our mates, Jordan Gatley. Our mates finally came and said there was a tank around the corner (T72 modified) and was about 50 meters away. They opened up with suppressing fire, we got out. I got one in a window covering my teammate and being the last one down other friendly's hit the T72 with a rocket and it fucked off. We got our boy along with one other KIA to safety and exfilled.

In total we lost two and got 20 of them. (Friendlies moved into the area later and confirmed the enemy dead) They also were not a Russian OP we found out, it was about 50 ABU (Russian/Chechen/Spetsnaz), and it was a hell of a gun fight. I'll leave it at this, Jordan was a part of black team, he was the best fucking soldier I've ever known, and he gave it his all until the last.

Ukrainian Soldier
Battle of Severodonetsk
June 19th

Leaving Severodonetsk was a difficult task. The last bridge was destroyed over a week ago. The territory we controlled was our back to the river, with the enemy in front of us. We had to leave on small boats or by swimming.

Before I left, the fighting in the city was very intense. Oh yes. It was frightening sometimes. Chechen soldiers are not the ones from Mariupol I saw on TikTok or telegram. The Chechens here wanted to fight.

For me the worst part of fighting was the exhaustion. Moving around was very difficult and being alerted to the enemy day and night was at times too much. There was little time to rest. I have been seen by the doctor for my ears.

My ears have constant ringing and now any noise louder than a speaking volume causes pain. A BTR shot its gun into the building we were in an explosion on the other side of the wall injured my hearing. I will recover.

Ukrainian Soldier
Battle of Severodonetsk
June 20th

Having soldiers killed is for me heartbreaking. It is like losing a child. You have to be strong for the others. Having soldiers captured and not having guaranteed fates is different.

As a commander, you worry for them. You allowed them to be prisoners of the enemy. I cannot guess their fate. They could be treated as honorable soldiers. They could be executed or beaten. I do not know. Not knowing is what hurts me.

I would rather not surrender. I cannot make that decision for them. If the moment comes that is a choice I believe most men need to make for themselves. No matter military code. To fight and die for our country or to give up after having fought honorably and possibly live in captivity or worse.

The effect it has on the soldiers still here is extremely negative. They are all friends with each other. And it is hard on them. They want to know where they are. They want to know where they are taken and being treated well or poorly. I do not have these answers.

It is just difficult. For me it is as bad as having soldiers killed because at least the condition of the dead is known. I cannot really say more than this. I hope these thoughts I have can help some understand the stress of leadership in these situations. People want officers to know everything but the situations on the battlefield rarely allow us to know more than the soldiers themselves.

"Viking"
Georgian Volunteer – International Legion
Battle of Severodonetsk
June 21st

We crossed the river early in the morning. Didn't really help because there was light, and our infiltration was spotted. Moving to your point of entry building was under fire, from that tank crew I praised before.

Nevertheless, we made it to our building. From there, we cleared the building on the left, that all on video. We recovered some equipment from there too. After that we went to complete our objective and clear the whole sector ahead of us. 4 giant hangars and a building. It was very hot, we had to move fast, and we took AT launchers with us so it was really, really exhausting. Took us good 30-40 minutes to do all that and we came back, 4 of us, the other 4 were holding the building. So, we could take a rest.

I removed my equipment and found a corner to sleep in. I was exhausted. Few minutes later our tank rolled up and began firing right next to us. Can't catch a god damn break. Russians responded with artillery. It's a full orchestra dedicated to not letting me sleep.

So, I do the only reasonable thing and put on my Peltor ear protection, switched off, shutting off all noise. Mind you, our tank is covering behind our building, so we get hit a lot but that can't get in the way of my nap.

By the time they woke me up to let others rest, apparently, I missed a Russian tank coming out to duel our tank for like 30 minutes, back and forth. Plus, artillery. Plus, aircraft trying to bomb the tank right behind our building. Also, our guys firing bunker busters into enemy buildings from inside our building legit 10 meters from me.

I slept through all of that.

When I woke up, I almost opened a grenade I was so mad they didn't wake me up. Exhaustion catches up with you man when you exert as much as I did. It's always wise to bow out and let someone take over because you make mistakes. Or sleep while you shouldn't. Battle Fatigue is real.

Week Eighteen: June 23 - 29

Ukrainian Soldier
June 23rd

Weeks ago, I was part of a team that investigated the site of a shot down Russian helicopter. We approach the area with guns up in case someone survived and ready to retaliate. But we all know that no one survives crashes like that. I had never seen a helicopter crash, but I knew from the sound no one survived.

We go through the area and on the ground is someone's body still on fire. It is mostly bones and other material.

We stay until the fire is out and search what we can. The body is a skeleton now and it made me wonder what his mission was. Why he was here. Three hours before he was a living and breathing pilot. Now he is a skeleton, and no one will ever know who he was.

This made me think how many bodies are decaying or burnt in the cities and trees that will never be found and identified. For me it does not bother me. A body is just a body. But I do think of the soldier's families.

Zura
Georgian Volunteer – International Legion
Marksman Community
Battle of Severodonetsk
June 24th

I was in the first team of the international legion who deployed in Severodonetsk. We knew it would be rough, we knew it would be a very difficult mission, but we still went in. We numbered 24 guys and unfortunately, we lost some good men there. The worst part I remember from going in was the city was already kind of on fire. A lot of buildings were destroyed, and we went into one of the forward positions. There was a reporter with us, and I said, "The most important part for us is for all of us to go back home", but the worst part is not all of us went back home.

As soon as we went in, they started shelling us. We lost one of our commanders and had three wounded in the first ten minutes. At the moment we thought all of us were going to fucking die there, but I started making jokes like, "Don't worry boys, I ordered KFC and it'll be here in 15 minutes." The boys started looking at me like I was a Special Ed student. One funny thing I remember is when we were going in, one of my Canadian teammates, he was not wearing a helmet. I was like, "What the fuck bro, you're going to need it." And he was like, "No man, I know what I'm doing."

So as soon as we went in and all that fucked up stuff happened, a lot of artillery. Then we went into one building and were holding it. As soon as I entered, I look at my left and I see that guy wearing a helmet. I laughed and he said, "Yeah, seems like I'm going to need it."

Even through all those hard times, we still tried to keep it positive. I'm one of the lucky ones who survived that. We had several wounded and two dead after that mission. That interview of mine with the reporter was shown in almost every country in the world, but unfortunately no one has mentioned the brave warriors lost. They were some of the most fearless men I have seen in my life, they knew what they were fighting for and what the cost was. They didn't back down and will always be remembered.

"Viking"
Georgian Volunteer - International Legion
Battle of Severodonetsk
June 24

We were on some FOB OP Using drones to walk in artillery on the enemy positions. At some point our position got hit by something. I believe it was a tank shell, because it had a lot of pressure and not much shrapnel. That shrapnel found one Ukrainian guy though. I was about 10-15 meters from it. The explosion kicked up a lot of dust, so l rushed towards the Ukrainians and asked where the guy was. I could hear his screams but due to dust I couldn't see anything.

They said they couldn't see, and they would wait for dust to settle to get him. Naturally that didn't sit with me. Besides, I saw my Commander's silhouette in the dust, he wears all black uniform. I could see him struggling to drag the wounded guy towards us, so I ran towards him and helped. Lifting heavy things is like 70% of my life so, it turned out useful.

I brought him to relative safety and applied a tourniquet on his arm. He had shrapnel wounds to his arm. Then I brought him down to the basement, where they had a female medic.

She was absolutely freaking out man. Hands shaking, body trembling. It was odd to see medic lose it that easily. I checked his wounds, he had a shrapnel wound on his ass, I cut his pants, saw the wound, and told her to patch him, and she started to just gently put a bandage on top.

At that point I knew she wasn't up to it. So, I got proper gauze out of my pouch and pushed it in, inflicting a lot of pain on the guy but clotted the blood flow. Then I applied pressure dressing everywhere that was needed. He was evacuated soon after.

Turns out this guy was the medic's husband. That's why she was freaking out. It's understandable. Guy will be fine. It wasn't anything too bad. It's a whole different feeling to save a life, man. Funny enough, I was given a crash course on doing first aid by a friend of mine here just couple of days back. He showed me how to properly dress a wound. Came in a clutch. He definitely gets the assist points.

Vlad
Russian Soldier
June 24th

We were in an accidental ambush. I won't give away where but it's busy right now. We were in a position in forest doing some advancement work for the infantryman, and one Ukrainian tank come down the road but doesn't see me or out team.

We had some more men down the way on the right in more forest and they were able to neutralize and capture the crew, soon later the rest of the Ukrainians came through on foot.

The ambush turned into a fight, and we used all the stuff we had with us, the machine guns, PKM the grenades and all our ammo. We had to send a man back to get more because we only packed small to do the reconnaissance work.

I've lost my hearing for a few days, and we had no losses and no injured yet, but we have captured 16 soldiers and there many dead right now. These soldiers are different than the ones in Mariupol. They have less experience. I don't see many of their officers here.

Western Volunteer
Eastern Front
June 25th

Right away the difference between Russian regulars and the DPR is apparent. Russian troops are typically better trained, better equipped, and have more assets available to them such as air, artillery and drones. The DPR guys though, it's like looking at a time machine across the battlefield. They're wearing helmets and body armor from the 90's or earlier. Carrying captured Ukrainian weapons or surplus weapons from WW2.

We had a sniper problem not too long ago on a part of the front, so we sent a team to find him and get him. Our snipers got him, and they brought back his equipment. It was a pair of binoculars and a Mosin Nagant 91/30 with a bent bolt fitted with a PU optic. Manufactured 1944.

This brought me back to my Afghan days. You don't go to war with equipment like this unless you are motivated. And he actually got two guys with this thing from a considerable distance in the twilight hours. The DPR guys aren't the guys to be laughing about. They're equipped poorly, trained poorly, but their morale seems ultra-high, and they are motivated to get into fights. From what I understand a bunch of them are hardcore fighters who've spent time in trenches since 2014-15.

Some of the hard-fuck Ukrainian guys I've met have fought them for years and even they warned us about how deadly these guys can be. I made the mistake in Afghan of thinking guys in sandals with 50-year-old AKs would be easy to fight against. That lesson transferred well here.

Art by João "J-Dot" Alves

"Zura"
Georgian Volunteer – Ukrainian Foreign Legion
Marksman Community
Battle of Severodonetsk
June 25th

On our last mission, finally me and Viking got a chance to work together. Can't say the location but it was a heavy artillery fight from both sides.

We were resting in one building. I was laying on a chair and looking outside, tired...kind of falling asleep and suddenly fuckin SU25 dropped A huge bomb on a building next to us about 40 meters from us.

All of us rushed to the bunker right away, we heard a second explosion. I looked around and couldn't see Viking. I went back upstairs, and I found him relaxing, laying on a couch smoking a cigarette and enjoying his first-class ticket to the show.

I was yelling, 'Get your ass in the bunker!' and he goes: 'Relax kid, it's normal and beautiful!'

He's the craziest badass mother fucker I know and I'm proud he is my friend and my mentor.

Ukrainian Soldier
June 26th

Every video or picture you see of dead soldiers makes you a small bit numb to death. It is worse seeing it for yourself. I had seen dead people at funerals before the war but not like this.

I was a civilian not long ago. Now I am a soldier and already numb to it. I think to myself every dead person I see is a person. A person who had a mother and a father. Maybe a pet. A person who had people and animals who loved him.

That is hard for me to keep thinking about. I hate thinking about it because it makes the war harder. I wish I could see the bodies as not people, but I cannot help it. So many families will be missing a person and so many cemeteries will be full of new occupants.

I have not killed anyone, and I hope I do not have to. I told this to my commander, and he threatened to have me removed for cowardice. I understand that soldiers need to kill to defend our homeland, but I would not want to kill anyone.

I am not a tough man like other soldiers. I do not want to kill someone. I have fired less than 100 shots in training and don't know if I could do it in real life at a person. I am a patriotic soldier. I believe in our country and its goals I just do not want to hurt someone even if they are our enemy. I don't understand this war.

Ivan
Ukrainian Civilian
Kyiv
June 26th

Russians killed my brother. My name is Ivan. I lived in Ukraine, Kyiv. I went to the 10th form and had to graduate from school in one year, in 2023. We all lived in peaceful city. Kyiv was becoming better and better every day. But everything had stopped in the early morning of 24th of February. On that day, Putin gave a speech in which he announced the starting of "Special Operation in Donbass".

All people in Ukraine woke up because of a great number of explosions. I was in Kyiv at that moment. I woke up at 5AM because all my family were in a panic and my mum told me that the war started. I came near the window and saw and heard explosions. I can't even explain what I felt in that moment and an air siren started to sound.

We started taking the most essential things and left house. We spent one hour in the car park under our building. Then our parents decided to send us to a village near Kyiv. When we were leaving Kyiv, we all cried. We didn't want to leave home and our, but it was very dangerous for us to be in Kyiv.

We were all very frightened and didn't know what would happen next. We were near a big city - Borispol, when they again threw a bomb at a military base. Our car jumped into the air and stopped. I had never been so scared before. After that we continued driving to that village. During our drive, we saw a lot of tanks and ambulances which were going to the war.

When we came to that village, I could not even talk or eat. Closer to the evening, it was more and more tanks in that village blocking streets because it was a huge military base near it. On the next day, my parents came, and we decided to go to the Carpathians where I spent all 4 moths of the war.

My brother Yuri was a real patriot. He had been defending Ukraine since 2014, but he was badly injured before the big war and then had to be taken to a rehabilitation. When the all-out war started, he was the first one in the village to go and defend Ukraine. He was killed four days ago. We will never forgive Russia for my brother's death and killed defenders and civilians. Glory to Ukraine!

Ukrainian Soldier
June 28th

You can see many things with a drone. Some are changed to accommodate grenades or mortars to drop on the enemy. For me, mostly I use a drone to observe and report what is seen at the front.

Enemy movement. Tracking tanks, supplies being moved. It is like being a bird and my job is to watch. Sometimes I see some funny things. Russians don't think they are being watched but they are. My partner watched a Russian finish himself (touch himself) in a shed. Other times we see them lay in the sun without clothes or throw rocks at each other when in defensive positions.

To be trusted with a drone is for me an honor. They are highly needed at the front and losing one can be extremely negative for the unit. I have never used a mortar or a grenade with one but have watched some do this and learn how to aim them.

Ukrainian Soldier
Eastern Front
June 29th

I have not experienced dead bodies before February. Not even family members or friends who are old. Not even a funeral ceremony. I saw the first dead body of my life in March. It was a dead Ukrainian soldier in a truck. They took his body away. I saw him and was disgusted and very sad. He must have a family.

I have been at war since March as a frontline soldier and have seen many bodies. They do not do anything to me anymore. Dead Russians.

Dead Ukrainians. Dead animals. I see them all and walk past them as someone would walk past a dead bird.

I see it but don't feel anything. My senses to death have been removed. Many people I care about (fellow soldiers) are gone. Someone said it was like a phone obituary. I look at my phone and see names who I can no longer speak to.

It makes me grateful I am still walking. The memories of our friends and family cannot die because some of us will survive and speak about them. Ukraine is not unaware of death. The last 100 years has seen many holes dug for our people. But we are not gone yet!

Week Nineteen: June 30 - July 6

Ukrainian Soldier
June 30th

I wanted to be a soldier since I was small. 2014 my father was a patriot and fought for Ukraine. I joined the army two years ago. I had fun during the trainings. I liked to sleep outside, to rappel, the tanks, the guns, it seems like a man's task, and I enjoyed it.

Then the war began and all of these things I enjoyed I do not enjoy anymore. I try to stay away from tanks because they attract drones and rockets. Sleeping outside in a trench is cold and wet and I never feel like I sleep.

It is hard to be a soldier in war. It is easy to be a soldier in relative peace. I did not have a rotation to the Donbas before it started. I was a peacetime soldier in the interior. I am a good soldier. I am not afraid. I do my job and fight with the rest. But I do not enjoy it anymore.

To be a soldier is to pretend you are an actor. To fight cheerfully for the others near you. Even if you do not mean it. To bring morale down is a crime to soldiers. We must all do our part no matter how much we hate this.

In training no one dies. Here people die all the time. Most of the soldiers I trained with before are dead or in other places. I have new people with me all the time and I don't know anyone. It is lonely sometimes being an older soldier. I am 24 and the oldest man sometimes.

In the position is usually two or more soldiers. We bring water, food, and other things to survive daily that we need. A hole is dug behind the position for shitting if you need, or if a battle is happening, you hold it, shit yourself, or shit in the hole dug for grenades they can land in the position.

Equipment we bring are rifles, 3 - 10 reloads for each man, at least one rocket if available to fight tanks, grenades, batteries if available. A tool for digging. One blanket per soldier, waterproof if possible, and several other things.

If there is time, we connect the positions with others to make trenches. I try to be near the hole with the machine gun to be close to its huge amount of bullets it can fire at the enemy. I don't want to be too close because it can attract lots of attention from the occupants.

The best advice for living in these positions come from soldiers who fought in them before February 24th. Before February 24th, most soldiers had not lived in the positions. Their experience is the best to follow because it makes things easier for us.

The best advice I learned is to use a wooden board to cover the position and to have dirt and plants on top to look like the land around it. It hides you from drones and soldiers. Dead grass can be used on the floor to soak water and to give better warmth when you are able to sleep. Living in positions is like an animal, but you can do small things to make it better.

Ukrainian Soldier
Azov Regiment
Former POW from Azovstal
Repatriated to Ukraine
June 29th

We left the factory (Azovstal) in groups. I helped carry a wounded man almost 1km from the factory to the designated point. We were told to get in lines. The only voices were the Russian soldiers telling soldiers to raise their arms or take their jackets off. None of us said anything other than our names.

A Russian soldier came up to me in line, told me to remove my jacket. I removed it. He searched me and went to the next man. Once our group was searched and had given names we stood.

We were told to turn right and walk to a bus. We were told to get on the bus and four Russians came on with us. We sat there for over an hour before we left. Not anyone looked back at the factory.

*Surrender at Azovstal. May 20th. Interviewed after repatriation to Ukraine on June 29th.

Art by João "J-Dot" Alves

Ukrainian Soldier
June 29th

My grandfather was a soldier in the Red Army at Sevastopol. He told my father stories about the German invaders and his fighting in the trenches. This history in our family lead me to become a history major and study abroad.

Now I am a soldier, back in my homeland I'm in trenches not far from where my grandfather once fought. My father told me that the war tormented my grandfather. He took lives. German lives, but lives still. I have also followed his footsteps in this experience. It makes me want to cry.

"Viking"
Georgian Volunteer – International Legion
Battle of Severodonetsk
July 1st

Last operation was a disaster from the start. We went to locate and assault some tanks and ended up spending the nights in a trench. I hate trenches. I'd rather be breaking down doors and breaching than to wait in a pre-made mass grave to get bombed.

In the morning Russians had brought up a massive concentration of armor and attacked. One of our sister units, made of Belarusians was smashed completely. We were told to evacuate them. They already had three wounded and two dead by the time we began movement.

It was a thick, impassable brush that destroyed my kit. Branches were literally ripping off my pouches. We didn't know where we were. They had no map with them, no GPS...Nothing. We spent two hours looking for them in enemy controlled territory and never found them.

Some of this shit is just basics man. Like having a radio on you when you recon; or having a map with you or a GPS to locate yourself. We could've saved some of them if we knew their exact location.

The only guy talking on the radio was hopeful. We were coming. His last words were:
"Tank came for me." Then silence.

It was heartbreaking. We couldn't find them in time. We tried our best, but with the massive open fields in Eastern Ukraine without exact coordinates we were looking for a needle in a haystack.

Besides, we could never carry the wounded out through that forest. It was an impossible mission from the start. On our way back to base, we had a head-on collision at high speed due to bombardment and consequent low visibility through smoke. I almost died in a car crash. My injuries are not severe, but it will take time to rehabilitate. I hope to get back into action soon. There's still work to do.

Former Russian Soldier
Russia
July 3rd

The army in Russia is very unfair. Especially for conscript soldiers. We are used as free slave labor. We had very little real combat training. Hazing and hatred rules the barracks. We also had problems because of ethnicities.

Those people who could not avoid getting into the army go as conscripts. Very often from the southern republics of Russia. Included in this are the Muslims from the Caucasus.

Muslims from the south of Russia are a bit physically stronger than most other Russian soldiers. And so, they built a prison hierarchy in the barracks, and their own laws. They beat other soldiers. Humiliate them. Treat them like animals, and the officers encourage this treatment because it keeps conscripts afraid and obedient.

Most soldiers will try to go to hospital for as long as they can, even years, to get away from the barracks. Soldiers will make up illnesses or suicidal thoughts to get themselves into the hospitals. I knew a friend in there for a year.

Ruslan
Ukrainian Soldier
Azov Regiment
Former POW from Azovstal
Repatriated to Ukraine
July 3rd

I left for war because I could not sit at home when my brothers died as heroes. I am not a perfect person, but I am not a traitor, and it was a matter of honor for me to go into battle without any conscience. Each person is individual, and everyone behaves differently in battle, but there were guys with me who went into battle without hesitation. Some were already wounded, and still ran from the hospital to stand shoulder to shoulder with their brothers.

Fear is a normal phenomenon, it must be controlled, if you do not manage it, it will eat you, and it will not lead to any good consequences. I'm not saying that I'm a brave person, it's just that the bravest hearts were with me.

There were many funny cases, it is difficult to fight and survive without humor. You must not think about the bad, but when you find out that your friend died, it's depressing, but we understand that the death of a man, as a warrior, is a great feat.

We are on our land, we did not fall to anyone, and it is our duty to protect our relatives, we are a brave nation, I do not want to be a slave, I want to live in a free and strong country.

I personally did not see any Russian prisoners, but I know that nothing bad was done to them, because we have military dignity and honor, and a prisoner is a person who will not harm you. What is most memorable about the battle is the chaos that surrounds you, and you see things that very few people are used to. Also, the faces of the fallen heroes remain in my head forever, and you know, you have to go to the end.

I lost my leg from being hit by an anti-tank missile (ATGM), which just cut off my leg like a knife. I was helped by my brave comrade, who saved my life and gave me his tourniquet, because my tourniquets and pockets were just blown away by the blast wave.

When I was wounded, we first we ran across the road, taking with us an ammunition kit, then I heard a whistle and in a split second I saw a bright fire flying straight at me, and that was it. I lost consciousness three times, lost three liters of blood, but still something made me think, I needed to get out of this mess. I remembered my friends, my relatives, my heroic soldiers in combat, and my girlfriend. I promised myself to get to the basement, where I was operated on.

I did not lose a drop of humor, I joked all the time, it was very it hurts, but the doctors, honor and praise, did everything to keep me alive.

Western Volunteer
Eastern Front
July 5th

What Can I say, man? This is the biggest, weirdest mix of soldiers you will ever see in any theater of war ever. We have former Green Berets, Navy SEALs, Royal Marines, French Foreign Legion, Marines, Rangers and everything in-between running around out here fighting a war; and then you also have guys who were literally civilians like a month ago doing the exact same thing as these hard-fuck experienced guys.

It's crazy, man. The level of organization is low, but the fighting spirit is all there. No two soldiers look alike. It's extremely rare that two guys are wearing the same uniforms with the same gear and the same rifles. Fuck, it's even rare if they speak the same language sometimes! It's a biiiiiiig difference from the US military where it looks like Attack of the Multi-Racial Clones. In the US military, every single dude looks like the guy next to him.

I will say though, the Ukrainian soldiers have got some balls. Especially the ones who were civilians not too long ago. They work as hard as they can, they learn as much as they can, and they fight as hard as they can. There was one Ukrainian who spoke English, so he was our translator or handler. Whatever you want to call him. Anyway, we were going to ambush this group of guys and their trucks, and this dude just nonchalantly stands up from our position and lobs an RPG their way. He gets back down and just smiles.

These dudes are crazy, man. American Non-Commissioned Officers would lose their minds over here. It's like working with the ANA but they actually return fire and move aggressively.

Week Twenty: July 7 - 13

Ukrainian Civilian
Girlfriend of Former Azovstal Soldier
Repatriated to Ukraine
July 7th

My boyfriend returned. He was a defender of Azovstal. I had never cried so much seeing him. My defender and my hero was alive, and right in front of me. I prayed and begged every God in as many heavens to keep him safe and bring him home, and now he is home.

He came back thin but smiling. He is a true hero. Our dog was so happy to see and play with him again. It made me so happy to see the two boys playing together again. I know the cost of this reunion and I acknowledge it with a sad heart.

He doesn't talk about what happened and I won't ask. He has kept a clean glass of water on the table since coming back. I asked him why he does this every day and he said it was for 'Them' and for him to remember. I don't know exactly what he means but I remember him telling me he would sell his car for a clean glass of water in Azovstal. I think it is his way of remembering his brothers in combat who died. It makes me want to cry thinking of it. He will share what it is really for when he is ready.

Our family is just so happy to have him home with us again. When he came back, he spent several days in hospital. He was unwell because of months of bad nutrition, sleep and being a prisoner. I hope all people in Ukraine and the world can understand what these soldiers did for us. I hope soon that all the women waiting for their husbands and men and sons will see their men again so they can all feel as I do.

Hundreds are still not home, and our family speaks often to pray for their health and to return safely. I know our family has been unusually lucky. He will speak for himself when he is ready. Glory to the heroes!

Art by João "J-Dot" Alves

"South"
Ukrainian Soldier / Medic
SOCM
Lysychansk area
July 7th

My unit was on a scouting mission. We had no obligation to disclose ourselves to anybody, even to UAF guys.

On our way back suddenly my group commander (GC) got a distress call on a radio from somebody not far from us: "We've got a 300* (casualty), somebody help us!"

My GC made a decision very quickly and told me: "Get ready, doc, we've got a 300!"

Two of us run to a place where we believed the 300 was and found a unit of UAF infantry guys who were hiding from shelling in the trenches. The casualty was relatively fine, (If you can say that) and could walk. He was wounded in his chest with a broken rib. He was hit by a fracture from his armor plate and was very lucky.

I checked his wound, put a chest seal on and also put a 12-inch bandage above all of that so as to immobilize his broken rib. Afterwards I then inserted an IV catheter 18G in his arm right on the spot.

We then walked out of the trenches and went back together to an evacuation point, (TFC area) where I infused saline into the 300 casualty and then passed him to a medevac doctor.

I am always happy to do my job, but my story is not about that. As I wrote above, we have no right to disclose ourselves to anybody. When we entered the trenches, my GC just said to the infantry guys that we came just to evacuate the 300 and nothing else. The casualty kept asking me who we were, and we just told him that we were just volunteers. The same thing was said to a medevac Doc.

I will be always thankful to my GC for his decision. Well, I did my job as a medic, but in my opinion, it is to my GC's credit in saving the casualty. Oh, Lord, bless and preserve that commander and those like him.

"Texas Corpsman"
Western Medical Volunteer
Eastern Front
July 8th

A few stories from me and my time in Ukraine. I'm a Corpsman by trade, went to Ukraine to do my bit. I've got a few stories. The day I learned that Ukrainian medics sometimes have to let people die.

I was helping to teach a class on casualty care to Ukrainian medics. I drew up a scenario on the white board and asked them what they would do. A casualty is 100 meters from in a big field and under fire. They actually let people die if it comes down to it. Imagine a big open field with both sides shooting at each other with artillery and snipers.

One of the infantry guys gets shot. Their standard procedure is that the soldier should patch himself up and wait until the fight is over. If Russians zeroed on a guy they hit, the worry is they would shoot the next guy going to help them.

I asked them, 'Have you let men die?'
They didn't say anything, but you could just see it on their faces. They just didn't know how to reach those casualties. I told them about all the assets we had in Afghanistan. Convoys of vehicles, air support, artillery, superior firepower. I felt for those guys. They didn't have those assets most of the time and on top of it they had to fight against artillery and Russian snipers.

I never fought against that in Afghanistan. I just felt so bad for them that they had to experience this. They had to let their own guys die. Not because they were cowards. They just couldn't get to them.

A different story, a Russian POW gave my brother some interesting information. My brother and I were both in Ukraine functioning as medics and medical facilitators. My brother was at a hospital and received a bunch of casualties. In the batch of wounded Ukrainians was a wounded Russian prisoner of war. Because he's a human being and the rules of war said so, the Russian was patched up and received medical care. Afterwards they interrogated him.

We had all thought that there was no way the Russian people and soldiers actually believed the propaganda their government told them. The Russian told us that he was in Ukraine to fight the Nazis. We couldn't believe it. My brother was shocked. They tried to tell the Russian that there were no Nazis here. This Russian was just so solid in his belief that there were Nazis just running around everywhere and that the government was under control of this secret group of Nazis. Like every single Russian soldier believes fully that the country is just overrun by them. They truly believe they are on some righteous crusade to liberate their Ukrainian brethren from evil. We just couldn't believe that this guy was so far gone and so deep in the propaganda. And this was two months into the war.

Later on, I was in the Donbas, and I checked out some of the gear that the Ukrainian medics were using. I brought my own gear to Ukraine. I put my own plate carrier together with a crappy IFAK. It weighed like 13lbs. When I saw the equipment the Ukrainians were using, I was just shocked. They had these crappy vest things and plate carriers with jimmy rigged pieces of steel they cut themselves that literally weighed 90lbs some of them.

When they tried my stuff on, they said it was God-like equipment. These guys in the Luhansk area were wearing chunks of steel! These medics were literally low crawling up to wounded casualties with this heavy ass bullshit, carrying dudes. They asked where they could get equipment like this. I asked them where the 40 billion dollars' worth of aid was? One of them said, 'I haven't seen any foreign aid from any government. We get things smuggled from Romania.'

I just couldn't believe they were trying to save lives with these medieval, heavy ass suits of armor.

Let me tell you about this Ukrainian guy. He was my driver, and he went everywhere I went. This guy has zero mil experience, but we built this trust and bond together.

He asked why a guy like me would come to Ukraine to help his country and his countrymen out. I told him my personal reasons. The birthplace of mother fucking communism. Because of Russia we have two fucking Koreas, (I am Korean) and due to this families are broken up and dead.

So, he knew I had this fucking hate inside of me for it. One day we get this fucking call from a mil commander. Said we to get to x spot yesterday to pick up casualties. This dude drove like fast and the furious we hooked up with the Ukky and Georgian docs and waited for the wounded.

Ukky military was putting the fucking hurt on Russia this day. The skies were clear at night and as soon as the clouds covered the moon, the pain was sent. Anyway, long story short we stayed there for half a day and as soon as arty started to zero on us, this guy didn't budge till he got the go from me. I told him if we have all the wounded on board and taken care of, let me scope the area and ask the other docs, and then we bolted like sonic the hedgehog.

The balls on this guy is gangster. There are many Ukrainians like this man. A fuck ton. Volunteers to defend their country. Behind the scenes making shit happen and arguing with Ukky leadership to see western point of view to get shit wrecked. If it wasn't for these guys my life would have been more difficult.

'Jak'
Western Volunteer
July 9th

We were billeted in a farmhouse on the edge of town, it was July 9th and we'd been in Donbas 2 weeks at this point. I was walking out the door when I heard what I thought was a low flying jet like we'd been hearing regularly.

I looked up and saw it was a missile coming down. It hit the apartment complex 300 meters away housing soldiers and civilians. I grabbed my English-speaking Ukrainian buddy. We donned our fatigues and helmets Grabbed our medical bags and started running.

As we approached the building he stopped and said we have to go back, there will be a second missile. Other members of our team had already reached the buildings. Not a minute later a second missile struck, luckily, he said that and we had time to run and take cover.

Soldiers started coming down the road from the complex, black faces, desperately choking for air. We gave them what water we had, deemed nobody needed immediate medical aid and started back to the buildings.

Ten minutes had passed since the second missile. As we approached the burning rubble, and could see the confusion and chaos amongst the soldiers and civilians, a third missile screamed in. This time we had no time to run, we hit the deck…. we were in it this time.

The rest of summer was uneventful. Static line mostly. Lots of artillery. Couple wounded. Contusions and the like. Firing PKM at Russian hedgerows across fields. But no visuals.

Former Taliban Affiliate
Pakistan
July 10th

I fought NATO, the United States. I saw some Canadians in Qamdhar also. ISIS as well. I don't know the exact ground situations. But an insurgency will need support. If Ukraine loses this war, they must become insurgents. Do anything, even war crimes. Use women to recon, also children. The Russians have drones, so do Ukrainians. Use personal drones to do recon.

Do raids on checkpoints, make IED's. Drop leaflets and use brutality. Ambush a unit, behead them all and leave one man tied up and naked. Make a way for them to come; leave some cleared roads with no signs of movements. Draw them in. Use dead cows to hide bombs. PCV pipes to hide them in doorways. Must be triggered by kicking doors or else civilians will set them off. We did one like that in Kashmir.

More advice. Use ceramic plates to evade metal detectors, and red pepper to fuck with K9 dogs. Ukrainians must be brutal to force the Russians away from their homes. Just like we did to the Russians.

Week Twenty-One: July 14-20

Ukrainian Soldier
July 14th

To describe a battle with both sides shooting at once is like a feeling you cannot describe. This is an experience you need to do yourself to understand. You cannot be told what it is like. As a memory, it is hard to remember what happens. It is in pieces that you remember it.

I do not remember big parts of fights we are in. Example: moving from one position to another under fire. This is a blur memory. You remember big events. Such as explosions close to you, killing an enemy, or a friend being killed or wounded.

My most memorable moment in battle against the occupier is when my friends are hurt. A tank shot down a trench from the side, and it exploded several soldiers into the air. The tank was damaged, and it moved away from our position. I went into the trench with some others to help anyone who survived.

There was an arm on the ground. There were legs in bushes. One soldier was unhurt and had already tried to save others who were not killed immediately. The moment was one I think about often. Human beings in pieces is not something to be forgotten easily.

Past that position, 100 yards further, a soldier was hit directly with a tank shot. The shot had gone through the dirt, but not exploded. It had hit him in the chest and emptied his insides from his body. He appeared to die instantly. It was the worst day of wounded and killed soldiers I have seen so far. 5 soldiers killed in a single moment. 12 wounded in total that day.

What makes this so horrible is this is common. This is happening even worse along the front. Some units lose even more every day. I have been in the army a long time. Iraq and Afghanistan and even the worst days there are an average day here. Because of my experience, I lead soldiers. It is days like that where I wish I was in charge of no one."

Swedish Volunteer
Frontline MEDEVAC - Ukrainian Hospitallers.
Charkiv
July 13th

We had a casualty with a terrible leg wound. His BMP had been hit by a penetrating attack, but we didn't know by what. Tank? Mine? Anti-tank? It didn't matter. They'd put two tourniquets on his leg, but neither was effective. A third I put on was better, but couldn't stop the bleeding entirely, the wound was too far up on the thigh and too messy. I could fit more than two fists into the wound cavity.

I packed it, not with the finesse I had trained to, since it wasn't a neat hole with a squirting artery, but just to fill out the entire wound cavity to create a more even pressure with the trauma bandage. It worked. He lived until we reached the civilian ER in Charkiv.

Katya
Ukrainian Civilian
July 14th

My name is Katya. My father is military. He is a border guard. He served and lived in the city of Mariupol. He held the defense along with other military men at the Azovstal plant. When he called last time, in March, he asked me. If I have a son, then name him in honor of his grandfather as a sign of memory.

My father said, "Here, life is on the border with death." The Russian military is attacking every minute, attacking like ants. In each of his SMS there were a couple of words: "Everything is fine, I love everyone." I was always surprised by these words, because how could it be good there?

Despite everything, they were ready to go and stand to the end. They understood that they might not return alive. Now he is a prisoner like the others. We are waiting for him; we miss him very much. We hope that soon the father will be exchanged, and we will be a family together.

I wanted to write because people think that there was one regiment of Azov. This is not so, there were many divisions.

Ukrainian Partisan
Behind Russian Lines
July 14th

I am a civilian. Some may call me partisan. Before the invasion on Feb 24, I was a normal Ukrainian man. Now, I carry SVD taken from Russian soldiers in an ambush.

My great grandfather was a partisan when the German occupier was here. Now I am a partisan while the Russian occupier is here. We joke that my children will see the next, Chinese occupier.

I cannot say what we are doing, too much will give us away. I can say we are always working. Always against the occupiers. They believe they are safe in their camps and buildings they take. Their convoys. Sleeping and bathing in our homes and properties. But we are always watching.

Russian soldiers know this. Just because you are not at the front, does not mean we will not make a new front for you in your sleep. We are watching always. Go home.

Art by João "J-Dot" Alves

Tarasenko D.V.
Russian/LPR Soldier
July 17th

PRE-DEATH LETTER

Tarasenko D.V.,

Husband and Father. This is a letter for the future if I die or get captured or become disabled! July 17th, 2022.

It's very hard to write this. I am crying, but I have to. Lera, darling. Tell him (their son) what dad was like. We were sent away like cannon fodder! Without armored vehicles. Without ammunition and without normal weapons - I am talking about our situation. When our son grows up, tell him that dad really wanted to come home and be the best dad.

I drank. I write emotionally, I know that everything will be forgotten, and you will live your life. You will find yourself a new husband, and I will simply disappear in the war, like all the boys. It's a shame that I didn't even have a normal life. Tell our son that dad was an athlete, did not smoke or drink. Too bad everyone forgot about me!

It is very difficult to reconcile, but everyone dies, and this cycle cannot be changed. It is bad to die. I would be better at the sea this summer.

*Letter was captured by Ukrainian Forces in September, and it circulated on social media

Mike Dunn
Western Volunteer
Grigorivka
July 18th

My name is Mike Dunn, and this is my firsthand account of the sacrifice of American, Swedish, and Canadian volunteer lives in Grigorivka.

One early day in July, a team of volunteers were assembled from the Ivan Bohun Special Purpose Brigade of the Ukrainian Army. These volunteers were English speaking fighters from around the world, particularly America, Canada, Sweden, Finland, Israel, Belarus, and England.

These volunteers all had combat experience in either Afghanistan, Iraq, or Ukraine. Our job? Defend the village and road in Grigorivka at all costs. If the 79th Brigade line broke, we were to repel the attackers. This village was crucial to the defense of Siversk and the rest of the Donetsk Region. On July 10th this Special Operations team was delivered to the Village of Grigorivka, which no longer stands due to Russia's constant shelling. We arrived early in the day under artillery fire as they tried to hit our delivery vehicle. We dismounted with our gear and immediately entered one of the few bunkers left standing in the village, as many others had been destroyed due to Russia using drones to help them zero in on the targets.

Our first 8 days were long and boring. We counted over 700 explosions in one day into our little village, and this continued every day we were there. Any time we exited our bunkers, we received shelling. We had a road we called Hamburger Hill, because a tank would shoot at you while you ran this road to the HQ, and you would just pray you didn't get shot.

On July 18 at 0800 hours, we received an order from our commanders that Russians had broken through the line, and we needed to run the 700 meters down this nightmarish road to stop them. Myself, my team leader Bjorn, my machine gunner Dave, and my assistant Grenadier Leevi began to run this road with two other fire teams. 700 meters through hell we ran. Explosions. Drones targeting us. Nowhere to hide. About 400 meters in we took heavy artillery to the road, and we immediately spread out and tried to take some form of cover and lay down. During this 20 minute of shelling, I received my first concussion and lost all hearing in my left ear.

The shelling stopped and we all got up and began running again into the mouth of the enemy. At almost exactly 700 meters we once again took fire to our position. The rear team took a casualty. Luke Lucyszyn (American of Ukrainian descent). He lost his arm in the blast. We immediately tried to take cover while his team attempted to render first aid. In the following blasts, our squad leader Finn was injured in the arm and leg, Oscar was wounded in the leg, and Luke Lucyszyn, Brian K Young (American) Edvard Selander Patrignani (Swedish) and Emile-Antoine Roy Sirois (Canadian) were killed instantly.

For almost 2 hours as we laid there, artillery and mortar and tank fire destroyed the road and what was left of the buildings around us. We were unable to help our friends. One of our bravest, Solomon, tried to run to help but was unable to do so.

After two hours the shelling stopped. We checked the bodies to see if they were alive, and they were not. No Russian's had broken through the line, and we realized it had been miscommunication that had led us into this trap. Not the fault of our company commander, but the fault of those who issued the information. We immediately began running this road of hellfire back to our bunkers. Every time for the next 5 hours that someone attempted to recover the bodies, they were shelled. At around 1800 that evening, we received the same order. Russians had broken through the line, and we were needed to stop them. One team was dead. One team had rotated out. That left only me, my team leader Bjorn, Dave, and Leevi.

Without hesitation, Bjorn accepted the mission, and we followed him. The 4 of us joined around 7 other Belarusians and ran through that hellish road to the original position where we lost our friends. Except this time, there was a difference. Russians. 4 tanks. 4 APCs. About 70 Russian infantry had broken through the lines with heavy armor. Our anger for our earlier losses was unmatched. Dave opened up on the M240. The rest of us on AKs. Our drone guy at HQ was directing our artillery into the tanks.

The firefight lasted for almost 2 hours. I have been in firefights before, and 6 to 7 minutes seems average. This lasted 2 hours, documented, on camera. One tank and one APC were destroyed. Around 17-20 Russians were killed, and we only took one wounded. We avenged the deaths of our fallen brothers, and then some. We held that road against all odds, and we broke the Russian advance, forcing them to withdraw. 2 days later they tried Phospher bombs onto our position with no luck.

After 15 days we all were rotated out, and I had been med evacuated to a hospital for emergency medical care due to major concussions and loss of balance and blurry vision. We will never forget July 18th. We will never forget our heartbreaking losses and we will never forget our victory. Our men ran into the mouth of hell and drove Satan back inside. We saved Siversk, regardless of what may happen in the future.

Art by João "J-Dot" Alves

Ukrainian Soldier
Eastern Front
July 18th

There are many choices to make in battles. Some are easy choices where you decide to move right or left. Some choices are different and have bigger consequences. To leave a wounded soldier behind or not, that is a difficult one.

People cannot imagine the situations that we get in. To say one choice is more honorable or right than another, these are all privileges of safety, not a battlefield. It is never that easy to make choices in battle. Right or wrong.

Sometimes you have to make tough decisions as an individual. Do you run out of cover to evacuate a wounded comrade? Maybe you be wounded yourself? And others try to rescue you and they also die. Do you stay? Leave a man to fight for his own life and you for yours?

People who are not soldiers cannot understand these decisions made by each soldier on the battlefield. It is not fair that we need to make these decisions at all. These are not decisions human beings should be making but that is not the way of this.

This is the war and, in the war, we have to do things that may upset us. We may feel ourselves are cowards, but we are alive. It is good to be brave, but bravery is wasted when it results in the meaningless death of you and someone else. Why should two die when only one has to?

I have made such a choice. I chose not to leave the position to save a wounded soldier. He was going to die, lost both legs. I would have died too should I go to get him. I won't say any more about this story. Some may judge me that is okay. They were not there. Most would make the same choice.

Ukrainian Soldier
Eastern Front
July 20th

Ukrainian soldiers do not like that the inhabitants of Donbass wish them death, surrender Ukrainian positions to Russian troops and believe that the war on their land is the fault of Ukraine.

"I don't love Bakhmut.
I don't love Lisichansk.
I don't love Severodonetsk."

Here don't live *our* people. They don't love Ukraine. They rat out our positions to the enemy. They run out of their homes and yell "may you all die". This is not the same as Kiev, where they greeted us with hugs and tears. We don't feel welcome here. To the residents of all these cities it doesn't matter who is here, Russia or Ukraine, they just don't want their homes destroyed. They believe that the war on their land is the fault of Ukraine. This is the reality of the war in this region.

Lyubomyr Suharyna
Ukrainian Soldier
Kherson/Mykolayiv Border
July 18th

Me and my volunteer friends were delivering critical supplies to our soldiers near Kherson border. As we approached our destination, a Russian drone might have seen us, and we came under severe artillery fire. We had to retreat to the nearby village called Limany to seek cover. When we got to the village, we found an elderly lady near her house whose feet have been torn off from either mortar shelling or a butterfly mine (PFM-1).

We got there too late to put tourniquets on her because she had already bled out. There was also her dead neighbor, an elderly gentleman, 50 meters from us down the road, with his guts all over the sidewalk, but we did not approach him too close, knowing there could me more mines down the road.

Week Twenty-Two: July 21-24

Western Volunteer
Eastern Front
July 21st

Teach soldiers to camouflage themselves and their positions and they are instantly better offensive and defensive soldiers. Before I was actively rolling with Ukrainian squads, I was teaching them about camouflage and concealment. The difference between cover and concealment, etc.

I had taught a class of soldiers about basic reconnaissance and shit like that, and as soon as they 'graduated' I accompanied them out to the front. Can't teach these guys skills and then leave them out to dry, you know?

Anyway, two go out on an LP/OP (listening post, observation posts) and they come back a few hours later. I guess they had concealed themselves exceptionally well in their OP, and a patrol of Russian soldiers had walked right up to them in the brush. I guess that the Russians had even stopped to smoke some cigarettes less than 10 meters from them, and the Ukrainian soldiers had to remove the batteries from their radios because they didn't want any radio traffic to come across to get them killed.

After a few minutes the Russians moved on, and the two soldiers crept back to our positions and told us the direction they had moved in. Discipline, good use of vegetation and concealment kept them alive and I'm glad that my classes could help in some small way.

Plus, the balls, man. Imagine being 10 meters from a group of enemy soldiers. Knowing that something as small as bad breathing can get you killed. Crazy stuff, man. This war is nuts.

Ukrainian Soldier
Eastern Front
July 22nd

It is artillery and snipers that makes working in these positions so difficult. New soldiers come to the front not knowing how life and war in trenches. The artillery is something that skill in battle can only save you from so many times. It is sometimes only luck that you survive.

Artillery working on your position for hours or days, the odds of your survival get smaller. It is a matter of time before the high number of shells come closer to you.

Trenches in new condition become unserviceable after bombardments. They become piles and holes of unorganized dirt that become hard to move through. Trenches are the best way to survive an artillery attack. You lay in the bottom or a dugout and just hope one doesn't land in the trench directly.

Wounds from the explosions are worse than bullets in almost every case. As a medic in the trenches, bullets make fine wounds mostly. Shrapnel from explosions is like a wound from jagged metal flying fast into you. Snipers are also to me a high threat.

Three things will be the most dangerous for you at the frontline. Artillery, drones and soldiers who are snipers. Soldiers who are snipers that are well trained, well equipped with night and thermal scopes, and with communication resources are to me one of worst part of the front.

Artillery is not personal. Snipers are. They are directly shooting for you. Untrained soldiers at the front who are not taught how to conceal themselves will not last long if they are working in the same part of the battlefield as an active and well-trained sniper.

Nighttime is bad, especially with thermal. (Thermal optics) Soldiers think it is safe to sit up and smoke cigarettes like the daytime, but they are just signaling where they are. Because of this an unproportional number of soldiers are shot in the neck and head.

The best way for us to find their snipers with ours is to create dummy positions to draw their fire. The enemy shots are then calculated by our own snipers until they are found.

Russian Paratrooper, VDV

Deserter

(Same soldier who communicated with a former Russian soldier on March 1st)

July 22nd

I couldn't invade that country in my right mind. I have family in Ukraine, you know? I've got cousins and relatives not too far away, I've been there. Been to the capitol, beautiful city, the night life there was great. If I had been on that plane, I would have done it. If I hadn't broken my leg, I would've had to be there for my friends. I wouldn't have thought about it. You know what I mean? Breaking my leg gave me time to think.

Because of our unit, we had foresight into this. All of those conscripts, those motorized rifle guys that got marched in there and died. They didn't know, but we did. Plans of airfields and drop zones were marked out. I knew. But I broke my leg training, that's what saved me. Gave me time to think.

I felt and feel like I may have let down my guys, my leg had started to heal, and I feel like I could be there. I don't betray people, but I feel like I did to them. But they can handle themselves, Crow is in charge now, he's a good man and I'm sure they'll be fine. How did I feel on the run? I'm going to be honest, it's a lot scarier than being in a firefight. It's just me, I'm on the run alone, but for now I think I'm okay.

Before I left, I stole a bunch of things. Mostly heavy painkillers, but I also took a knife, some money, and a Grach (pistol) from an officer's desk before I left. I had my normal phone for a little bit I ditched it when I remembered I could be tracked. I popped a lot of painkillers at first, to the point where I couldn't feel anything. I was on foot for a long time, I couldn't tell you how many kilometers I walked. I found a farmer's clothing line and I took his shit.

I looked like a country bumpkin, but it made me look less suspicious because I'm limping around in drunkard's clothes. I didn't take any public transportation because I was afraid the GAI (Russian public transport police) would check my papers and fuck me royally. Then it's off to the Black Dolphin for me (prison in Siberia). Those fuckers are seizing transport vehicles around the country to move supplies, I watched them confiscate old ZILs in civilian service. I carjacked a guy near Kharabali.

I wouldn't have done it, but he was an asshole. I asked him for a ride, but he refused and then he threatened to call the cops on me for being a vagrant. So, I pulled out my pistol and I smacked his face, then I pulled him out and I took off. Luckily it was secluded, so I just drove off on a country road and lost him pretty quickly.

I ran out of petrol close to Volgograd and started to walk again. I made it around Volgograd, it's a big city with too much attention that I couldn't handle. My body had been chaffing because I had my pistol riding my dick and my knife was running in my pant leg. To eat, I'd ask the old women to spare bread, or fruit and cheese. In return I'd do a chore or two, cut wood, collect eggs from chickens, broom a doorway or two.

There was a nice older woman, she lived near Lake Baskunchak. I stayed with her a few days to heal up my leg. She was nice. She let me bathe and fed me good meals for a few days. She didn't know much about the war, she just believed Ukraine had started it. She thought we were just liberating captured Russians. I left her in peace, her neighbors started to get nosy when they saw a new man in the house, they came to visit and asked me lots of questions. I said I was just traveling to see some family and my bus left me too far.

I stole a bike from some kids, they had left it sit out and it was rusted so I showed them a lesson for not taking care of their things. I was able to ride a bike to a roadway where I hitched a ride with a trucker, he was a drunk old man missing a lot of teeth. Simple guy, he asked me why I was heading to Kazakhstan, and I told him I was heading there to give him money, so he took it as it was. I think he knew what I was, I was afraid at that point. He stayed quiet until we got to the border, when the border patrol asked him who I was he said I was his nephew learning the trade after my father died from tuberculosis.

He said I didn't have papers because I was supposed to get off, but I wanted to stay on for the job. The whole time he talked I was feeling up my pistol, ready to do what gangsters do, man. But everything was fine, and we drove to Shungay. He dropped me off there and I gave him almost all my money, he looked at me and said, "Don't think I don't know what you are." Then he drives off.

The Kazakhs are very nice people, everyone was willing to share, and I got many car rides to them. You say not to give my current location, so I won't. But I made it to a bigger city, from car to car. Very friendly, I

360

may live here forever and find a wife. When I was in a village, I ditched the pistol in a well, but I kept the knife because it's innocent enough. I helped load some crates onto a truck and got paid some money for new clothes. Now I live in a whore house, in the back rooms where the ladies undress so that is pretty nice.

I provide security sometimes and get paid enough that I don't have to scrounge and beg like a worm on the streets. I'm looking for more permanent work right now. As you can see, I've acquired a new phone and that's how I'm contacting you. For now, I'm okay, but I would like to see my family again. I'm afraid they would say something if I contact them though. This is life for now, I could be dead.

Western Volunteer
Southern Front
July 22nd

There's no way to confirm what I think happened, but we found a Russian with a gunshot wound under his chin going out the top of his skull. We found him behind some trenches inside the underground cellar type of thing in building with the roof blown off.

He'd been dead nearly 2 days (a guess) by then we thought. His weapon was gone, and we were the first to come to this area and actually clear it. We didn't do this. It didn't look like anyone did it to him. We assume he took his own life for one reason or another.

What we think happened is he must have left his mates in the trenches, meandered behind their line, found a spot in this house and done it quick. Others must have found him and taken his rifle and ammunition before they left.

I haven't any idea why they didn't bury him. But I can't help but feel shit for the man. Come all the way from home just to die in a dirty room presumably alone, and then get left to rot. God only knows why he did that.

Western Volunteer
July 22nd

You wouldn't believe the different kinds of weapons coming out of storage and making their way into the frontlines. It's like Build-A-War Workshop for infantry units out here.

Everything from bolt action Mosin Nagants, MP40 submachine guns, hand grenades literally from WW2 packaging, and everything in between.

I've seen more than one machine gun position manned by a PKM and a WW2 era Maxim Machine Gun, or a DP-28 Saucer gun. It's honestly crazy, man. Like it's not uncommon to see a drone operator manning his drone armed with a PPSH or something like that.

What's even crazier is this happens on both sides. Soldiers on both sides are armed randomly with whatever they could find it seems. Even though these weapons are outdated and there are newer and better alternatives, they are still effective and dangerous.

I've seen and heard of more than one soldier killed by a sniper armed with a Mosin Nagant. If it goes boom, it can still ventilate your skull.

Ukrainian Soldier
Azov Regiment
Former Prisoner of War
Repatriated to Ukraine
July 24th

Battle of Mariupol and in the city itself: The battle for Mariupol was very difficult. The enemy had an advantage in the number of both manpower and equipment - literally dozens of times. We practically did not sleep and every minute we did everything so that the Russian soldiers did not advance a single centimeter. But they, regardless of civilians and children, went forward, destroying everything in their path.

A shootout in which I participated: Russians decided once again to carry out reconnaissance by battle (sending men to fight our people without body armor - not sparing their own people) - sent a tank and a detachment of infantry, about 10-12 people; to break through. They were like in a dash.

362

Working on the enemy and destroying him in the very center of the city, we thought that it would be an "easy job", but instead of animals that decided to stop breathing and remained to fertilize the ground, another tank arrived and started working precisely on our position.

This was the most fun shootout with rpg-22 and machine guns on a tank. After that, the anti-tank missile group arrived and destroyed the enemy's equipment.

When we found out that we were in a completely encircled environment - there was no surprise. All that mattered was only a matter of time. I understood that this is the same "last outpost". The guys from my unit were also ready and we didn't doubt the commander's decision for a second - we're here to the end! The fighting spirit did not leave us. We stood firmly on our feet and knew what we were fighting for. They carried out the assigned task, no matter what. Protected our Earth, protected our Nation!

It is difficult to single out someone for courage. After all, every day enemy equipment and food was destroyed by different people (in large numbers). A huge amount of enemy manpower was liquidated every day. In Mariupol - everyone became heroes.

But still, I would like to tell about the warrior with the call sign "Cabbage". He was an artilleryman. At the beginning of March, "The artillery ran out." Because of the intense fire, the barrels of the guns were deformed, and the shells began to run out...Especially if you are surrounded and there is no supply.

Artillery soldiers actually became infantry. Kapusta adapted to the realities of urban warfare - he developed and honed infantry skills. While in positions in broken houses of the private sector, he changed into civilian clothes and walked the street, knocking on houses, asking for water 'allegedly as a civilian.'

Because there was no civilian population there - the doors were opened by Russian soldiers. The night was a time of rest for them. In the morning, all intelligence from Kapusta was processed, and he and his group could eliminate the enemy much more effectively without suffering losses, because they had an understanding of the locations of the enemy's deployment.

He died on May 4th while moving towards the position on Azovstal, he came under fire from enemy artillery. Fragments from the projectile did not give life a chance. Cabbage will stay with us forever! He was a hero and deserves to be remembered.

What is it like to be a prisoner of war: We carried out the order and removed the defense and surrendered. The Ukrainian garrison was evacuated from Azovstal. Some of the fighters (wounded and seriously wounded) ended up in the hospital, the other part in the pre-trial detention center in the temporarily occupied territories.

We did not expect anything good from the enemy. But our task was to, "Hold on and not bend."
To be a prisoner of war is to live one day and not know what will happen next. This is when you don't decide anything, you don't have any rights, and you can't influence anything.

Every day passed like the last, and only hopes comforted me. Hopes for a return to the native land in Ukraine.

Western Volunteer
July 24th

Some perspective. I just left the US Marines not too long ago. Coming from the US, an infantryman has all the toys he needs to be successful. It's not top of the line stuff, but it beats most of our competitors.

The average American Marine or soldier who's in combat arms is equipped with something like $28,000 - $40,000 worth of gear and equipment. Everything from helmets, rifle optics, to IR strobes and drones.

The average Ukrainian soldier is equipped with something like $1,450 - $2,200 worth of gear and equipment. To me, I find this absolutely insane. The first time I was around Ukrainian soldiers, they had just gotten back from the front.

Their gear and equipment looked like it had been through the ringer and on its last legs. They're out here fighting the most conventional war that the world has seen in the last 30 years, and the majority of them are doing it with scraps. It's either extremely impressive or extremely depressing. Probably both.

Olena
Ukrainian Civilian
Wife of Azovstal Soldier
July 24th

My name is Olena, I'm from Ukraine and this is my story. Before the war, I lived in Mariupol with my husband and a five-year-old son from a previous marriage. On the morning of February 24, I woke up to the sound of explosions, like the whole people of Ukraine. For the previous few days, until February 24th, my husband had to stay at the base. We didn't see each other, and he convinced me to leave the city, but I didn't want to. It seemed to me that everything will be fine, and these are just unnecessary measures. I thought that everything would be about the same as in 2014-15, but I collected a backpack with documents, essentials and a first aid kit.

In general, on the morning of February 24th, my work was canceled, the kindergarten was also canceled, the windows were shaking, and my son and I spent several hours in the corridor between two walls, reading the horrible news about war in all country. Then I decided to leave the apartment for my mother's house. There was a basement there and it seemed safer than sitting on the 6th floor.

It was incredibly scary to be outside, the shelling was very frequent. It seemed that the shells were hitting simultaneously from all types of weapons, and that day for the first time I heard an anti-aircraft siren. The road to my mother is quite close, but to go and constantly think, "Where is the shelter?" And "Where can I lie down if a shell comes very close", etc. It was very tiring. I can't imagine how the military lives in this 24/7.

About an hour later, my husband called me and said that the last evacuation bus that the Azov regiment had organized for wives and children was leaving soon. On it, my son and I left Mariupol for Zaporozhye. From there a friend of my husband took us at night and took us to my mother-in-law in the Dnipro. We stayed there for several weeks, but I practically don't remember anything from those days. I cried all the time, I really missed home and my life and also, I was very angry that my ideal happy life was cut short at one moment.

Meanwhile, the situation in Ukraine did not improve. The front expanded, and in mid-March, my husband told me to leave further to western Ukraine, closer to the border. Since then, we have been here. Well, something important happened in Dnipro: I found out that I was pregnant, obviously it happened right before war start and seems the wrong time, but we were happy anyway. So now my safety and comfort are very important.

Of course, there were no words about the whereabouts, their tasks or movements of my husband. Basically, we talked about how we miss each other, love and other romantic things. The first days the connection was regular, but we spoke very little, because he was really busy. There were tough battles in Mariupol, as you know. Over time, getting in touch became more difficult, but he still found the opportunity to at least text to me. Then there was a moment when there was no connection for more than two weeks. Sometimes his comrade in arms sent me messages that he was fine.

At first, he wrote about the situation in Mariupol that everything is complicated, but they are in full control. I got the details from the news. My husband had combat experience even before Mariupol, because before the Azov Regiment, he served in the Marine Corps, but one day he admitted that he had never seen such combat like this.

Anyway, the only thing he complained about was the lack of bread and often said that he misses the food I cook, especially desserts. There was even a list of what I would have to cook when he returned - a lot of carbos and sugar!

His mood was always cheerful, until the exit from the Azovsteel, we joked, made plans for the future, chose a name for the baby.
Once he found an internet connection and we texted, I asked for a photo. He said that he had not washed for a month and a half, and it was better for me not to see this, because there was not even water to wash gunpowder dust off his face. But then he sent it anyway. I have never seen him so tired.

The news of the "evacuation" from Azovsteel into captivity was terrible for me. Until the last moment, I hoped that there would be an extraction to a third country, or a breakthrough, or some other miracle. It is one thing to fight, die in battle, on your own land, with your guys, and quite another to suffer from torture and other hardships in the captivity of the enemy. We need to exchange guys as soon as possible, while there is still someone to exchange. Unfortunately, Russia is not interested in the exchange and, in general, they do not comply with any rules of warfare, and international organizations only express concern, without providing real assistance to prisoners of war.

Most of all I wish that the exchange of prisoners took place as soon as possible. Azov people are strong, brave and tough, but they need medical help, they are exhausted from the struggle at Azovsteel, injuries, poor nutrition and related diseases. And I am really worried about my husband's life because we didn't speak about two months, from the moment they leave from Mariupol. The only thing I know that he was alive and not seriously injured at the moment they evacuated to Olenivka, that's official information came from his military organization.

"Fox"
Ukrainian Soldier
Eastern Front
July 24th

In April I was shot in the stomach. My unit of 20 soldiers was doing a patrol to find the enemy in their territory with the help of a drone. The trees were too thick for our drone, so we went on foot to find them. This made me very nervous, and I didn't like the idea.

We moved down a trail in trees, and we came to a clear area. The area was looking like a big open circle surrounded by trees. It made me feel unsafe to be standing here on the edge of this area, and it was unsafe.

I didn't hear anything. I just felt it. It felt like a person had run and kicked me in the stomach and I fell down. The next thing I saw was the ground from a point zero view, and then the sky as I was rolled over. Two of my comrades were standing over me yelling and speaking something I could not understand. Then I felt them put their hands on my bulletproof vest and I began to move.

They dragged me back into the trees and this is when I remember hearing things. Our other comrades were kneeling behind trees working on the enemy positions on the other side of the clear area. Someone put me on their shoulders to carry me away, but I screamed because of how much pain this caused me. I asked them not to carry me like that.

They laid a blanket on the ground, and me on top of the blanket. One man grabbed each corner and carried me back like that. I found out later a sniper had shot me below my vest and above my belt.

Art by João "J-Dot" Alves

Nicholas Laidlaw

Former US Marine Rifleman

Author of the What War Did To Us series

"You don't have to like it, but you have to show up."

Ilya Rudyak

US Marine Rifleman

Co-Author

Война дело молодых,

Лекарство против морщин.

João "J-Dot" Alves

Artist

Mike Liu

Arist

ACKNOWLEDGEMENTS

I would like to thank some very special people who helped encourage and support me during the documentation process for this book. Many people helped to make this book a reality.

First and foremost, I would like to thank my family. Specifically, my Mom and Dad. Their love and encouragement has been my rock through many rough storms.

A big, "Thank you!" To my beautiful and supportive girlfriend, Isabelle, who has supported, encouraged, and helped me put together two books in less than a year. Wherever you are, give her a round of applause.

I would also like to thank a fellow author and mentor, Adam Makos. Without his guidance and advice, this book would be headed your way in far worse shape than it is now. Adam is a true professional in this art, and I am grateful to have worked alongside him during our collaborative efforts to support and document the stories of the soldiers inside of Azovstal during the Siege of Mariupol.

A huge THANK YOU to the followers and supporters of my platform, Battles and Beers: War Stories. Without the following's help, absolutely none of this would have been possible. Hundreds of leads and stories were given to me by followers. They are the real MVP's.

Finally, I'd like to thank in no particular order people or social media pages which helped me in some way or another in making this book possible through leads, direct actions, or support online. There are too many to count, but here are a few who stood out.

Oleksandra Fischer	@CossackGundi
Chase Baker	@OAFNation
@Tales_From_The_Grid_Square	@Task&Purpose
@SaintJavelin	@ApparitionGroup
Chris Naganuma	@Spetsnazer2.0
Collin Mayfield	So...so many more.

RESOURCES AND REFERENCES

Extensive oral interviews form the bedrock and foundation of this collection. Because of the conditions on the ground in Ukraine, and the nature of warfare, the vast majority of these interviews were conducted through social media applications such as Instagram messenger, Telegram, Signal, and other communication methods such as texting, email, phone calls and video chats.

Ukrainian Soldier, 51st Guards Mechanized Brigade, Battle of Ilovaisk. 2014
    Page 26. Documented on Instagram Direct Messenger. January 2nd, 2022
"Krusader", Western Volunteer, Ukrainian Marines, Svitlodarsk Sector. 2017
    Page 26. Documented on Instagram Direct Messenger. March 28th, 2022
"Carlo", British Army Veteran from Northern Ireland. Donbas 2015-17
    Page 27. Documented on Facebook Messenger, March 22nd, 2022
Ukrainian Soldier. Svitlodarsk Frontline Trenches, January 2022
    Page 28. Documented on Instagram/Telegram, January 26th, 2022
Russian Soldier. Russian-Ukrainian Border. January 2022
    Page 30. Documented on Instagram Direct Messenger. February 13th, 2022
Ukrainian Soldier. Donbas Frontline, January 2022
    Page 30. Documented on Instagram/Telegram. February 13th, 2022
Ukrainian Soldier, Donbas Frontline, January 2022
    Page 30. Documented on Facebook Messenger, January 20th, 2022
Aiden Aslin, Western Volunteer – Ukrainian Marine, Donbas Frontline/Mariupol. January 2022
    Page 31. Documented on Instagram. January 22nd, 2022
Ukrainian Soldier, Frontline, January 2022
    Page 31. Documented on Instagram Direct Messenger. January 21st, 2022
Ukrainian Soldier. 79th Air Assault Brigade. Frontline. February 20th
    Page 32. Documented on Telegram. February 20th, 2022
Russian Soldier. Logistics Unit. Ukrainian-Russian Border. February 22nd
    Page 32. Documented on Instagram Direct Messenger. February 22nd, 2022
Ukrainian Soldier. Frontline. February 23rd
    Page 33. Documented on Telegram. February 23rd, 2022
Dymtrus, Ukrainian Civilian. February 23rd
    Page 34. Documented on Instagram Direct Messenger. February 23rd, 2022
Hadeon. Ukrainian Civilian, Kyiv, February 24th
    Page 35. Documented on Facebook/Telegram. February 24th, 2022
Anastasiia. Ukrainian Civilian. Kyiv Suburbs. February 24th
    Page 35. Documented through text message. February 24th, 2022
Ukrainian Soldier - Reservist. Frontline. February 24th
    Page 36. Documented on Telegram. February 24th, 2022
Mychajlo. Ukrainian Civilian. February 24th
    Page 36. Documented on Instagram Direct Messenger. February 24th, 2022
Alina. Ukrainian Civilian. February 24th
    Page 36. Documented on Instagram Direct Messenger. February 24th, 2022
"Bumblebee" Russian Soldier. Kharkov Area. February 24th
    Page 37. Documented on Telegram. July 30th, 2022
Ukrainian Soldier. Donbas Frontline. February 24th
    Page 43. Documented through phone call. February 24th, 2022
Pavel Filatyev. Russian Soldier. VDV Paratrooper. February 24th

378

Page 194. Documented on Instagram Direct Messenger. April 5th, 2022
Ukrainian Soldier. Eastern Front. April 7th
    Page 196. Documented on Instagram Direct Messenger/Telegram. April 7th, 2022
Ukrainian Special Operations Soldier. April 7th
    Page 196. Documented on Instagram Direct Messenger. April 7th, 2022
Ukrainian Soldier. Sumy Oblast. April 7th
    Page 199. Documented on Telegram/Facebook Messenger. April 7th, 2022
Western Civilian/Volunteer. Odessa. February 26th – April 8th
    Page 199. Documented on Instagram Direct Messenger. April 8th, 2022
Western Civilian. Abroad. April 12th
    Page 201. Documented on Instagram Direct Messenger. April 12th, 2022
Aiden Aslin. Western Volunteer-Ukrainian Marine. Siege of Mariupol. April 12th
    Page 201. Documented on Aiden's personal Instagram account. April 12th, 2022
Ukrainian Civilian. April 12th
    Page 203. Documented on Facebook Messenger/Telegram. April 12th, 2022
David. Azov Regiment. Siege of Mariupol. April 13th
    Page 203. Documented on Telegram. July 22nd, 2022
Ukrainian Civilian. April 13th
    Page 206. Documented on Instagram Direct Messenger/Email. April 13th, 2022
Ukrainian Soldier. Border Guard. Siege of Mariupol. April 13th
    Page 207. Documented on Instagram Direct Messenger/Telegram. April 13th, 2022
Maria Petrovna. Ukrainian Civilian. Siege of Mariupol. April 13th
    Page 207. Documented on Instagram Direct Messenger/Telegram. April 13th, 2022
"Gandalf" Ukrainian Soldier. Azov Intelligence Officer. Siege of Mariupol, Azovstal. April 15th
    Page 211. Documented on Telegram. April 15th, 2022
Ukrainian Soldier. Azov Regiment. Siege of Mariupol. Azovstal. April 17th
    Page 213. Documented on Telegram. April 17th, 2022
Western Volunteer. Former Azov Regiment Member. April 19th
    Page 214. Documented on Facebook Messenger. April 19th, 2022
Russian Soldier. Siege of Mariupol. April 20th
    Page 214. Documented on Telegram. April 20th, 2022
Ukrainian Soldier. April 22nd
    Page 217. Documented on Telegram. April 22nd, 2022
Ukrainian Soldier. April 23rd
    Page 217. Documented on Instagram Direct Messenger. April 23rd, 2022
Ukrainian Civilian. April 23rd
    Page 218. Documented on Telegram/Email. April 23rd, 2022
Ukrainian Soldier. Eastern Front. April 24th
    Page 221. Documented on Telegram. April 24th, 2022
Ukrainian Civilian. April 25th
    Page 221. Documented on Instagram Direct Messenger. April 25th, 2022
DPR Soldier/Separatist. Siege of Mariupol. April 25th
    Page 222. Documented on Telegram. April 25th, 2022
Ukrainian Soldier/ Medic. Siege of Mariupol, Azovstal. April 26th
    Page 224. Documented on Telegram. April 26th, 2022
Ukrainian Soldier/Medic. Siege of Mariupol, Azovstal. April 26th
    Page 224. Documented on Telegram. April 26th, 2022
Ukrainian Soldier. Azov Regiment. Siege of Mariupol, Azovstal. April 26th
    Page 224. Documented on Instagram Direct Messenger. April 26th
DPR Soldier/Separatist. Izyum Front. April 26th
    Page 225. Documented on Telegram/Instagram Direct Messenger. April 26th, 2022
Ukrainian Soldier. Azov Regiment. Siege of Mariupol, Azovstal. April 27th
    Page 226. Documented on Instagram Direct Messenger/Telegram. April 27th, 2022
Ukrainian Soldier. Azov Regiment. Siege of Mariupol. April 27th
    Page 227. Documented on Telegram. April 27th, 2022
Major Bohdan Krotevich. Chief of Staff, Azov Regiment. Siege of Mariupol, Azovstal. April 27th
    Page 229. Documented on Instagram Direct Messenger/Telegram. April 27th, 2022
Ukrainian Marine. Siege of Mariupol. Azovstal. April 27th
    Page 231. Documented on Telegram. April 27th, 2022

Works Cited (Preface):

Applebaum, A. (2022, March 27). The victory of Ukraine: Anne Applebaum. Retrieved from https://www.nybooks.com/articles/2016/04/07/the-victory-of-ukraine/

Arnold, K. (2020, September 30). "There is no Ukraine": Fact-checking the Kremlin's version of Ukrainian history. Retrieved from https://blogs.lse.ac.uk/lseih/2020/07/01/there-is-no-ukraine-fact-checking-the-kremlins-

version-of-ukrainian-history/Auty, R. (1964). Community and Divergence in the History of the Slavonic Languages. *The Slavonic and East*

European Review, 42(99), 257–273. http://www.jstor.org/stable/4205561
Bechtel, D., Brooks, C., Dean, M., Desbois, P., Eikel, M., Kunz, N., . . . Sukovata, V. (2013, April). The Holocaust

In Ukraine: New Sources and Perspectives. Retrieved from https://collections.ushmm.org/search/catalog/bib243350

Budnitskii, O. (2001). Jews, Pogroms, and the White Movement: A Historiographical Critique. *Kritika: Explorations in Russian and Eurasian History 2*(4), 1-23.

Carlton, T. R. (1991). *Introduction to the Phonological History of the Slavic languages*. Columbus, OH: Slavica.

Conflict in Ukraine's Donbas: A Visual Explainer. (2022, March 28). Retrieved from https://www.crisisgroup.org/ content/conflict-ukraines-donbas-visual-explainer

Hosking, G. A. (2011). *Russia and the Russians: A History*. Cambridge, MA: Belknap Press of Harvard University Press.

Krause, T. B., & Slocum, J. (n.d.). The University of Texas at Austin, Linguistics Research Center: Old Russian Online. Retrieved from https://lrc.la.utexas.edu/eieol/oruol

Malloryk. (2022, January 23). The "Holocaust by bullets" in Ukraine: The National WWII Museum: New Orleans. Retrieved September 15, 2022, from https://www.nationalww2museum.org/war/articles/ukraine-holocaust

Myers, D. (2022, March 9). The Ironies of History: The Ukraine crisis through the lens of Jewish history. Retrieved from https://katz.sas.upenn.edu/resources/blog/ironies-history-ukraine-crisis-through-lens-jewish-history

Pelenski, J. (1998). *The Contest for the Legacy of Kievan Rus'*. Boulder (Colo.): East European Monographs.

Peterson, B. (2014, March 16). The long war over the Ukrainian language - The Boston Globe. Retrieved from

https://www.bostonglobe.com/ideas/2014/03/15/the-long-war-over-ukrainian-language/HXllLbK9wVnhwGSHNVPKIUP/story.html

Pritsak, O. (1977). The Origin of Rus'. *The Russian Review, 36*(3), 249–273. https://doi.org/10.2307/128848

Service, R. (2022, January 01). Hundreds of Ukrainians march to honor controversial Nationalist leader. Retrieved September, from https://www.rferl.org/a/ukraine-march-stepan-bandera/31635671.html

Shapiro, A. (2014, May 20). Hero or villain? historical Ukrainian figure symbolizes today's Feud. Retrieved from

https://www.npr.org/sections/parallels/2014/05/20/312719066/hero-or-villain-historical-ukrainian-figure-symbolizes-todays-feud

Veidlinger, J. (2019, November 4). The 1919 Pogroms in Ukraine and Poland: One Hundred Years Later. Retrieved from https://www.wilsoncenter.org/event/the-1919-pogroms-ukraine-and-poland-one-hundred-years-later

Гордон, Д. (2014, July 04). *Борис Немцов. "В гостях у Дмитрия Гордона". 1/2 (2008)* [Video file]. Retrieved from https://www.youtube.com/watch?

Haring, M. (2019, August 29). The truth behind Ukraine's language policy. Retrieved from https://www.atlanticcouncil.org/blogs/ ukrainealert/the-truth-behind-ukraine-s-language-policy/

Made in the USA
Monee, IL
22 December 2023

50176603R00226